A Complete Life of
General George A. Custer

VOLUME 1: THROUGH THE CIVIL WAR

G. A. Custer.

A Complete Life of General George A. Custer

VOLUME 1: THROUGH THE CIVIL WAR

BY

Frederick Whittaker,

BREVET CAPTAIN SIXTH NEW YORK VETERAN CAVALRY.

Introduction by Gregory J. W. Urwin

University of Nebraska Press
Lincoln and London

Introduction copyright © 1993 by the University of Nebraska
Press
Manufactured in the United States of America

First Bison Book printing: 1993
Most recent printing indicated by the last digit below:
10   9   8   7   6   5   4   3   2   1

Library of Congress Cataloging-in-Publication Data
Whittaker, Frederick, 1838–1889.
A complete life of general George A. Custer / by Frederick
Whittaker; introduction by Gregory J.W. Urwin.
p. cm.
Originally published: New York: Sheldon, 1876.
"Bison."
Includes bibliographical references (p.   ) and index.
Contents: v. 1. Through the Civil War— v. 2. From Appomattox to
the Little Big Horn.
ISBN 0-8032-4766-4 (cloth: v. 1).—ISBN 0-8032-9742-4 (pbk.: v. 1).—
ISBN 0-8032-4767-2 (cloth: v. 2).—ISBN 0-8032-9743-2 (pbk.: v. 2).—
ISBN 0-8032-9744-0 (set)
1. Custer, George Armstrong, 1839–1876. 2. Generals—United
States—Biography. 3. United States. Army—Biography. I. Title.
E467.1.C99W6   1993
973.8'2'092—dc20
[B]
92-37701   CIP

Reprinted from the original 1876 edition published by Sheldon &
Company, New York. This Bison Book edition has been divided
into two volumes. Volume 2 begins with the Seventh Book, "On
the Plains," and, like Volume 1, carries a new introduction.

♾

TO THE AMERICAN PEOPLE,

WHOSE LIBERTIES HE SO GALLANTLY DEFENDED,

AND ESPECIALLY TO THE

AMERICAN CAVALRY, PAST AND PRESENT

WHOSE GREATEST PRIDE AND BRIGHTEST ORNAMENT HE WAS,

I DEDICATE THIS MEMOIR.

CONTENTS.

FIRST BOOK.—THE BOY.

CHAPTER I.
EARLY LIFE.

CHAPTER II.
PLEBE CUSTER.

CHAPTER III.
CADET CUSTER.

SECOND BOOK.—THE SUBALTERN.

CHAPTER I.
LIEUTENANT CUSTER, SECOND CAVALRY.

CHAPTER II.
BULL RUN.

CHAPTER III.
ORGANIZING AN ARMY.

THIRD BOOK.—THE CAPTAIN.

FOURTH BOOK.—THE MICHIGAN BRIGADE.

FIFTH BOOK.—THE THIRD CAVALRY DIVISION.

CHAPTER VI.
THE GREAT PARADE.

SIXTH BOOK.—AFTER THE WAR.

CHAPTER I.
THE VOLUNTEERS IN TEXAS.

CHAPTER II.
THE REGULAR ARMY.

CHAPTER III.
THE SEVENTH CAVALRY.

LIST OF ILLUSTRATIONS.

STEEL PLATE OF GENERAL CUSTER AS HE AP-⎫
PEARED THE SUMMER OF HIS DEATH..........⎬ FRONTISPIECE.
⎭

Mrs. Custer says of this likeness: "I cannot say how pleased I am with the steel plate engraving you sent me. It grows upon me, and I think it gives the General's intellectual look better than any portrait I have."

INTRODUCTION
by Gregory J. W. Urwin

Shoppers scanning the December 16, 1876, edition of the *New York Times* for holiday gift ideas would have found this item among the notices of new publications:

THE COMPLETE LIFE OF
GEN. G. A. CUSTER
Elegantly Illustrated.
EMBRACING HIS BRILLIANT ARMY LIFE.
And .
HIS WONDERFUL EXPLOITS IN INDIAN WARFARE.
He was the best purely Cavalry Officer this country
has ever seen.
He was the ablest Indian Fighter we have ever had.
His life was a perfect romance. His name recalls
nothing but brilliant deeds of daring and romantic
courage, and all that is noble and charming.
Every one will read this book! It is elegantly illus-
trated.
PRICE, $4 25.[1]

This immodest blurb alerted the reading public to the release of the book that spawned the phenomenon known as the "Custer Myth." More than any other printed work, Frederick Whittaker's *A Complete Life of Gen. George A. Custer* laid the groundwork for the passionate debate that continues to rage over America's most famous frontier soldier and his unforgettable defeat at the Little Big Horn.[2]

Some Custer-hating pundits have dismissed Whittaker as simply a mean-spirited opportunist who deliberately courted controversy to boost the sales of his magnum opus. Others view him as a naive hero-worshiper who erred spectacularly in his choice of subject. Be that as it may, anyone who reads, writes, or publishes a Custer book today is an heir to Whittaker's legacy. His influence is still deeply felt, even by those who do not share his exalted opinion of the United States Army's last cavalier.[3]

The road that led Frederick Whittaker to become the founding father of Custeriana was neither smooth nor straight. He was born in London, England, on December 12, 1838, fifty-one weeks before George Armstrong Custer's birth at New Rumley, Ohio. Frederick's father, Henry Whittaker, was a respected solicitor, but he made the mistake of endorsing a loan taken out by a noble client. When the nobleman defaulted, the elder Whittaker had to flee to the Continent to avoid a stay in debtor's prison. In 1850, Henry moved his family to New York City, where he secured employment as managing clerk in a law office.[4]

Due to his family's wanderings, young Frederick received little formal education, spending only six months in a private school in Brooklyn. He grew up in a cultured household, however, and developed into an avid reader with an amazingly wide range of interests. After the lad turned sixteen, Henry found him a job as an office boy in the law office of N. Dane Ellingwood, there to train for a legal career. Frederick rebelled against following in his father's footsteps, however, and went to work for an architect. But a slight defect in his eyesight soon forced the headstrong youth to search for another means of earning a living. Just prior to the Civil War, he published an article in the *Great Republic Monthly*, and that success inclined him to try his hand at a literary career.[5]

Before Whittaker could prove himself as a professional writer, the Civil War erupted. Youthful patriotism overcame personal ambition, and Whittaker joined with hun-

dreds of thousands of other Northerners in answering
Abraham Lincoln's appeal for troops to save the Union. On
November 11, 1861, Whittaker enlisted as a private in Company L of the Sixth New York Cavalry, a regiment which
drew its recruits from the Empire State, Massachusetts,
and Washington, D.C. Whittaker and the other ninety-one
original members of his company were all city boys, fresh
from the streets of New York. Like the English solicitor's
son, the other men of Company L regarded the cavalry as
the most glamorous branch of the service, and all aspired to
be swashbuckling cavaliers. But a prolonged shortage of
horseflesh nearly blasted that dream to pieces. Union authorities were unable to mount the entire regiment until
July 11, 1862, a full year after the Sixth signed up its first recruits. During Whittaker's first few months in uniform, he
heard unfounded but persistent rumors that the Sixth New
York would be converted into infantry. While Whittaker
and his comrades prayed for horses, Colonel Thomas C. Devin, a gifted and diligent citizen soldier, subjected them to
long hours of drill and instruction. Under Devin's strict
tutelage and steady leadership, the Sixth New York
evolved into one of the Union Army's most trustworthy cavalry units.[6]

Colonel Devin issued sabers to his troopers on December 16, 1861. For Private Whittaker, that day marked the
beginning of a lifelong love affair. Nothing thrilled him
more than plunging headlong into a cut-and-slash melee on
horseback. Years later, Whittaker would describe such en-
counters as combat "of the most inspiring, romantic and
thoroughly delightful kind." In fact, he was as much a war
lover as Custer. "Glorious days were those," Whittaker
wrote of his experiences in the Gettysburg campaign, "and
green to the memory of those who shared in them." To the
end of his days, Whittaker preached that dexterity with
the saber and a willingness to close with the enemy were
the traits of well-trained cavalrymen—a quaint conviction
that surfaced repeatedly in his biography of Custer.[7]

The Sixth New York Cavalry finally took the field in
piecemeal fashion between March and July 1862—as

horses became available for its various companies. Elements of the regiment took part in nearly every major battle of the Army of the Potomac, and the New Yorkers particularly distinguished themselves at Chancellorsville, Brandy Station, and Gettysburg. Whittaker distinguished himself as well, rising through the ranks to corporal and sergeant. A Confederate shot him through the left lung at the Battle of the Wilderness in May 1864, but Whittaker recovered from his wound and returned to the Sixth New York to finish out the war in the Eastern Theater. On February 12, 1865, he received a promotion to second lieutenant of Company A, a position he held until he was discharged and mustered out of service on August 9.[8]

Although Custer and Whittaker never actually met during the Civil War, they both served in the Army of the Potomac's Cavalry Corps. The young New Yorker had plenty of opportunities to watch the "Boy General" in action. For a brief while, the two men even served in the same division. When the Army of the Potomac launched its sustained drive against Richmond, Virginia, in the spring of 1864, Brigadier General Custer commanded the First Brigade of the First Cavalry Division. Whittaker's Sixth New York Cavalry occupied a slot in the division's Second Brigade. Consequently, Whittaker was eminently qualified to assess Custer's performance in the Civil War and to compare him with other cavalry commanders in both blue and gray.[9]

Following the war, Whittaker landed a job as a book agent and then switched to teaching school. He returned to writing in 1869, turning out poetry, sketches, and stories for a variety of magazines and newspapers. An inheritance from some English relatives provided him with enough financial security to marry and buy a house in Mount Vernon, New York, where he would devote the remainder of his life to literary pursuits. Never outgrowing his fascination with military affairs, Whittaker published a lengthy article, "Volunteer Cavalry, the Lessons of the Decade, by a Volunteer Cavalryman," in the January 21 and June 3, 1871, issues of the *Army and Navy Journal*. He was so proud of this effort that he repackaged it as a limited edition book of one hundred copies. For the historian, *Volunteer Cavalry* is probably the most valuable of all Whittaker's works. Based on first-hand experience, the slim volume represents a vivid and reasonable analysis of the use of mounted troops in the Civil War.[10]

Whittaker's career took another great leap forward in 1871 when he started writing for Beadle and Adams, then the leading American publisher of pulp fiction. Beadle and Adams employed the best minor popular writers of the day, and Whittaker was one of the firm's most prized talents. Over the next fifteen years, he wrote eighty-two dime and nickel novels, many of which were printed two or more times. Whittaker's short fiction was produced too quickly to rank as real literature, but his work was as good as anything churned out by his peers. He set his action-packed tales in exotic locales—the Wild West, the colonial frontier, the high seas, the courts and battlefields of Napoleonic Europe, the steppes of Russia, and the Orient. His heroes were fearless and dashing, and the values they embodied dovetailed nicely with the mores of polite Victorian society.[11]

While toiling over dozens of brief potboilers for Beadle and Adams, Whittaker took the time to create several full-length novels. The first of these, *The Cadet Button: A Novel of American Army Life*, appeared in 1878. He also placed articles in such popular magazines as the *Fireside Companion* and the *Galaxy*, and continued to contribute to the *Army and Navy Journal*. That last-named publication appointed him as its National Guard editor in 1874 and later promoted him to assistant editor. To enhance his status as a military commentator and a general man of letters, the rising writer resorted to a minor fraud. He began signing his work as "Frederick Whittaker, Brevet Captain Sixth New York Veteran Cavalry."[12]

Whittaker's life took a dramatic turn in the summer of 1876 with George Armstrong Custer's debacle at the Little Big Horn. The thirty-seven-year-old writer already admired Custer for his daring exploits in the Civil War. The two cavalrymen had finally met face to face in the winter of

1875–76, when Custer visited the offices of the *Galaxy* to discuss the publication of his Civil War memoirs. Whittaker apparently came away from that interview more impressed with his celebrated contemporary than ever.[13]

The news of Custer's Last Stand stunned and saddened Whittaker, as it did much of America. He promptly expressed his grief by eulogizing Custer in a nine-page article in the September 1876 issue of the *Galaxy*.[14] That same month, he published an epic poem, "Custer's Last Charge," in the *Army and Navy Journal*. Its first stanza set the tone for all his subsequent writings on the fallen Indian fighter:

"Dead! is it possible? He, the bold rider,
Custer, our hero, the first in the fight,
Charming the bullets of yore to fly wider,
Shunning our battle-king's ringlets of light!
Dead! our young chieftain, and dead all forsaken!
No one to tell us the way of his fall!
Slain in the desert, and never to waken,
Never, not even to victory's call?"[15]

Not content with these two flowery tributes, Whittaker relinquished his editorial duties at the *Army and Navy Journal* to devote himself to writing a comprehensive biography of Custer. Whittaker received invaluable assistance from his hero's widow, Elizabeth Bacon Custer, who allowed him to examine and copy portions of the general's voluminous private correspondence. Although she later denied charges of collaboration, "Libbie" Custer recognized Whittaker as a natural ally and gently guided him in exonerating the tarnished military reputation of her slain husband.[16]

Whittaker threw himself heart and soul into his new project, and completed it with incredible speed. He later boasted that his book appeared "just six months after the battle" which claimed Custer's life. Whittaker intended his thick volume to stand as a lasting monument to "one of the few really great men that America has produced." But Whittaker was too protective of Custer to sketch an objective portrait of the man, and he did not always take the time and care required to confirm his facts or mold his rambling narrative into memorable prose.[17]

Contrary to the sneering remarks of certain critics, Whittaker understood the elements of good writing. When Mrs. Custer disclosed her intention to write her own books about her beloved "Autie," Whittaker generously offered the following tips:

> Use *short* sentences preferably. Avoid using the *dash*. Be careful of your *pronouns*; they are the cause of much confusion to all young writers. Each must have its antecedent clearly indicated, or you must change your form of expression. Don't be afraid to correct. Don't be afraid to repeat a name for the sake of clearness in a sentence concerning two persons. Talk on paper as you talk viva voce, and you conquer all mankind.[18]

Unfortunately, Whittaker often ignored his own advice. He was too eager to publish his Custer biography while the memory of the Little Big Horn was fresh in the public mind. The manuscript he rushed to his publisher was padded with large chunks of Custer's Civil War memoirs and 1874 book, *My Life on the Plains*; the general's personal letters; newspaper articles of dubious historical worth; and excerpts from the reports and memoirs of other officers.

Nonetheless, Whittaker sprinkled his biography with enough astute observations on American cavalry operations, military life, and Indian relations to provide modern readers with substantial food for thought. Moreover, his treatment of Custer's final battle created a tremendous stir in both the press and the U.S. Army. The questions he raised more than a century ago are still being argued by legions of Custer buffs.

For this Bison Book reprint, Whittaker's weighty tome is divided into two volumes. The first volume follows Custer from his Ohio boyhood through his meteoric ascent to brigadier and major general in the latter half of the Civil War. Whittaker structured his version of Custer's rise according to the formula already perfected by Horatio Alger. Born to a humble village blacksmith, young Custer procures an appointment to West Point, proves himself a military genius on numerous battlefields, and emerges from his country's bloodiest war loaded with honors and universal acclaim. Whittaker's adulation is obvious, but it should be stated that this view of Custer was commonly held by those who served with the Boy General in the Civil War. Unlike Whittaker, those who soldiered with Custer in the West soon learned that even a national idol can have a dark side. [19]

Having created an image of Custer that would influence biographers until 1934 and inspire the 1941 film, *They Died with Their Boots On*, Whittaker returned to writing fiction. He dabbled in spiritualism for a while in the 1880s, and then developed an enthusiasm for Volapuk, the international language. His life ended in an unexpected and bizarre manner on May 13, 1889. Returning to his Mount Vernon home after a visit to the local newspaper, Whittaker accidentally fell down a staircase with a loaded revolver in his hand. The weapon discharged, and a .38-caliber bullet pierced his brain. He died within thirty minutes without regaining consciousness, leaving a wife, three daughters, one stepson, and a host of faithful readers to mourn his passing. Beadle and Adams and other firms continued to reissue Whittaker's adventure tales well into the twentieth century. As reading tastes changed, however, Whittaker's dime and nickel novels fell from favor. Few people recognize his name today, and they know him only as Custer's first biographer.[20]

Although Whittaker's treatment of the Little Big Horn caused a greater sensation than any other part of his Custer biography, he devoted 265 pages—nearly half the book—to his protagonist's Civil War exploits. Whittaker recognized the formative role that the Civil War played in Custer's development as a man and a soldier. Surprisingly, this basic truth was lost on many subsequent Custer scholars, who focused on the Last Stand to the virtual exclusion of almost every other aspect of his life.[21] The next major Custer biographer to take a close look at the Boy General's Civil War years was Jay Monaghan. First published in 1959, Monaghan's *Custer: The Life of General George Armstrong Custer* ranked as the most balanced and complete account of Custer's life until the publication of Robert M. Utley's *Cavalier in Buckskin* in 1988. Interestingly enough, the reasons Monaghan cited for Custer's elevation to high rank echoed many of the same themes first sounded by Whittaker. [22]

In preparing my own study of Custer's early career, *Custer Victorious: The Civil War Battles of General George Armstrong Custer*, I utilized many sources not available to either Whittaker or Monaghan. As it happened, my research revealed that most if not all of the Union soldiers who followed Custer in the Civil War regarded him as a peerless cavalryman and a genuine hero. This was something that Whittaker already knew from personal experience. Whittaker may have been blind to Custer's faults, but he knew his hero's strengths and many of his assertions have been vindicated by recent scholarship.

Whittaker's treatment of the Civil War years is significant in another respect. *A Complete Life of General George A. Custer* represents one of the earliest analyses of the war in the Eastern Theater to appear in book form. It was published at a time when most Americans considered the Civil War as a harrowing and divisive nightmare that deserved to be forgotten. Even veterans were trying to suppress their memories of the conflict. In both his Custer biography and his treatise on *Volunteer Cavalry*, Whittaker assumed a pioneering role in examining the war's conduct and military legacy. Whittaker wrote about the Civil War just as Jubal Early and other Confederate apologists were launching their concerted campaign to transform Robert E. Lee into the object of a rabid personality cult. Whittaker's views were untainted by the clichés, literary formulas, and maudlin sentiments that Early and his cohorts would inject into Civil War literature. Indeed, some of Whittaker's observations make for a refreshing change from the pro-Lee interpretations that have held sway in Civil War historiography since the 1870s.[23]

NOTES

1. *New York Times,* December 16, 1876.
2. For a detailed examination of Whittaker's effect on Custer studies, see Robert M. Utley, *Custer and the Great Controversy: The Origin and Development of a Legend* (Pasadena: Westernlore Press, 1980).
3. *Philadelphia Times,* March 13, 1879; Fred Dustin to Theodore W. Goldin, February 26, 1934, and Frederick W. Benteen to Theodore W. Goldin, March 14, 1896, in John M. Carroll, ed., *The Benteen-Goldin Letters on Custer and His Last Battle* (Lincoln: University of Nebraska Press, 1991), 114, 332.
4. Albert Johannsen, *The House of Beadle and Adams and Its Dime and Nickel Novels: The Story of a Vanished Literature,* 3 vols. (Norman: University of Oklahoma Press, 1950–62) 2: 301; *New York Times,* May 14, 1879.
5. Johannsen, *The House of Beadle and Adams,* 2: 301.
6. Hillman Hall, *History of the Sixth New York Calvary* (Worcester: Blanchard Press, 1908), 17–21, 31–43; Stephen Z. Starr, *The Union Calvary in the Civil War,* 3 vols. (Baton Rouge: Louisiana State University Press, 1979–85) 1: 112, 136.
7. Hall, *Sixth New York Cavalry,* 32; Frederick Whittaker, *Volunteer Cavalry; The Lessons of the Decade, by a Volunteer Cavalryman* (New York: Printed for the Author, 1871), 18–19.
8. Hall, *Sixth New York Cavalry,* 23–30, 37, 43, 99–120, 127–28, 133–50, 319, 348; Johannsen, *House of Beadle and Adams,* 2: 301.
9. Gregory J. W. Urwin, *Custer Victorious: The Civil War Battles of General George Armstrong Custer* (Lincoln: University of Nebraska Press, 1990), 125–27, 131; Robert Underwood Johnson and Clarence Clough Buel, *Battles and Leaders of the Civil War,* 4 vols. (New York: Century Co., 1889), 4: 186–87.
10. Stephen Z. Starr made repeated use of Whittaker's *Volunteer Cavalry* in his magisterial three-volume history of the Union Cavalry in the Civil War. Johannsen, *House of Beadle and Adams,* 2: 301.
11. For a thorough critique of Whittaker's short fiction, see Bruce A. Rosenberg, *Custer and the Epic of Defeat* (University Park: Pennsylvania State University Press, 1974), 53, 93–100. Rosenberg credited Whittaker with writing over one hundred dime and nickel novels, a mistake caused by not distinguishing between the original titles and subsequent reprints. Johannsen, *House of Beadle and Adams,* 1: 94–98, 102–4, 178–79, 181, 186, 189, 205–17, 220–22, 230, 243, 248–50, 257–58, 262–63, 265, 267–68,

271, 273, 301–2, 321–23, 325, 329–31, 333, 335, 339, 341, 344–45, 348–51, 356, 425, 428–32, 434–36, 439–44, 446, 448–49, 451, 457, 461–65, 473, 476.

12. Sheldon & Company, the publisher of Whittaker's Custer biography, also published *The Cadet Button*. His other full-length novels did not appear in print until after his death. They include the following: *The Great Kenton Feud, A Novel* (New York: R. Bonner's Sons, 1891); *Bel Rubio, A Novel* (New York: R. Bonner's Sons, 1891); *The Black Tiger, A Novel* (New York: R. Bonner's Sons, 1892); *Transgressing the Law, A Novel* (New York: R. Bonner's Sons, 1893). In addition, Whittaker wrote a short biography of Custer and an exercise manual. He aimed both of these publications at young readers. See Frederick Whittaker, *The Dashing Dragoon; or, The Story of Gen. George A. Custer from West Point to the Big Horn* (New York: Beadle and Adams, 1882) and *Handbook of Summer Athletic Sports, Comprising Walking, Running, Jumping, Hare and Hounds, Archery, Etc. with Complete American and English Athletic Rules* (New York: Beadle and Adams, 1880).

13. The *Galaxy* originally carried Custer's articles on his early Indian campaigns, which Sheldon & Company then published as a book, *My Life on the Plains*. Lawrence A. Frost, "Two Sides of a General," in Gregory J. W. Urwin and Roberta E. Fagan, eds., *Custer and His Times: Book Three* (Conway: University of Central Arkansas Press, 1987), 131–34; Rosenberg, *Custer and the Epic of Defeat*, 53; Utley, *Custer and the Great Controversy*, 52.

14. Frederick Whittaker, "General George A. Custer," *Galaxy* 22 (September 1876): 362–71.

15. Frederick Whittaker, "Custer's Last Charge," *Army and Navy Journal*, September 1876, special page.

16. Mrs. Custer pertly declared that she never saw any part of Whittaker's manuscript or read the finished volume. But Whittaker openly acknowledged her assistance and his text contains information and opinions that could have come only from her. Furthermore, the extensive Custer collection of the late Lawrence A. Frost contains letters from Whittaker in which he updated Libbie on his efforts to absolve her husband of blame for the Little Big Horn disaster. Lawrence A. Frost, *General Custer's Libbie* (Seattle: Superior Publishing Company, 1976), 236–37; John Upton Terrell and George Walton, *Faint the Trumpet Sounds: The Life and Trial of Major Reno* (New York: David McKay Company, Inc., 1966), 194–95, 199–200; Utley, *Custer and the Great Controversy*, 52–53.

17. For instance, one of the myths Whittaker created was his

claim that Custer was descended from a Hessian officer who was captured during the Saratoga campaign in 1777 and chose to stay in America. *New York Times,* December 16, 1876; Frost, *General Custer's Libbie,* 236; James Joseph Talbot, "Custer's Last Battle," *Penn Monthly* 13 (September 1877): 679–99; Frederick Whittaker, *A Complete Life of Gen. George A. Custer* (New York: Sheldon & Company, 1876), 1, 5; *New York Sun,* February 26, 1879.

18. Frederick Whittaker to Elizabeth Bacon Custer, March 31, 1877, quoted in Frost, *General Custer's Libbie,* 240.

19. For an excellent analysis of Whittaker's literary influences, see Richard Slotkin, *The Fatal Environment: The Myth of the Frontier in the Age of Industrialization, 1800–1890* (New York: Atheneum, 1985), 501–11. For a more objective account of Custer's success in the Civil War, see Gregory J. W. Urwin, "Custer: The Civil War Years," in Paul A. Hutton, ed., *The Custer Reader* (Lincoln: University of Nebraska Press, 1992), 7–32.

20. Johannsen, *House of Beadle and Adams,* 2: 301–2; *New York Times,* May 14, 1889; Utley, *Custer and the Great Controversy,* 56, 121, 155–58; Rosenberg, *Custer and the Epic of Defeat,* 53; Slotkin, *Fatal Environment,* 510–11.

21. For an intriguing critique of the narrow scope of Custer studies, see Don Russell, "Custer's First Charge," *By Valor & Arms: The Journal of American Military History* 1 (October 1974): 20–29. Frederic F. Van De Water covered Custer's Civil War career in ten short chapters in his classic revisionist work, *Glory-Hunter: A Life of General Custer* (Indianapolis: Bobbs-Merrill Company, 1934). But Van De Water deliberately skewed the facts in an effort to make Custer's every success look like dumb luck or newspaper propaganda.

22. See Jay Monaghan, *Custer: The Life of General George Armstrong Custer* (Boston: Little, Brown and Company, 1959) and Robert M. Utley, *Cavalier in Buckskin: George Armstrong Custer and the Western Military Frontier* (Norman: University of Oklahoma Press, 1988).

23. For the efforts of the Civil War generation to forget the conflict, see Gerald F. Linderman, *Embattled Courage: The Experience of Combat in the American Civil War* (New York: Free Press, 1987). For a detailed account of the rise of the Robert E. Lee cult, see Thomas L. Connelly, *The Marble Man: Robert E. Lee and His Image in American Society* (Baton Rouge: Louisiana State University Press, 1977).

LIFE OF

GEN. GEORGE A. CUSTER.

PRELIMINARY REMARKS.

THIS book aims to give to the world the life of a great man, one of the few really great men that America has produced. Beginning at the foot of the social ladder, with no advantages beyond those, physical and mental, given to him by the GOD who made him, he rose to the top. His upward career was so rapid and phenomenal in its success as to deceive the world in general as to the means by which he rose, and none more completely for a time than the present writer of his biography. Much of Custer's success has been attributed to good fortune, while it was really the result of a wonderful capacity for hard and energetic work, and a rapidity of intuition which is seldom found apart from military genius of the highest order. It is only after a careful and complete examination of the character of the *man*, and the perusal of a mass of private correspondence, beginning in his days of obscurity, after the unconscious revelation by himself of his inmost thoughts and aspirations, that the author has learned aright to appreciate the personality of the subject of this biography. Few men had more enemies than Custer, and no man deserved them less. The world has never known half the real nobility of his life nor a tithe of the difficulties under which he struggled. It will be the author's endeavor to remedy this want of knowledge, to paint in sober earnest colors the truthful portrait of such a knight of romance as has not honored the world with his presence since the days of Bayard.

This may sound exaggerated praise to some. A few short weeks ago it would have sounded so to the writer. He only asks the world to accept it to-day, as the honest conviction and sober testimony, arrived at after very thorough and careful examination, of one who entered on the task with very different impressions. The current idea on the subject, largely due to the expression set afloat by Custer himself, has been embodied in the words, "Custer's Luck," but never has there been a more mistaken impression. To remove that impression, to show to the world the dead as he really was—not as an ideal hero,—is the object of these pages, which seek to show the truth, the whole truth, and nothing but the truth, limited only by such knowledge of facts as may be accessible at the time of writing. The author earnestly hopes his efforts may be successful.

FIRST BOOK.—THE BOY.

CHAPTER I.

EARLY LIFE.

GEORGE ARMSTRONG CUSTER was born in New Rumley, Ohio, December 5, 1839. New Rumley is a group of houses, an old established settlement, in Harrison County, on the border of Pennsylvania, and peopled from thence early in the last century. It is a small place, not set down on any but very large scale maps, and most of the population of the township is scattered in farm houses about the country. The family history, gleaned from the family Bible, is plain and simple. It is that of an honest group of hard workers, not ashamed of work, and it shows that the stock of which the future general came was good, such as made frontiersmen and pioneers in the last century.

Emmanuel H. Custer, father of the general, was born in Cryssoptown, Alleghany County, Maryland, December 10th, 1806. To-day, a hale hearty old man of seventy, somewhat bowed, but well as ever to all seeming, he stands a living instance of the strong physique and keen wits of the determined men who made the wild forests of Ohio to bloom like the rose, He was brought up as a smith, and worked at his trade for many years, till he had saved enough money to buy a farm, when he became a cultivator. All he knows he taught himself, but he gave his children the best education that could be obtained in those early days in Ohio. When quite a young man, he left

Maryland and settled in New Rumley, being the only smith for many miles. He prospered so well that he was able to get married when twenty-two years of age. He married Matilda Viers, August 7th, 1828, and their marriage lasted six years, during which time three children were born, of whom only one, Brice W. Custer, of Columbus, Ohio, is now living. He is bridge inspector on one of the railroads leading from that place. The first Mrs. Custer died July 18th, 1834.

The maiden name of the second Mrs. Custer, mother of the general, was Maria Ward. She was born in Burgettstown, Pennsylvania, May 31st, 1807, and was first married, when only a girl of sixteen, to Mr. Israel R. Kirkpatrick. Her husband died in 1835, a year after the death of the first Mrs. Custer. The widow Kirkpatrick had then three children, whereof two are now alive. David Kirkpatrick lives in Wood County, Ohio, some forty miles south from Toledo. Lydia A. Kirkpatrick married Mr. David Reed, of Monroe, Michigan, and in after life became more than a sister, a second mother, to the subject of our biography.

After two years widowhood, Mrs. Kirkpatrick married Emmanuel Custer, April 14th, 1837, and became the mother of the general, two years later, as the second Mrs. Custer. She is still, at the present date of writing, living, but in very feeble health.

The children of this second marriage were born as follows:

1. George Armstrong Custer, December 5, 1839.
2. Nevin J. Custer, July 29, 1842.
3. Thomas W. Custer, March 15, 1845.
4. Boston Custer, October 31, 1848.
5. Margaret Emma Custer, January 5, 1852.

All were born in Harrison County, in or near New Rumley. Nevin and Margaret alone now survive, the latter the widow of Lieutenant Calhoun, who was killed on the field of battle with his three brothers-in-law, June 25th, 1876. Nevin Custer now lives on a farm near Monroe, Michigan. During the late war he enlisted as a private soldier, but was thrown out for physical disability, in spite of his anxiety to serve his country. He had all the spirit of the Custers, but lacked the good physique of the other members of the family.

I have been thus particular in giving the family record, because little is known to the world on that subject. It is the record of a plain yeoman family, such as constitutes the bone and sinew of the country. The name of Custer was originally Küster, and the grandfather of Emmanuel Custer came from Germany, but Emmanuel's father was born in America. The grandfather was one of those same Hessian officers over whom the colonists wasted so many curses in the Revolutionary war, and who were yet so innocent of harm and such patient, faithful soldiers. After Burgoyne's surrender in 1778, many of the paroled Hessians seized the opportunity to settle in the country they came to conquer, and amongst these the grandfather of Emmanuel Custer, captivated by the bright eyes of a frontier damsel, captivated her in turn with his flaxen hair and sturdy Saxon figure, and settled down in Pennsylvania, afterwards moving to Maryland. It is something romantic and pleasing after all, that stubborn George Guelph, in striving to conquer the colonies, should have given them the ancestor of George Custer, who was to become one of their greatest glories.

Of this family the boy George Armstrong was born, and grew up a sturdy, flaxen-headed youngster, full of life and frolic, always in mischief, and yet, strange to say, of the gentlest and most lovable disposition. The closest inquiry fails to reveal a single instance of ill-temper during Custer's boyhood. All his playmates speak of him as the most mischievous and frolicsome of boys, but never as quarrelsome. There is actually not a single record of a fight in all his school life, though the practical jokes are without number. He was very early, however, imbued with a passion for soldiering, how early he could not tell himself. In those days Emmanuel Custer, like most countrymen, was in the militia, and very fond of his uniform and his little son. When "Armstrong," or "Autie," as the boy was always called, was only about four years old, a miniature military suit,* was made for him. Whenever father Custer went to training, Autie went with him, and marched after the soldiers as well as he could, his small legs doing their best to make big strides. After drill it was a favorite pastime of the "New Rumley Invincibles" to see little Autie go through the old Scott manual of arms with a toy musket, and thus the boy became imbued from his earliest years with the soldier spirit.

As Autie grew older, like all the Custer boys, he was sent to school—district school—where he learned, in the good old fashioned way, how to read, write and cipher. The winter schooling over, in the summer he worked on the farm, like all the Custer boys, ploughing, mowing, chopping wood, "doing chores," and developing into a strong hearty boy. It was this early farm life, the constant and vigorous exercise that he underwent, that laid the foundation of that iron constitution which he afterwards possessed, and gave him that capacity for bearing fatigue, which made him such a tremendous marcher in days to come. He could handle an axe when he was a general officer, as well as any pioneer, and has been known on more than one occasion to set to work to help the fatigue parties, when clearing a way over fallen timber in the forests of Virginia and the coppices that fringe the Black Hills.

When Armstrong was about ten years old, an event happened in the family which changed the current of his life to an extent which no one at the time expected would happen. His half sister Lydia was married to Mr. Reed, a young man who came from Monroe, Michigan, and after her marriage departed to live at Monroe. Now in those days Monroe was a long way off from New Rumley. There were very few railroads in the United States, and none between the two towns. The

---

* This tiny soldier-suit still exists, in the keeping of General Custer's mother.

State of Michigan was then sparsely settled. The act admitting it into the Union was only passed the year in which young Custer was born. The site of Lansing, the present capital of the State, was, in 1846, only a few years before Mrs. Reed's marriage, occupied by a single log cabin, and the population of the State was not quite four hundred thousand people. The only old settled places were Detroit and Monroe. The former dated from the days of the fur-posts, before the Revolution, and it was very near Monroe (then called Frenchtown) that the massacre of 1813, known as the battle of Raisin River, took place, in which the British General Proctor, and Tecumseh with his Indians, annihilated eight hundred mounted riflemen of Kentucky.

Mrs. Reed felt that she was going away among strangers, with none of her own kin near her, and she begged that Armstrong might go with her to her new home. The boy, like all boys, was only too glad to see new scenes, and went to Monroe with his sister and her husband, remaining there for two years. Newly settled as was the State of Michigan in those days, it was already becoming noted for its excellent educational advantages, which have since expanded into one of the best school systems in the Union. When young Custer went there, he was at once put to school in Stebbins' Academy, where he remained till about twelve years old.

Of those early days the records and reminiscences are many and amusing, and we shall quote a few of them. Custer's chum at school, the boy who sat at the same desk with him, was named Bulkley, and the friendship that then began has since continued through life. In the case of Mr. Bulkley, who still lives in Monroe, it survives in the form of an ardent love and appreciation of his quondam desk-mate. Many years after, when the old Stebbins' Academy was broken up and the property sold at auction, Mr. Bulkley found the same old desk at which he and Custer used to sit, with their names carved on it in school-boy fashion. He bought it in, and it now stands in his store, the receptacle of the various papers connected with the " Custer Monument Fund Society" of which Bulkley is the Secretary, General Sheridan being President. How little those two boys thought, a quarter of a century ago, what would be the ultimate fate of that old desk, as they furtively whittled away at its corners.

Young Custer was a smart lad, with very quick appreciation, a remarkably rapid student, but one who hated study. He seldom or never looked at a lesson out of school, trusting to the short period before recitation to skim over his task, and yet rarely failing to have a creditable lesson. He was always smuggling novels into school and reading them furtively, and his old comrade cannot help, even at this late date, a chuckle of lawless satisfaction, as he recalls the way in which he and Custer used to cheat the old schoolmaster, in " geography hour." Custer used to have his geography wide open, while beneath it lay " Charles O'Malley," also wide open. With a pencil in his hand, he would be earnestly tracing the course of a river on the map when old Stebbins came round behind him, it being the habit of that worthy man to wear list slippers and to be on the watch at all times for surreptitious amusements among the boys. Sly as he was, however, Custer was slyer. His senses were as sharp as those of an Indian even then, and Stebbins never found him otherwise than busy and studying intently, to the worthy pedagogue's great satisfaction. As he passed, he would pat the boy's head and pronounce him a credit to the school, a compliment received by the youngster with an edifying air of virtuous humility. No sooner was Stebbins gone, however, than the end of the geography was lifted, while Armstrong returned to the perusal of the humors of Mr. Michael Free and the gallant charges of the Fourteenth Light Dragoons, with renewed zest.

His passion was reading military novels, his chief ambition to be a soldier. Even then, he had made up his mind to go to West Point when he got old enough. One thing that tended to inflame his martial spirit in those days, was the Mexican war, just then closed. The heroes of that war were almost all West-Pointers, and the little regular army made a very considerable figure therein. However that may be, he had formed the firm resolve to go to West Point when old enough.

Out of school, he was always in the midst of rough horse play with the other boys, fond of practical jokes, a great wrestler and runner, and the strongest lad of his age in the place. He became an acknowledged leader in all the athletic sports of the day, the only thing in which he did not excel being swimming. Curiously enough, he never liked the water much, to the day of his death, and though he could swim, seldom did so. Boating was also one of his dislikes. He would do anything on land, but had no aspirations as a sailor. At home, he was chiefly distinguished, according to the account of Mrs. Reed, by his extreme gentleness and kindness of heart. To her he was the most docile of boys, obeying her slightest wish the moment it was expressed. He was exceedingly tender-hearted also ; so much so that he never could bear even to see a chicken killed; and the sight of suffering of any kind completely unnerved him. He was very fond of nursing Mrs. Reed's children, as they successively arrived, and was especially proud of her first boy who was named Armstrong, after himself. Poor little Autie Reed, he died on the same field with Custer, together with Custer's youngest brother, on that last fated expedition.

A strange compound of qualities was this lad in those days, gentle and brave, with an overflowing sense of humor, hating his books, and yet working to the head of his class by fits and starts when he took a notion, obstinate under harsh treatment, opposing the constituted authorities at school with all ingenious evasions, meeting the wily tricks of his pedagogue with tricks still wilier, but ruled by his gentle sister with an absolute sway. He reminds us of one of Thackeray's schoolboys, full of vague poetical yearnings, tempered by the savage free-

dom of overflowing physical strength and health, a boy all over,
a boy to the backbone, with the promise and potency of—who
knows what?—of manhood.   The ruling traits of his character,
as they struck his family, were those of great goodness, of duty
performed, of kindness, love, and devotion.   To this day, they
seem to think of him, not as the brilliant warrior, but as the
exemplary son and brother, who never omitted a duty, never
abated in his love.   Inside of all the rough play of the cham-
pion wrestler of the school, lay this hidden kernel of surpassing
gentleness and love, that was to make the foundation of the
future knight.   And yet he was a plain American boy, who
knew little or nothing of mediæval lore, and less of European
history, as was the necessary consequence of the habitual American education.   He was then, and remained to the last, a
thorough American, a Western boy at that.

After spending two years at Stebbins' Academy, he returned
to New Rumley, and passed some time there, on his father's
farm.   When about fourteen, he was again sent to Monroe,
this time to the " Seminary," the principal school of that place,
then and now kept by the Rev. Mr. Boyd.   The Seminary is
a fine old brick mansion, large and irregular, stretching out its
wings in the midst of shady grounds, a pleasant and picturesque
home.   Here Custer finished his education in the English
branches, remaining there two years.   It was a far better school
than the old Academy, Mr. Boyd being a man of much greater
refinement and taste than was then common in the west, and
young Custer worked under him to more advantage.   He left
school at the age of sixteen, and went back to New Rumley.

It was, however, while at the Seminary, that a little incident
occurred, which subsequently influenced his whole life, as Mrs.
Reed's marriage had done when he was a child.   The incident
is so small and trifling that it seems nothing, and yet on such
trifles hang human lives.   Coming from school one day to Mrs.
Reed's, the rough, flaxen-headed, freckled-faced boy, was pertly
accosted by a little girl with black eyes.   She was a pretty little

creature, rounded and plump, her father's pet, an only child and naturally spoiled. Like most little children, she was proud to show all she knew, and she knew that Custer was a stranger. She said archly as she swung on the gate, her pretty face dimpling with smiles, "Hello! you Custer boy!" then frightened at her own temerity, turned and fled into the house.

A trifle, you will say, not worth recording; yet it was the beginning of Custer's first and last love. The sweet arch face of that little girl was the first revelation to the wild young savage, whose whole idea of life was that of physical exercise, war, and the chase, of *something else*, of another side to life. It was to him, love at first sight, and he then and there recorded an inward vow, that some day that little girl should be his wife. He kept the vow through many obstacles.

This little girl was Libbie Bacon, only child of Judge Daniel S. Bacon, one of the oldest settlers of Monroe. The Judge had come there long before Emmanuel Custer's first marriage, and fifteen years before Armstrong was born. Beginning as a school teacher, he had become a lawyer, a member of the Territorial Legislature before Michigan was yet erected into a State, Judge of Probate, President of the Monroe Bank, director of the first Michigan Railroad—in short he was one of the first men of the little town, and the centre of its "upper ten." To young Custer, poor and obscure, it might have then seemed as if a great gulf divided him from the little girl whose arch beauty flashed on him for the first time. It was characteristic of the determination which afterwards marked his whole career that he should make such a vow and keep it. To this we shall afterwards return.

Custer had now lived at Monroe, off and on, for four years. His return to Ohio must have seemed to him an exile, for he ever after seems to have looked on Monroe as his home. He went back to New Rumley, and soon after obtained a place as teacher at Hopedale, Ohio, not far from his native place. Here he earned his first money—not much to our notions now, but a little fortune to him in those days. Twenty-six dollars a month and his board were the terms, and he brought the whole of his first month's salary and poured it into his mother's lap. In after years he often referred to the joy he then experienced as being the greatest he had ever known, as being his first opportunity to repay in a measure the love of his parents, for whom he ever cherished the fondest affection. That affection was well deserved. Hitherto we have spoken but little of Custer's father and mother, but when we reflect on the fact that out of the savings of a small farm, and burdened with the support of a large family, they had managed to pay for the best education then to be found in the Western country for their eldest son, we can understand much of the spring of that son's energy and goodness of character.

Long years after, when Custer was distinguished among men, an eminent warrior, courted and petted by all, he wrote his father and mother a letter, which is worthy of being printed in letters of gold. It shows what parents and what a son combined to make the perfect knight that Custer became. We quote but a fragment, in answer to one of their letters, in which the modest parents have disclaimed any merit of their own in the success of their brilliant son. Custer writes:

You do yourself injustice when you say you did but little for me. You may forget it, but I never can. There is not a day but I think with deep gratitude of the many sacrifices, the love and devotion you and mother have constantly bestowed upon me. You could not have done more for me than you have. A fortune would be nothing to me with what I am indebted to you for. I never wanted for any thing necessary, and if you did not give me a fortune in money, you did what was infinitely better. You and mother instilled into my mind correct principles of industry honesty, self-reliance; I was taught the distinction between wrong and right; I was taught the value of temperate habits; and I now look back to my childhood and the days spent under the home roof, as a period of the purest happiness; and I feel thankful for such noble parents. I know but few if any boys are so blessed as I have been, by having such kind, self-sacrificing parents to train and guide them as I have had. I know I might heap millions of dollars at your feet, and still the debt of gratitude on my part would be undiminished.

All honor to parents and son. In that letter lies much of the secret of Custer's success.

At Hopedale, young Custer remained for a year, teaching; but he was not the man to stagnate into a pedagogue. Teaching was to him, as to many another man in the United States, a mere stepping-stone to better things, a temporary means of support. He had determined to go to West Point : the question remained, how was he to get there. Father Custer was a stanch old Jacksonian Democrat, double-dyed and twisted in the wool; the member for the district was an equally stanch Republican. It was now the year 1856, the time when Fremonters began to be enthusiastic and aggressive, when the burden of the campaign songs was "Free speech, free press, free soil, free men, Fremont and Victory!" The member for the district was an enthusiastic republican, what chance was there that he would use his influence to advance the son of an equally enthusiastic democrat? So Emmanuel Custer thought, when his son pressed him to try and get Mr. Bingham to nominate him to West Point. He said frankly that it was no use trying, that the young fellow might try if he wished, but he could not help him. He had no influence, and none but humble friends. But Armstrong would not give up. He would try for himself, and trust to his own efforts alone. He had one advantage, habits of study, and facility in using his knowledge. Teaching had given him that, as it has many others. No way to master a science so good as to undertake to teach it. One *must* know it then. So he sat down and wrote the following letter :

HOPEDALE, OHIO, MAY 27th, 1856.

To THE HON. JOHN A. BINGHAM.

SIR :—Wishing to learn something in relation to the matter of appointment of cadets to the West Point Military Academy, I have taken the liberty of addressing you on the subject. My only apology for thus intruding on your notice is, that I cannot obtain such information here. And as the matter is to be finally settled in Washington, I have thought better to make application at head-quarters from the beginning. If in the multiplicity of your duties, which I know you must have on hand, you can find time to inform me as to the necessary qualifications for admission, and if our congressional district is unrepresented there or not, or at least when there will be a vacancy, you will confer a great favor on me.

I am desirous of going to West Point, and I think my age and tastes would be in accordance with its requirements. But I must forbear on that point for the present. I am now in attendance at the McNeely Normal School in Hopedale, and could obtain from the principal, if necessary, testimonials of moral character. I would also say that I have the consent of my parents in the course which I have in view. Wishing to hear from you as soon as convenient,

I remain,
Yours respectfully,
G. A. CUSTER.

It will be seen from this letter that Custer had at the time ceased teaching for awhile, to further perfect his education. The handwriting is very strongly contrasted with that of his later years, which is rather light and pointed, resembling a lady's hand in many respects. In the Bingham letter it is that of a particularly careful schoolboy of the old time, with down-strokes of portentous weight and blackness, with fine hair lines for upstrokes. The letter brought forth a reply from Bingham, in which the requisite information was given, and it appeared that others were after the place. In answer to this, Custer wrote again. He would not be denied, if persistency would effect his purpose. There was another young man after the place, but he wrote as follows:

McNEELY NORMAL SCHOOL, Thursday, June 11, 1856.
HON. JOHN A. BINGHAM.

DEAR SIR—Yours of the fourth was duly received and I feel myself compelled to write again to express my sincere thanks for

your prompt attention, explicit information as to qualifications, etc.
I will also add that in all the points specified I would come under
the requirements set forth in your communication, being about seventeen years of age, above the medium height and of remarkably
strong constitution and vigorous frame. If that young man from
Jeff. County of whom you spoke does not push the matter, or if
you hear of any other vacancy, I should be glad to hear from you.

Yours with great respect,

G. A. CUSTER.

Nothing came of it that year, however. The young man
from Jefferson County got the place, but there was still time
during the next year. That summer Mr. Bingham came home
at the close of the session of Congress, and young Custer went
to see him. The result of the interview was that Bingham,
pleased with the frank face of the boy, his modest determination,
and something in his looks that told that he would yet be a
credit to his nominator, promised that he would give him the
next year's vacancy, and Custer went home happy.

The rest of the year 1856 was passed by him partly at the
Normal School, partly teaching, partly on his father's farm.
At last came the eventful day when he received his commission, and was ordered to report at West Point. The die was
cast. He had longed to be a soldier. From henceforth to the
day of his death he was a soldier to the core.

This period of Custer's life may be regarded as that of his
first awakening to the consciousness of his own powers and of
the deficiencies of his early education. One evidence of this is
the fact of his attendance at the Normal school and his selection
of teaching for an occupation. He had already received more
than enough education to fit him for such a life as his father or
any of his relatives led, and the fact of his voluntarily entering the
Normal school to avail himself of its further advantages shows
that he was already looking forward to a change in his prospects
before he applied to Mr. Bingham. The latter had told him of all
the difficulties besetting an applicant for a cadetship, and espe-

cially of the preliminary examination, and Custer occupied all
the rest of the year in fitting himself therefor. The result was
that, when he went to West Point, he had already mastered as
much mathematics as any one of the one year cadets, and was
so far ahead of his class that he found all his subsequent studies
as easy as he had his earlier labors at Stebbins' Academy. Of
the other troubles of a cadet, lessons apart, he was now to gain
his first experience. He found his troubles there, much the
same as at school, in the irksomeness of discipline, not the severity of study. Such as he was, a headlong, impulsive, generous lad, full of life and spirits he entered West Point. Would
there were hundreds more to-day there, like him.

CHAPTER II.

PLEBE CUSTER.

A TALL, slender lad of seventeen, with frank, handsome face and fair hair, landed on the wharf at West Point, in the summer of 1857. A certain free, careless air told of the Western man, so different in his surroundings and bearing from the town-bred citizen of the East. It was our young hero, fresh from the independent merry life of the West, and plunged all alone into the peculiar life of West Point—a *Plebe*, with all his sorrows to come.

A great change for the careless young fellow, overflowing with the fun and frolic that comes of magnificent physical organization and keen intellect. There is something in the atmosphere of Western life that seems to rebel against rules and restrictions and everything narrow. It goes straight to its purpose, whatever it be, by direct common sense methods, original in their simplicity, but appears awkward and rough when contrasted with Eastern polish. With all his differences of race and education, come from the most perfectly republican part of the Union, young Custer was dropped into the midst of one of the most absolute despotisms on earth, the Military Academy at West Point. What the change is, for a young fellow fresh from home life, and especially from country home life, it is difficult to picture, without a knowledge of that curious microcosm, "the Point."

There is something in the Military Academy so totally different from the usual life of America, that it has fixed a great gulf between West Pointers and the outside world, none the less real because impalpable. It shows itself in the reception

2

accorded to the "Plebe" when he first enters the Academy, so different from that accorded to a Freshman at college, the nearest person to a Plebe in condition. The poor Plebe comes from the world of freedom, and enters another world, where implicit obedience is the unflinching rule. Instantly, every one seems to set on him to make his life miserable. From time immemorial it seems to have been the tradition at the Academy, that every new-comer should be made to suffer all the discomforts possible, during his first months, without a possibility of escape. His ordinary treatment has been embalmed in some very truthful, though undeniably doggerel verses, in the "West Point Scrap Book," entitled "West Point Life." The composition from which they are taken was written for the Dialectic Society of West Point in 1859, and therefore may be said to portray very accurately the state of society at the "Point," when Custer was a cadet. The minstrel, describing the Plebe, breaks out:

When landed at the Point, you ask a man where you report,
And ten to one you get from him a withering retort.
He'll say, "Subordination, Plebe's, of discipline the root;
When you address an old Cadet, forget not to salute."
He sends you to a room and says, "Report and then come back."
You enter and discover there only the old boot-black.
You wander like Telemachus; at last you find the place
And see the dread INSTRUCTOR—yes, and meet him face to face.
He shouts out, "Stand attention, sir! hands close upon your pants,
And stand erect. Hold up your head! There—steady! don't advance;
Turn out your toes still further, look straight toward the front,
Draw in your chin! Throw out your chest! Now steady! Don't you grunt."
Says the Instructor "Where's my pen? this old one doesn't suit me."
"There it is, sir." "You hold your tongue! How dare you talk on duty?
I'm not surprised to see you quail and flutter like a partridge,
But soldiers' mouths must only open when they tear a cartridge."
He wants to know all things you've brought, your clothes of every kind;
(You think the gentleman's endowed with an enquiring mind)
You get a broom, some matches, and a bed made up of patches,
Though little do you think such schools could ever have their matches.
A comforter you also get, a thing that most you need,
A comforter! It's one of Job's, a sorry one indeed!

" On your return, report yourself," they earnestly exhort you.
Report *yourself ! ! !* when twenty men are eager to report you !
You're now assigned to quarters—there deposit bed and broom,
And though in want of shelter, wish for you there was no room.
Are these the luxuries on which our Senators agree ?
You do not fancy this " hot-bed of aristocracy."
The drill drum beats, so does your heart, and down the stairs you scud,
You slip before you reach the ranks, fall full length in the mud ;
How strange you think it when next night reported you have been,
In spite of all your efforts, for neglecting to " fall in."

.   .   .   .

When reading in your room, absorbed in prison discipline,
You suddenly hear some one knock ; jump up, and cry " Come in !"
You find the dread INSTRUCTOR already in the door,
He says " Did you give that command to your SUPERIOR ? "
You ask to be forgiven, say you'll never do't no more,
You didn't yet know all the rules and articles of war.
Next day they march you into camp.   How pretty it does look !
That you may fare the better, you have brought a cookery book.
You get in camp, an old cadet cries, " Come put up this tent."
And with the aid he renders you, you're very well content.
You thank him, take possession ; when you find that all is done,
He coolly tells you " Plebe, that's mine; go, get another one.
What you have done is only *play ;* Plebes always make mistakes."
Foul play you think it is, when you have put down all the *stakes,*
You possibly are six feet high ; some officer you dread
Arrests you at the break of day for lying *long* in bed.

.   .   .   .

July the Fourth at last arrives ; you think it rather hard,
When on this day of liberty, the Plebes must go on guard.
You go on post, the night arrives, you scarcely are alive,
But still a lonely watch you keep, way down on " No. 5."
At first you like the lonely post, the path's so nicely levelled,
But soon you share the fate of ham—that is, you're nicely " devilled "
Bodies vast of men approach, and sound their rude alarms—
From divers punches you receive, you find they all have arms—
Baggage wagons, ropes, and ghosts, upon your post appear—
Teeth begin to chatter—though, of course, it's not through **fear,**
A spirit white you seize upon; and hold it on your post,
Until the corporal arrives, when you give up the ghost.
When in a wheel-barrow you fall, that's moving up behind,
To rapidly desert your post, you're forcibly *inclined.*

Then you swear that you'll resign, the climate is too damp,
But once within the tented field, you find you can't decamp.
Resolving then to be content, there's no more hesitation,
You find more satisfaction in this kind of resignation.
Spartan like, you stay until encampment has an end,
And when that time is closing up, your times begin to mend.

The woes of the poor Plebe on first joining, as recited in
the above pathetic ballad, are by no means over-strained. An
old graduate says of the new comers very feelingly : " We can
not but feel an involuntary pity for the new cadet who is just
landing at the old wharf, where a sentinel is waiting to conduct
him to the adjutant's office, there to record his entrance on—
he knows not what small and great tribulations.

" The poor fellow has just left the endearments of home, and
by a rapid transition has become a stranger among the mighty
hills. But worst of all, instead of receiving kindly hospitality,
he becomes, for a time, one of an inferior caste, toward whom,
too often, the finger of derision is pointed, and over whom the
Fourth Class drill-master flourishes, with too snobbish zeal, his
new-born authority. Then too, to be called a " conditional
thing," a " thing " and a " plebe " in slow promotion ; to be
crowded five in a room, with the floor and a blanket for a bed ;
to be drummed up, drummed to meals, and drummed to bed, all
with arithmetic for chief diversion ; this is indeed a severe ordeal
for a young man who is not blessed with good nature and good
sense ; but with these excellent endowments, it soon and smoothly
glides on into a harmless memory. People are found who contend that West Point is a hot-bed of aristocracy, where caste and
titles rule. It would be pleasing to exhibit to such an one, the
ununiformed new class, presenting a line of about one hundred
young men of all types, at least in externals. Side by side are
seen the flabby Kentucky jeans, and the substantial homespun,
the ancient long-tailed, high-collared coat of the farmer's boy,
and the exquisite fit of the fashionable New York tailor. We
have known two presidents' sons, two protegés of General Jackson, several sons of secretaries, and other high functionaries,

found deficient, for the simple reason that they *were* deficient. Before us lies a little volume, by a Vermont farmer's son, who successfully competed for the headship of his class, with a talented son of Henry Clay."

Into the midst of West Point, dropped young Custer. As far as temperament went, he was just the one to get on among his comrades and be happy; and we find accordingly, that he was soon a general favorite. The hardships of Plebe life passed over him lightly. He had the advantage of being a tall strong young fellow, not easily brow-beaten, or physically oppressed, and his good-nature and jolly ways saved him from the more annoying kinds of small persecution. The first week's squad drills and the preliminary examination being safely passed, young George Custer at last received his full appointment, was permitted to don the uniform, and became a full-fledged cadet. The happy day arrived when he, with the other Plebes, shed the badges of their servitude, and all the black coats vanished from the cadet battalion. Then, at the close of June, the barracks were abandoned; and Cadet Custer, along with his comrades, marched out for the annual encampment. This takes place every year at the same time after graduation. The first class of 1857 was examined and graduated while the Plebes were joining, the second class became the first, the fourth became the third, and went on furlough for the summer; and the " June Plebes " blossomed out into the fourth class. Then, at dress parade, the order was read out to go into camp, the barracks being vacated. The young cadets turned into May-day carmen, without any carts. Not even a wheelbarrow was to be obtained. Mattresses, tables, chairs, trunks, every article had to be cleared out, the furniture placed in the empty recitation rooms, leaving only iron bedsteads in the dormitories, which were to be thoroughly cleaned by the workmen. The camp ground on the northeast of the plain was laid out, and the tents all pitched before breakfast; then at the exact hour indicated in the order, the companies formed on the parade ground, and marched out to the camp, with band playing.

The cadets at West Point are divided into four companies. During the June examinations, the Plebes, being an additional class, had been of course stinted for space in the barracks, but in camp there was plenty of room. There were eight rows of tents, two opening on each street, company officers in a row at the end of the streets of their companies, commandant's marquee opposite the centre of the camp, which was the same as that of a small battalion of infantry. The guard tents, six in number, were at the other end of the streets, and there were six sentries on duty round the camp. Each walked his beat two hours, being then relieved for four hours, after which he went on again, his tour of duty being six hours out of twenty-four, the guard having three " reliefs," or eighteen cadets, besides a corporal to each relief, a sergeant, and an officer of the guard.

During the encampment, the duties of the cadets were wholly military. It was a relief from the long course of hard mathematical studies which they had pursued when in barracks, served to maintain their health, and especially to accustom them to the daily routine of soldier's life. During the time the camp lasted, from the end of June to the end of August, the drills were constant and unintermitting in infantry evolutions, with artillery drill for the upper classes. The result was a most wonderful perfection of mechanical movement, from which even the newly joined Plebes were not exempt, the nearest approach to which is to-day seen in the street parades and drills, on grand occasions, of the celebrated New York Seventh Regiment, when put on its mettle. During the summer encampment, the vicinity of West Point is always crowded with visitors, and as the members of the upper classes are allowed considerable liberty at this time, it becomes to them a season of comparative enjoyment.

At last came the close of August. The barracks were awaiting their occupants, and the time of serious work for the Fourth Class had come. On the 29th the cadets carried off their blankets and clothing to the rooms soon to be occupied for the fall, leaving in camp only their muskets and full dress uniforms. The order for breaking camp had been read on dress parade the previous evening, and at the fixed hour the drums were heard beating "the general," the signal to pack up and be off. Then came one of the most imposing sights in military life, and one which always impresses the civilian spectator with a certain feeling of desolation when it is over.

Before us stands the populous little town, that for two months has been the scene of such picturesque activity, with all the "pride, pomp and circumstance of glorious war." The cadets fly to their tents at the beating of the "general," and await three taps of the drum amid breathless silence. " *Tap !* " comes the first, and the whole camp is alive in a moment, the men flinging themselves on the stakes, which are pulled up, leaving the tents supported only by the four corners. Then comes another breathless hush, every one waiting. " *Tap !* " comes the second signal, and up come the corner pegs, while the canvas is swept into the centre, and a man stands at each pole, all the tents still up, and hiding the view. Another hush, and then—

" *Tap !* "

In a moment, ere the sound has time to die away, down goes every tent with a single clap, and the lately populous town has vanished, leaving behind it nothing but a bare plain, while the men, like a swarm of bees, fling themselves on the prostrate tents, withdraw the poles, and roll up the canvas in long rolls, which are piled in heaps for the quartermaster's people to take away. Then comes the "Assembly," and the companies take their stacked arms, while the battalion is formed and marched to the barracks.

Cadet Custer had seen his first camp, and it was over.

This West Point camp is one of the very best features of

academic life. It serves as a wholesome relaxation to the cadets, who are necessarily working at books all the rest of the year; and it tends to remind them of what they might otherwise easily forget, that they are soldiers, not school-boys. The influence of academic life at other times, on both officers and students, is very injurious to breadth of mind. To the officers it is indescribably narrowing. They generally become, after a long residence at the "Point" more like school-masters than soldiers, fond of espionage, with sympathies and tastes confined to the small circle of a class-room, as contracted in their views of life as so many school-teachers, besides being strongly inclined to petty tyranny. The camp comes to remind them that there is a whole world outside of West Point, and that the end of the academic course is to make officers, not pedants.

To the incoming cadets it serves as a good introduction to what follows, and gives them courage to attack their winter studies, which commence as soon as the encampment is over. So it was now with Cadet Custer. His work was beginning.

CHAPTER III.

CADET CUSTER.

THE Fourth Class, to which Cadet Custer belonged, was now safely ensconced in the barracks, and entering on the unvarying routine of cadet life. What that routine is, has been pictured by more than one old graduate, in that same storehouse of information from which we have already quoted, and it will serve, in addition to the personal reminiscences of his classmates, to complete the picture of Cadet Custer's life at West Point.

Let us commence at early dawn, when the faint grey light first steals over the heavens. The rounded tops of the encircling mountains are cut clearly against the bright sky, old Cro'nest brooding protectingly over the little settlement. The sentry by the gate looks northward over the plain, and hears through the silence the distant thunder of paddles, as the Albany night boat comes sweeping down the river on her way to the city below. There is a gay twittering of birds, growing louder and louder, from the woods that clothe the mountains from base to summit. The river in the distance gleams white in the dawn, and the lights of the steamer, not yet extinguished, glide slowly along. The edge of the plateau cuts the view, and it would hardly seem possible that the same river sweeps almost beneath our feet, black and glistening in little eddies, surrounded by the bold Highlands that form the bay at West Point. Nestled at the foot of those Highlands, on the opposite side of the river, are the white cottages of Cold Spring, and the distant murmur of Buttermilk Falls can be heard through the stillness. Now the faint white light of dawn grows stronger, and a crimson flush is on the east, while the little floating clouds overhead are speckled with gold and rose color. Louder grows the sweet clamor of the birds in the early morning, and the barking of dogs from the village below announces the increasing stir of life. Anon the crimson flushes into scarlet, the scarlet flames into gold, and a bright shaft of light bathes the top of old Cro'nest and comes creeping down the mountain side.

Boom ! ! !

A bright flash and a volume of snow white smoke, as the morning gun awakens the echoes. The smoke goes drifting away on the breeze towards the water, and the sharp boom of the gun reverberates from hill to hill all round the bay, ending in a dull grumble far up the river. Simultaneously, the long roll of the drum-corps, mingled with the sweet notes of the fifes, softened by the distance into a strain of perfect sweetness, comes gaily out on the morning air, as the drummers beat the long reveillé.

Cadet Custer and his room-mate are sleeping the sound sleep of the tired plebe, in their little room in the North Barrack, when the loud boom of the gun comes through the open window. Up they spring, for the two months of camp life have already inured both to the soldier's habit of coming broad awake in a moment. No rubbing of eyes, stretching or yawning. Outside, the reveillé is beating, and the fifes are piping sweetly forth the first tune of the three that constitute the morning call. Each tune lasts about two minutes, and at the end of six minutes, every cadet knows that the orderly sergeant will be standing on the company parade ground, book in hand, ready to call the roll. Into their clothes as hastily as possible, little time for toilet comforts, and down the barrack staircase send Custer and Parker. As the rollicking notes of the last quickstep are in full progress, they dart to their places, and a moment later reveillé ceases. There are the four companies, each on its own ground, the stiff orderly sergeant in front, book in hand, the cadet captain behind him, while the officer of the day, arms folded, solemnly surveys the scene from his distant post. The cadets are standing at "parade rest," the weight resting on the right leg, hands crossed in front.

Hardly has the last strain of the fife, the final roll of the drum died away, when we hear the sharp voices of the First Class men, who act as sergeants, all together, " Attention, company ! "

In an instant every cadet has stiffened into a statue, in "position of a soldier," eyes staring straight to the front, with that vacant glare which marks the modern soldier in ranks. Out come the books, and each sergeant rattles off the names of his men in alphabetical order, having the list by heart. He knows every voice in his company, and is as sharp as a needle. Not a late man can slink into his place but the sergeant notices him, and checks a mark against him in that inexorable roll-book. If a head turns, or a whisper mars the perfect stillness, the sergeant can pick out the guilty one in a moment; even the shelter of the rear rank is no protection for the offender, for the Second and Third Class sergeants and corporals are ready to report *him*, in terror lest that lynx-eyed sergeant should report *them*, for neglect of duty. The roll call is rattled off in a minute and a half, and the sergeant faces around, stiff as a stake, salutes, and says to the captain, " Sir, all are present or accounted for," or " Sir, so many absent." The young captain touches his hat, and proceeds forthwith to the cadet adjutant, where the same formality of report takes place for each company, the adjutant standing, book in hand, to receive the reports. Finally, the adjutant in his turn proceeds to the officer of the day, and reports the result of the whole battalion roll call to that mighty official, whose place it is to report the absentees at the end of his tour of duty. The ser geants then warn the cadets detailed for guard on that day, and ranks are broken. Now Cadets Custer and Parker are to be seen hastening to their little barrack room, having time to wash and comb, and clean up their room. Reveillé, during summer, is at five, and by half past five, every room must be in perfect order, for the captain and lieutenants of each company come round for morning inspection.

From this time till seven o'clock the two cadets are hard at work at their books, studying for the morning recitations. At half past six they can hear the drummers beating the " sick call," when all the sick, lame and lazy troop to the surgeon, to be excused from duty or dosed as the case may be. Custer and Parker are healthy young fellows and the life of the Point leaves little excuse for sickness. Besides, both are yet Plebes, and have not learned so thoroughly as they will some day, how to play " old soldier." Very amusing stories are told of the efforts of older cadets, to appear terribly sick all of a sudden, when the day's lessons promise to be uncommonly hard. The Academy surgeon is no exception to army medical officers in time of peace ; half of his time is wasted in detecting fraudulent cases of sickness, feigned to evade duty. One very ingenious trick by which a surgeon was completely deceived, was once played by a cadet who was out all night, and whose pulse was consequently feverish and irregular. He put a piece of chalk in his mouth which he chewed, and when his turn came to go to the doctor, complained of having a sunstroke. The pulse indicated not much the matter, and the doctor was about to put him off with a dose, when his forlorn aspect induced the functionary to ask to see his tongue. Its white and furry aspect alarmed the doctor, who pronounced it a clear case of high fever, and Cadet Foxey was excused from duty.

These and similar mean tricks were entirely uncongenial to the frank nature of Custer. His pranks at the Academy were those of a high-spirited boy anxious to escape from restraint, but he was always ready to take the consequences. The sick call this morning passes away, and he and Parker are hard at work on geometry and algebra, tactics and French, fortification and gunnery, till the welcome notes of " Peas upon the Trencher" echo through the quadrangle, calling to breakfast. Now another roll call, and the companies are marched to the mess hall; from thence till eight o'clock there is leisure to study or look around one and watch guard mount. At eight, old Rentz, the Academy bugler for thirty years, calls the cadets to quarters, and now, for five mortal hours, the routine of study and recitation is unvarying. Now another roll call. The classes that recite are marched to the recitation rooms by the section marchers, and reported to the Instructor. The first half of the corps works till half past nine, when the second half relieves them, while the fencing classes are called up.

At one o'clock dinner call is beaten : and for this and re-creation an hour is allowed. From two till four more reci-tations, after which afternoon drill for an hour and a half, then liberty till sunset.

Sunset is the signal for dress parade of the battalion, when there are more roll calls, and retreat is beaten by the drum corps, while the band plays, and everything puts on its most imposing and martial aspect. As the band paces up and down the front of the motionless line of cadets, the setting sun gleam-ing on the fixed bayonets, officers at parade rest, the solitary figure of the commandant standing with folded arms in front of the centre, the scene attracts multitudes of spectators, and the effect on the imagination is romantic and warlike in the highest degree. The band wheels into its place, the gorgeous drum major flings up his staff, and as the melancholy notes of "retreat" echo on the evening air they are interrupted by the sudden boom of the evening gun. Down comes the great standard, fluttering on its way from the summit of the lofty flagstaff. As the last roll of "retreat" ceases, the line springs into sudden life at the sharp voice of the adjutant, and the brief formality of dress parade proceeds on its way. A few moments later, the companies are marching away to the sweet strains of the famous West Point band, and the day's work is over. Now comes supper and half an hour's time for recrea-tion, when the bugle is heard once more, calling "to quarters;" Every cadet must be in his room and studying, or at least quiet, and orderly, till tattoo at half past nine, when the beds are spread.

At ten o'clock the quadrangle is nearly silent, the subdued murmur of conversation dying away, the light in the different rooms twinkling like stars.

Tap !

A couple of drummers proceed slowly along round the barracks, and at every hundred steps or so, each gives a single tap. As if by magic, the twinkling lights disappear, and the Academy is silent as the grave, buried in sleep.

The duties of the guards during barrack time are much less onerous than when in camp. They walk post only at meal times, during drills, at dress parade, and during evening study hours. Each sentinel is responsible for the rooms on his post, which he is required to inspect. He must report all absentees, as well as suppress all noise and disturbances. Of course this part of his duty is the most onerous and delicate he can have during the day, as the strict restraints of discipline, irksome at any time to young men, are doubly so when night and darkness give them an opportunity to escape surveillance. This is the time when cadets fall into most of their scrapes, by getting out of quarters, either during study hours, or more commonly after taps. In the case of Cadets Custer and Parker, these escapades and frolics were born of that irrepressible spirit of fun so common in the West, for Parker was a Missourian. There seems to be something peculiarly enticing to a high-spirited cadet in the idea of getting out of bounds, and when to that is added the attractions of "Benny Havens," the temptations to the bold spirits were much greater than the cadets could resist.

Benny Havens has been for many years a famous character at the Point. Long before the Mexican War he was established within the lines, and under the guise of an honest seller of coffee and cakes, was wont to administer surreptitious egg-flip, when no officers were round, to the thirsty cadets. Expelled for this cause, he established himself about a mile from the Point, in a little cabin under a cliff, which has ever since been the rendezvous of innumerable pilgrims from the barracks. The attractions of Benny Havens' cabin did not seem, then nor now, to lie so much in the fact of his selling liquor. In the case of young Custer, who very seldom, except as hereinafter referred to, used spirits or tobacco, this could have been no temptation. But Benny has been so long at the Point, and seen so many generations of cadets, that he has become a perfect storehouse of interesting legends, and these constitute the charm which draws so many to his little cabin from far away.

Grey-headed general officers, distinguished in active service, come to-day to the Point, to revisit the scenes of their youth, and always pay a visit to Benny, and the old man knows them all, and can tell stories of the days when they were cadets. No wonder the cadets of all time have been fond of slipping out of quarters after taps, to visit Benny, to sit around his fire, to listen to stories of the day when Grant, Sherman, and Thomas were wild boys at the Point, to dream as they listen of the days when they perhaps may rival the fame of those great leaders. Meantime, they eat Benny's buckwheat cakes, for which he is famous, and drink his old wine, while at intervals they join in the time-honored song of " Benny Havens, oh ! " This is one of the regular institutions at Benny's. The song was written by Lieutenant O'Brien, of the 8th Infantry, assisted by others, many years ago, and set to the tune of " Wearing of the Green." When O'Brien afterward died in Florida, stanzas were added to commemorate his death. A very few verses will give an idea of the song, which is quite long. Imagine a group of young cadets, who have stolen away after taps, gathered in Benny's little parlor, awaiting the coming of the celebrated buckwheats. One stands up and cries:

" Come, fellows, fill your glasses and—
(*All join in.*)
Stand up in a row.
For sentimental drinking, we're going for to go,

In the army there's sobriety, promotion's very slow,
So we'll cheer our hearts with choruses at Benny Havens, oh !
Benny Havens, oh ! oh ! Benny Havens, oh !
We'll sing our reminiscences of Benny Havens, oh ! "

Then the song proceeds to describe the features of army life in various verses, till the chief breaks out rapturously :—

" To the ladies of our army, our cups shall ever flow,
Companions of our exile, and our shield against all woe,
May they see their husbands generals, with double pay also,
And join us in our choruses at Benny Havens, oh !
                                    Benny Havens, oh ! etc.

May the army be augmented, promotion be less slow,
May our country in her hour of need, be ready for the foe,
May we find a soldier's resting place beneath a soldier's blow,
With space enough beside our graves for Benny Havens, oh !
                                    Benny Havens, oh ! etc."

Year by year, as new generations of cadets have passed through the Academy, and former graduates attain fame, their names are embalmed in successive verses. In Custer's day the only heroes were Taylor and Scott, for the regular army, that within a few years was to produce so many distinguished names, was then sunk in the rust of peace, with little chance of distinction before it. It seems to us now, looking back at that indefinite period " before the war," as if a whole century had passed since then. The state of the army, its names and traditions, its very dress and appearance, are so different now, that in a few years all memory of that old army will have faded.

Quietly glided away the days and nights at West Point, in the monotonous round of duties that came to Cadet Custer and his room-mate, while in the fourth class; and the dreaded January examination came, when, if not successful, the Plebe would be " found deficient," and sent back to civil life. It was safely passed, however, and the spring wore on, bringing nearer and nearer the memorable June day that opened to Cadet Custer "third class encampment," when he ceased to be a Plebe, and became at one bound an "old cadet," no longer on probation, but only liable to be put back a class if he failed in studies.

Now came the real pleasures of camp, when visitors were present in crowds, when the evening balls were crowded with cadets on leave, when the new Plebes were to be drilled, and the old torments inflicted on a new generation. To join in these, young Custer was too good-natured and jovial, but at the balls he was in his element. His remarkably handsome face and figure were wonderfully effective among the ladies, as they continued to be all his life, and attracted no little of the envy of his brother cadets. In those days, before the heavy blonde moustache had come to lend an air of sternness to his features, his bright locks gave him a girlish appearance, which, coupled with the remarkable fact of his strictly temperate habits, procured him the nick-name of "Fanny." Boys always have good names for each other, indicative of character or personal appearance, and the name "Fanny" stuck to Custer through his academic life and long after, when he met his former classmates as enemies in the field. "That's just like Fanny," said one of them, when he received a note from Custer, left at a farm house, informing him politely that he had just whipped such an one (a former classmate) handsomely, and was coming next day to repeat the operation on the recipient of the letter.

Camp wore its way out, and the Third Class went into barracks once again for the same routine, the studies being advanced and much more severe than before, the principal recreation being mounted drill in the riding hall. Here it was that Cadet Custer developed that perfection in horsemanship which distinguished him afterward, with the more ease as every Western boy knows something of riding early in life. To those who do not, the riding school of West Point is a hard one, but very effective. The Third Class men take up riding

3

in November, and are exercised by platoons of about twenty at a time, the same old troop horses being used from year to year, in the riding hall. The floor is strewn with tanbark several inches in depth, so that there is no danger to life or limb in a fall, and the animals are caparisoned in full army rig at the close of the course. Usually the class commences on blankets alone, without stirrups, and when this is the case the lesson is comparatively easy ; but sometimes the riding master orders on saddles, and gives the command to the cadets " Cross-Stirrups ! " Those who have ever tried to ride in a large McClellan saddle without stirrups, on a hard trotting horse, can imagine the torments of the poor boys on strange animals. In the army a man gets used to his own steed and inured to his paces, but where rider and horse are frequently changed, as at West Point, it is a very different thing. The constant alterations spoil the horses' tempers, and most of them get to be hard-mouthed, unruly brutes, full of bad tricks, and always on the watch for a chance to unseat a rider.

Put a lot of green riders on such animals, and make them cross stirrups, then let the platoon start at a walk, and all is well, but when the command is given " Trot—March ! " what a jolting and pounding ensues, the unlucky cadets trying to hold on with knees and thighs to a saddle flap that seems as slippery as glass ! And yet two-thirds of the practice in the riding hall is done at the same trot, and the unfeeling riding master sits on his horse in the centre, cool as a cucumber. *His* stirrups are not crossed, you may be sure, or he could not smile so sweetly over the miseries of the poor pupils, bumping about. One of the late cadets—a young fellow, too, promoted from the ranks of the army during the war, and who had served in battle with the volunteer cavalry before he came to West Point, says : " It is one of the most cruel things that can be thought of, to be obliged to ride without stirrups for the first time on such perfect devils as some of these horses are. There were upwards of thirty in my class who were thrown, though only three or four of them were injured—none severely. One had his foot stepped on in a playful manner by one of the incarnate fiends, mashing his big toe to a jelly; but that was not of much consequence, as it has now recovered. Many were severely bruised, but in ninety-nine cases out of a hundred it is impossible for a cadet to be hurt badly by being thrown in the riding hall. The only way is to ride right through and take the pounding and bruises, and get used to it. The remedy is a rough one, but the only one effectual."

Through all the troubles of the riding hall passed Cadet Custer, as blithe and debonair as ever. His length of limb gave him great advantage, his rough Western life still more. A tall wiry built man has greater ease in riding than a shorter aspirant; and it was not long before "Fanny" was known as one of the best riders at the Point, emulating the fame that belonged in by-gone times to Cadet Grant, whose famous leap on "Old York" is traditional to this day.

The winter passed away and another spring, and then the airs of June were felt once more, blowing over "Second Class Camp" and—blessed news—furlough to see home for the first time in two years.

Furlough lasts till the Second Class goes to work again in barracks, and there is no need to say how it was enjoyed by Cadet Custer at his home, nor how many of his buttons he exchanged for locks of hair and vows of affection. In this he was not peculiar. All cadets have done it from time immemorial, and Cadet Custer, nearly twenty, handsome as Apollo, was by no means behind the fashion. How he enjoyed his furlough, how he hated to go back, how his work during the winter seemed duller and harder than ever, all these things are understood. The daily routine of his further life was a repetition of the past.

But the time was coming, as Custer approached First Class and graduation, when a change passed over the spirit of West Point, such as it had never seen before and is never likely to see again. This it was which rendered the experiences of

Custer's classmates unique in the annals of the Academy, and from henceforth it is fitting that Custer himself should take up the story, as he has done in the opening chapters of his War Memoirs, wherein he rapidly summarizes his Academic career, in the following fashion :

The first official notification received by me of my appointment to the Military Academy bore the signature of Jefferson Davis, then Secretary of War in the cabinet of President James Buchanan. Colonel Richard Delafield, one of the ablest and most accomplished officers of the Engineer Corps, occupied the position of superintendent of the Academy, and Lieutenant-Colonel William J. Hardee, of the cavalry, afterward lieutenant-general in the Confederate army, was the commandant of the Corps of Cadets.

Among the noticeable feature of cadet life as then impressed upon me, and still present in my memory, were the sectional lines voluntarily established by the cadets themselves ; at first barely distinguishable, but in the later years immediately preceding the war as clearly defined and strongly drawn as were the lines separating the extremes of the various sections in the national Congress. Nor was this fact a strange or remarkable one. As each Congressional district and territory of the United States had a representative in Congress, so each had its representatives at the Military Academy.

In looking back over the few months and years passed at West Point immediately preceding the war, some strange incidents recur to my mind. When the various State conventions were called by the different States of the South with a view to the adoption of the ordinance of secession, it became only a question of time as to the attempted withdrawal of the seceding States. And while there were those representing both sections in Congress who professed to believe that war would not necessarily or probably follow, this opinion was not shared in even by persons as young and inexperienced as the cadets. War was anticipated by them at that time, and discussed and looked forward to as an event of the future, with as much certainty as if speaking of an approaching season. The cadets from the South were in constant receipt of letters from their friends at home, keeping them fully advised of the real situation and promising them suitable positions in the military force yet to be organized to defend the ordinance of secession. All this was a topic of daily if not hourly conversation. Particularly was this true when we assembled together at meal-time, when, grouped in squads of half-a-dozen or more, each usually found himself in the midst of his personal friends.

I remember a conversation held at the table at which I sat during the winter of '60–'61. I was seated next to Cadet P. M. B. Young, a gallant young fellow from Georgia, a classmate of mine, then and since the war an intimate and valued friend—a major-general in the Confederate forces during the war and a member of Congress from his native State at a later date. The approaching war was as usual the subject of conversation in which all participated, and in the freest and most friendly manner; the lads from the North discoursing earnestly upon the power and rectitude of the National Government, the impulsive Southron holding up pictures of invaded rights and future independence. Finally, in a half jocular, half earnest manner, Young turned to me and delivered himself as follows: " Custer, my boy, we're going to have war. It's no use talking; I see it coming. All the Crittenden compromises that can be patched up won't avert it. Now let me prophesy what will happen to you and me. You will go home, and your abolition Governor will probably make you colonel of a cavalry regiment. 1 will go down to Georgia, and ask Governor Brown to give me a cavalry regiment. And who knows but we may move against each other during the war. You will probably get the advantage of us in the first few engagements, as your side will be rich and powerful, while we will be poor and weak. Your regiment will be armed with the best of weapons, the sharpest of sabres; mine will have only shot-guns and scythe blades; but for all that we'll get the best of the fight in the end, because we will fight for a principle, a cause, while you will fight only to perpetuate the abuse of power." Lightly as we both regarded this boyish prediction, it was destined to be fulfilled in a remarkable degree. Early in the war I did apply, not to the abolition Governor of my native State, but to that of Michigan, for a cavalry regiment. I was refused, but afterward obtained the regiment I desired as a part of my command. Young was chosen to lead one of the Georgia cavalry regiments. Both of us rose to higher commands, and confronted each other on the battle-field.

On December 20, 1860, South Carolina formally led the way by adopting the ordinance of secession ; an example which was followed within the next few weeks by Mississippi, Alabama, Florida, Georgia, Louisiana, and Texas, in the order named. As soon as it became evident that these States were determined to attempt secession, the cadets appointed therefrom, imitating the action of their Senators and representatives in Congress, and influenced by the appeals of friends at home, tendered their resignations, eager to return to their homes and take part in the organization of the volunteer forces which the increasing difficulties and dangers of the situation rendered necessary. Besides, as the Confederate Congress was called to meet for the first time at Montgomery, Alabama, February 6, 1861, and would undoubtedly authorize the appointment of a large number of officers in the formation of the Confederate armies, it was important that applicants for positions of this kind should be on the ground to properly present their claims.

One by one the places occupied by the cadets from the seceding States became vacant ; it cost many a bitter pang to disrupt the intimate relations existing between the hot-blooded Southron and his more phlegmatic schoolmate from the North. No school-girls could have been more demonstrative in their affectionate regard for each other than were some of the cadets about to separate for the last time, and under circumstances which made it painful to contemplate a future coming together. Those leaving for the South were impatient, enthusiastic, and hopeful. Visions filled their minds of a grand and glorious Confederacy, glittering with the pomp and pageantry which usually characterizes imperial power, and supported and surrounded by a mighty army, the officers of which would constitute a special aristocracy.

Their comrades from the North, whom they were leaving behind, were reserved almost to sullenness; were grave almost to stoicism. The representatives of the two sections had each resolved upon their course of action; and each in a manner characteristic of their widely different temperaments, as different as the latitudes from which they hailed. Among the first of the cadets to leave West Point and hasten to enroll themselves under the banner of the seceding States, were two of my classmates, Kelley and Ball, of Alabama. Kelley became prominent in the war, and was killed in battle. Ball also attained a high rank, and is now a prominent official in one of the most extensive business enterprises in this country. They took their departure from the Academy on Saturday. I remember the date the more readily as I was engaged in—to adopt the cadet term—"walking an extra," which consisted in performing the tiresome duties of a sentinel during the unemployed hours of Saturday, hours usually given to recreation. On this occasion I was pacing back and forth on my post, which for the time being extended along the path leading from the cadets' chapel toward the academic building, when I saw a party of from fifteen to twenty cadets emerge from the open space between the mess hall and the academic building, and direct their steps toward the steamboat landing below. That which particularly attracted my attention was the bearing aloft upon the shoulders of their comrades of my two classmates Ball and Kelley, as they were being carried in triumph from the doors of the Academy to the steamboat landing. Too far off to exchange verbal adieus, even if military discipline had permitted

it, they caught sight of me as, step by step, I reluctantly paid
the penalty of offended regulations, and raised their hats in
token of farewell, to which, first casting my eyes about to see
that no watchful superior was in view, I responded by bringing
my musket to a " present."

The comrades who escorted them were Southerners like
themselves, and only awaiting the formal action of their respect-
ive States on the adoption of the secession ordinance to follow
their example.   It was but a few weeks until there was scarcely
a cadet remaining at the Academy from the Southern States.
Many resigned from the border States without waiting to see
whether their State would follow in the attempt at secession or
not; some resigned who had been appointed from States which
never voted to leave the Union; while an insignificant few, who
had resolved to join the Confederate forces, but desired to
obtain their diplomas from the academic faculty, remained until
the date of their graduation.   Some remained until the declara-
tion and commencement of hostilities; then, allowing the
government to transport them to Washington, tendered their
resignations, and were dismissed for doing so in the face of the
enemy.   Happily the number that pursued this questionable
course did not exceed half a dozen.

At no point in the loyal States were the exciting events of
the spring of 1861 watched with more intense interest than at
West Point.   And after the departure of the Southern cadets,
the hearts of the people of no community, State, town, or village, beat with more patriotic impulse than did those of the
young cadets at West Point.   Casting aside all questions of
personal ambition or promotion; realizing only that the government which they had sworn to defend, the principles they
had been taught from childhood, were in danger, and threatened
by armed enemies, they would gladly have marched to battle as
private soldiers, rather than remain idle spectators in the great
conflict.

As the time for the inauguration of Mr. Lincoln approached,

rumors prevailed, and obtained wide belief, to the effect that a plot was on foot by which the inauguration of Mr. Lincoln was to be made the occasion on the part of the enemies of the government, of whom great numbers were known to be in Washington, for seizing or making away with the executive officers of the nation, and taking possession of the people's capital. Whether or not such a scheme was ever seriously contemplated, it was deemed prudent to provide against it. The available military resources of the government amounted to but little at that period. Lieutenant-General Scott, then Commander-in-Chief of the army, issued orders for the assembling at Washington of as large a military force as circumstances would permit. Under this order it became necessary to make a demand upon the regular military forces then employed at West Point. A battery of artillery was hastily organized from the war material kept at the Academy for the purpose of instruction to the cadets. The horses were supplied by taking those used by the cadets in their cavalry and artillery drills. The force thus organized hastened to Washington, where, under the command of Captain Griffin—afterward Major-General Griffin—it took part in the inaugural ceremonies. Then followed the firing upon Sumter, the intelligence of which waked the slumbering echoes of loyalty and patriotism in every home and hamlet throughout the North.

It is doubtful if the people of the North were ever, or will ever be again, so united in thought and impulse as when the attack on Sumter was flashed upon them. Opponents in politics became friends in patriotism ; all differences of opinion vanished or were laid aside, and a single purpose filled and animated the breast of the people as of one man—a purpose unflinching and unrestrained—to rush to the rescue of the government, to beat down its opposers, come from whence they may. In addition to sharing the common interest and anxiety of the public in the attack upon Sumter, the cadets felt a special concern, from the fact that among the little band of officers shut up in that fortress were two, Lieutenants Snyder and Hall, who had been our comrades as cadets only a few months before.

As already stated, the time of study and instruction at West Point at that period was five years, in the determination and fixing of which no one had exercised greater influence than Jefferson Davis—first as Secretary of War, afterward as United States Senator, and member of a special congressional committee to consider the question as to whether the course should extend to five years or only include four.

In the general demand in 1861, not only from the National Government, but from States, for competent and educated officers to instruct and command the new levies of troops then being raised, in response to the call of the President, to oppose the rebellion, it was decided by the authorities at Washington to abandon the five years' course of instruction at the Military Academy, and re-establish that of four years. The effect of this was to give to the service in that year, two classes of graduates for officers, instead of but one. By this change the class of which I was a member graduated, under the four years' system, in June, while the preceding class was graduated, under the five years' rule, only a couple of months in advance of us. The members of both classes, with but few exceptions, were at once ordered to Washington, where they were employed either in drilling raw volunteers, or serving on the staffs of general officers, engaged in organizing the new regiments into brigades and divisions. I was one of the exceptions referred to, and the causes which led me in a different direction may be worthy of mention.

My career as a cadet had but little to commend it to the study of those who came after me, unless as an example to be carefully avoided. The requirements of the academic regulations, a copy of which was placed in my hand the morning of my arrival at West Point, were not observed by me in such manner as at all times to commend me to the approval and good opinions of my instructors and superior officers. My offences against law and order were not great in enormity, but what they lacked in magnitude they made up in number. The forbidden locality of Benny Havens possessed stronger attractions than the study and demonstration of a problem in Euclid, or the prosy discussion of some abstract proposition of moral science. My class numbered, upon entering the Academy, about one hundred and twenty-five. Of this number, only thirty-four graduated, and of these thirty-three graduated above me. The resignation and departure of the Southern cadets took away from the Academy a few individuals who, had they remained, would probably have contested with me the debatable honor of bringing up the rear of the class.

We had passed our last examination as cadets, had exchanged barrack for camp life, and were awaiting the receipt of orders from Washington assigning us to the particular branches of the service for which we had been individually recommended by the academic faculty. The month of June had come, and we were full of impatience to hasten to the capital and join the forces preparing for the coming campaign. It is customary, or was then, to allow each cadet, prior to his graduation, to perform at least one tour of duty as an officer of the guard, instead of the ordinary duties of a private soldier on guard. I had not only had the usual experience in the latter capacity, extending over a period of four years, but in addition had been compelled, as punishment for violations of the academic regulations, to perform extra tours of guard duty on Saturdays—times which otherwise I should have been allowed for pleasure and recreation. If my memory serves me right, I devoted sixty-six Saturdays to this method of vindicating outraged military law, during my cadetship of four years. It so happened that it fell to my detail to perform the duties of officer of the guard in camp, at a time when the arrival of the order from Washington, officially transforming us from cadets to officers, was daily expected. I began my tour at the usual hour in the morning, and everything passed off satisfactorily in connection with the discharge of my new responsibilities, until, just at dusk, I heard a commotion near the guard tents. Upon hastening to the scene of the disturbance, which by the way was at a considerable distance from the main camp, I found two cadets engaged in a personal dispute which threatened to result in blows. Quite a group of cadets, as friends and spectators, had formed about the two bellicose disputants. I had hardly time to take in the situation, when the two principals of the group engaged in a regular set-to, and began belaboring each other vigorously with their fists. Some of their more prudent friends rushed forward and attempted to separate the two contestants. My duty as officer of the guard was plain and simple. I should have arrested the two combatants and sent them to the guard tents, for violating the peace and the regulations of the Academy. But the instincts of the boy prevailed over the obligation of the officer of the guard. I pushed my way through the surrounding line of cadets, dashed back those who were interfering in the struggle, and called out loudly, " Stand back, boys; let's have a fair fight."

I had occasion to remember, if not regret, the employment of these words. Scarcely had I uttered them when the crowd about me dispersed hurriedly, and fled to the concealment of their tents. Casting about me to ascertain the cause of this sudden dispersion, I beheld, approaching at a short distance, two officers of the army, Lieutenants Hazen and Merrill (now Major-General Hazen and Colonel Merrill of the Engineer Corps). I sought the tent of the officer of the guards promptly, but the mischief had been done. Lieutenant Hazen happened to be officer of the day on that particular day, whose duty it was to take cognizance of violations of the regulations. Summoning me to his presence, near the scene of the unfortunate disturbance, he asked me in stern tones if I was not the officer of the guard; to which I of course responded in the affirmative. He then overwhelmed me by inquiring in the same unrelenting voice, "Why did you not suppress the riot which occurred here a few minutes ago?" Now, it had never been suggested to me that the settlement of the personal difficulty between two boys, even by the administering of blows, could be considered or described as a riot. The following morning I was required to report at the tent of the commandant (Lieutenant-Colonel John F. Reynolds, afterward General Reynolds, killed at Gettysburg). Of course no explanation could satisfy the requirements of military justice. I was ordered to return to my tent in arrest. The facts in the case were reported to Washington, on formal charges and specifications, and a court-martial asked for to determine the degree of my punishment.

Within a few hours of my arrest the long-expected order came, relieving my class from further duty at West Point, and directing the members of it to proceed to Washington and report to the Adjutant-General of the army for further orders. My name, however, did not appear in this list. I was to be detained, to await the application of the commandant for a court-martial to sit on my case. The application received approval at the War Department, and the court was assembled at West Point, composed principally of officers who had recently arrived from Texas, where they served under General Twiggs, until his surrender to the Confederate forces. The judge advocate of the court was Lieutenant Benét, now Brigadier-General and Chief of the Ordnance Corps. I was arraigned with all the solemnity and gravity which might be looked for in a trial for high treason, the specification setting forth in stereotyped phraseology that "He, the said cadet Custer, did fail to suppress a riot or disturbance near the guard tent, and did fail to separate, etc., but, on the contrary, did cry out in a loud tone of voice, ' Stand back, boys ; let's have a fair fight,' or words to that effect."

To which accusations the accused pleaded "Guilty," as a matter of course, introducing as witnesses, by way of mitigation, the two cadets, the cause of my difficulty, to prove that neither was seriously injured in the fray. One of them is now a promising young captain in the Engineer Corps.

The trial was brief, scarcely occupying more time than did the primary difficulty.

I dreaded the long detention which I feared I must undergo while awaiting not only the verdict, but the subsequent action of the authorities at Washington, to whom the case must by law be submitted.

My classmates who had preceded me to Washington interested themselves earnestly in my behalf to secure my release from further arrest at West Point, and an order for me to join them at the national capital. Fortunately some of them had influential friends there, and it was but a few days after my trial that the superintendent of the Academy received a telegraphic order from Washington, directing him to release me at once, and order me to report to the Adjutant-General of the army for duty. This order practically rendered the action and proceedings of the court-martial in my case nugatory. The record, I presume, was forwarded to the War Department, where it probably lies safely stowed away in some pigeon-hole. What the proceeding of the court or their decision was, I have never learned.

———

Thus ends the record of Cadet Custer's life at West Point as traced by his own hand. It shows him as he was, but, as usual with the author, tells far less of himself than we should like to know. We see the generous impulsive boy before us, always doing the first thing that came to his hand, and never recking of the consequences. There is something in this wild free character that seems utterly unsuited to the pedantic martinetry and restraint of the Point. "Let's have a fair fight" smacks of the old days of chivalry. It was to be the watchword of the young cadet's future career. It seems plain, although Custer did not say so, that in his heart he had long chafed against the arrogant superciliousness of the Southern members of his class, who in those days thought to monopolize all the chivalry in America. As his first recorded escapade tells of the chivalrous spirit, so his early career was to be the very incarnation of chivalry, and he was fairly to eclipse the most romantic heroes of the South in brilliancy and dash. But after all, this was only one phase of his character, overlying the sterling sense at the bottom of it, as will appear in its place. During his career at West Point, Custer kept up a strict correspondence with his sister Mrs. Reed, and spent a large part of all his furloughs at her house in Monroe. He seems to have become much enamored of this sleepy little country town, with its broad streets planted with handsome trees, the brawling little river that runs through its midst, its old houses, and general air of quiet respectability. So fond was he of the place that he even persuaded his parents to move there, which they did, remaining for about a year. Not liking the place, they concluded to return to New Rumley, but afterwards compromised the matter by moving to the vicinity of Toledo, taking a farm in Wood County, near that of Mr. David Kirkpatrick, Mr. Custer's stepson. From his first entrance to Monroe, young Custer seems to have identified himself with it, to have been a "Monroe boy," to have loved all the "Monroe boys." Years after, we find his staff full of "Monroe boys," and right well they fought, too.

What was the magnet that drew him to Monroe? The place never did him any material good. He owed his cadetship to Ohio, and his parents lived there. Every thing seemed to point his way to his native state. Yet there was a little thing, a mere trifle in the world's eye, a secret vision locked in his own breast, which even his sister, who was his closest confidant in all else, never suspected : that was the magnet that drew him to Monroe. The vision of a little dark eyed maiden of only eight summers, swinging on a gate, and flinging him a careless salutation in very want of thought, then shyly fleeing into the house when she met his eye, and realized something strange and undefined in its glance. It was four, five, six, seven, eight years later, as he came home on his several vacations, that he saw the little maid shooting up into a shy, modest young lady, guarded around so closely by parental care that he could rarely catch a glimpse of her. No more salutations for him : she no longer recognized him. The innocent freedom of the child had been changed into the reserve and dignity of the young lady. She was either at home with her father, or at school in the Seminary (by this time a young lady's school), of which she was one of the most promising and pains-taking scholars. The gulf that divided the Judge's heiress from the penniless cadet seemed to grow wider and wider, and more impossible to leap, for as yet he had not even been introduced to the young lady.

All the same, Custer bided his time in silence. He felt that time was coming, and meantime his " vision " was out of danger from any one else, hedged round with every safeguard. To pass away the time, a candid biographer is compelled to admit that he flirted with other girls considerably, even what strict church members would call outrageously, but it was all only skin-deep. He was still, after all, only a boy. When we next come to him, it will be as a man among men.

SECOND BOOK.—THE SUBALTERN.

CHAPTER I.

LIEUTENANT CUSTER, SECOND CAVALRY.

THE introduction of the young officer to military life can hardly be told by any one so well as he has described it himself. It is unique. Probably no cadet ever experienced such a quick transition from school to active duty. Hear himself.

I left West Point on the 18th of July, 1861, for Washington, delaying a few hours that afternoon on my arrival in New York to enable me to purchase, of the well-known military firm of Horstmanns, my lieutenant's outfit of sabre, revolver, sash, spurs, etc. Taking the evening train for Washington, I found the cars crowded with troops, officers and men, hastening to the capital.

At each station we passed on the road at which a halt was made, crowds of citizens were assembled, provided bountifully with refreshments, which they distributed in the most lavish manner among the troops. Their enthusiasm knew no bounds; they received us with cheers and cheered us in parting. It was no unusual sight, on leaving a station surrounded by these loyal people, to see matrons and maidens embracing and kissing with patriotic fervor the men, entire strangers to them, whom they saw hastening to the defence of the nation.

Arriving at Washington soon after daylight, Saturday morning, the 20th of July, I made my way to the Ebbit House,

4

where I expected to find some of my classmates domiciled. Among others whom I found there was Parker, appointed from Missouri, who had been my room and tent-mate at West Point for years. He was one of the few members of my class who, while sympathizing with the South, had remained at the Academy long enough to graduate and secure a diploma. Proceeding to his room without going through the formality of announcing my arrival by sending up a card, I found him at that early hour still in bed. Briefly he responded to my anxious inquiry for news, that McDowell's army was confronting Beauregard's, and a general engagement was expected hourly. My next inquiry was as to his future plans and intentions, remembering his Southern sympathies. To this he replied by asking me to take from a table near by and read an official order to which he pointed.

Upon opening the document referred to, I found it to be an order from the War Department dismissing from the rolls of the army Second Lieutenant James P. Parker, for having tendered his resignation in the face of the enemy. The names of two others of my class-mates appeared in the same order. Both the latter have since sought and obtained commissions in the Egyptian army under the Khedive. After an hour or more spent in discussing the dark probabilities of the future as particularly affected by the clouds of impending war, I bade a fond farewell to my former friend and classmate, with whom I had lived on terms of closer intimacy and companionship than with any other being. We had eaten day by day at the same table, had struggled together in the effort to master the same problems of study; we had marched by each other's side year after year, elbow to elbow, when engaged in the duties of drill, parade, etc., and had shared our blankets with each other when learning the requirements of camp life. Henceforth this was all to be thrust from our memory as far as possible, and our paths and aims in life were to run counter to each other in the future. We separated; he to make his way, as he did immediately, to

the seat of the Confederate Government, and accept a commission under a flag raised in rebellion against the Government
that had educated him, and that he had sworn to defend; I to
proceed to the office of the Adjutant-General of the army and
report for such duty as might be assigned me in the great work
which was then dearest and uppermost in the mind of every
loyal citizen of the country.

It was not until after two o'clock in the morning that I
obtained an audience with the Adjutant-General of the army,
and reported to him formally for orders, as my instructions
directed me to do. I was greatly impressed by the number of
officials I saw, and the numerous messengers to be seen flitting
from room to room, bearing immense numbers of huge-looking
envelopes. The entire department had an air of busy occupation which, taken in connection with the important military
events then daily transpiring and hourly expected, and contrasted with the hum-drum life I had but lately led as a cadet,
added to the bewilderment I naturally felt.

Presenting my order of instructions to the officer who seemed
to be in charge of the office, he glanced at it, and was about to
give some directions to a subordinate near by to write out an
order assigning me to some duty, when, turning to me, he said,
" Perhaps you would like to be presented to General Scott, Mr.
Custer ? " To which of course I joyfully assented. I had
often beheld the towering form of the venerable chieftain during his summer visits to West Point, but that was the extent
of my personal acquaintance with him. So strict was the discipline at the Academy, that the gulf which separated cadets
from commissioned officers seemed greater in practice than that
which separated enlisted men from them. Hence it was rare
indeed that a cadet ever had an opportunity to address or be
addressed by officers, and it was still more rare to be brought
into personal conversation with an officer above the grade of
lieutenant or captain; if we except the superintendent of the
Academy and the commandant of the corps of cadets. The

sight of a general officer, let alone the privilege of speaking to one, was an event to be recounted to one's friend. In those days, the title of general was not so familiar as to be encountered on every hotel register. Besides, the renown of a long lifetime gallantly spent in his country's service, had gradually but justly placed General Scott far above all contemporary chieftains, in the admiration and hero worship of his fellow countrymen; and in the youthful minds of the West Point cadets of those days, Scott was looked up to as a leader whose military abilities were scarcely second to those of a Napoleon, and whose patriotism rivalled that of Washington.

Following the lead of the officer to whom I had reported, I was conducted to the room in which General Scott received his official visitors. I found him seated at a table over which were spread maps and other documents, which plainly showed their military character. In the room, and seated near the table, were several members of Congress, of whom I remember Senator Grimes, of Iowa. The topic of conversation was the approaching battle in which General McDowell's forces were about to engage. General Scott seemed to be explaining to the Congressmen the position, as shown by the map, of the contending armies. The Adjutant-General called General Scott's attention to me by saying, " General, this is Lieutenant Custer, of the Second Cavalry ; he has just reported from West Point, and I did not know but that you might have some special orders to give him." Looking at me a moment, the General shook me cordially by the hand, saying, " Well, my young friend, I am glad to welcome you to the service at this critical time. Our country has need of the strong arms of all her loyal sons in this emergency." Then, turning to the Adjutant-General, he inquired to what company I had been assigned. "To Company G, Second Cavalry, now under Major Innes Palmer, with General McDowell," was the reply. Then, addressing me, the General said, " We have had the assistance of quite a number of you young men from the Academy, drilling volunteers, etc. Now, what can I do for you? Would you prefer to be ordered to report to General Mansfield to aid in this work, or is your desire for something more active?"

Although overwhelmed by such condescension on the part of one so far superior in rank to any officer with whom I had been brought in immediate contact, I ventured to stammer out that I earnestly desired to be ordered to at once join my company, then with General McDowell, as I was anxious to see active service. "A very commendable resolution, young man," was the reply, then turning to the Adjutant-General, he added, "Make out Lieutenant Custer's orders directing him to proceed to his company at once"; then, as if a different project had presented itself, he inquired of me if I had been able to provide myself with a mount for the field. I replied that I had not, but would set myself about doing so at once. "I fear you have a difficult task before you, because, if rumor is correct, every serviceable horse in the city has been bought, borrowed, or begged by citizens who have gone or are going as spectators to witness the battle. I only hope Beauregard may capture some of them and teach them a lesson. However, what I desire to say to you is, go and provide yourself with a horse if possible, and call here at seven o'clock this evening. I desire to send some dispatches to General McDowell, and you can be the bearer of them. You are not afraid of a night ride, are you?" Exchanging salutations, I left the presence of the General-in-Chief, delighted at the prospect of being at once thrown into active service, perhaps participating in the great battle which every one there knew was on the eve of occurring; but more than this my pride as a soldier was not a little heightened by the fact that almost upon my first entering the service I was to be the bearer of important official dispatches from the General-in-Chief to the General commanding the principal army in the field.

I had yet a difficult task before me, in procuring a mount. I visited all the prominent livery stables, but received almost the same answer from each, the substance of which was, that I was too late; all the disposable horses had been let or engaged. I was almost in despair at the idea that I was not to be able to take advantage of the splendid opportunity for distinction opened before me, and was at a loss what to do, or to whom to apply for advice, when I met on Pennsylvania avenue a soldier in uniform, whom I at once recognized as one of the detachment formerly stationed at West Point, who left with those ordered suddenly to the defence of Washington at the time of Mr. Lincoln's inauguration, when it was feared that an attempt would be made to assassinate the President elect. Glad to encounter any one I had ever seen before, I approached and asked him what he was doing in Washington. He answered that he belonged to Griffin's battery, which was then with McDowell's forces at the front, and had returned to Washington, by Captain Griffin's order, to obtain and take back with him an extra horse left by the battery on its departure from the capital. Here then was my opportunity, and I at once availed myself of it. It was the intention of this man to set out on his return at once; but at my earnest solicitation he consented to defer his departure until after seven o'clock, agreeing also to have the extra horse saddled and in readiness for me.

Promptly at seven o'clock I reported at the Adjutant-General's office, obtained my dispatches, and with no baggage or extra clothing to weight down my horse, save what I carried on my person, I repaired to the point at which I was to find my horse and companion for the night. Upon arriving there I was both surprised and delighted to discover that the horse which accident seemed to have provided for me was a favorite one ridden by me often when learning the cavalry exercises at West Point. Those who were cadets just before the war will probably recall him to mind when I give the name, " Wellington," by which he was then known.

Crossing Long bridge about night-fall, and taking the Fairfax C. H. road for Centreville, the hours of night flew quickly past,

engrossed as my mind was with the excitement and serious novelty of the occasion, as well as occasionally diverted by the conversation of my companion.   I was particularly interested with his
description, given as we rode in the silent darkness, of a skirmish which had taken place only two days before at Blackburn's
Ford, between the forces of the enemy stationed there, and a
reconnoitring detachment sent from General McDowell's army;
especially when I learned that my company had borne an honorable part in the affair.

It was between two and three o'clock in the morning when
we reached the army near Centreville.   The men had already
breakfasted, and many of the regiments had been formed in column in the roads ready to resume the march; but owing to
delays in starting, most of the men were lying on the ground,
endeavoring to catch a few minutes more of sleep; others were
sitting or standing in small groups, smoking and chatting.   So
filled did I find the road with soldiers that it was with difficulty
my horse could pick his way among the sleeping bodies without disturbing them.   But for my companion I should have
had considerable difficulty in finding my way to headquarters;
but he seemed familiar with the localities even in the darkness,
and soon conducted me to a group of tents near which a large
log fire was blazing, throwing a bright light over the entire
scene for some distance around.   As I approached, the sound of
my horse's hoofs brought an officer from one of the tents nearest to where I halted.   Advancing toward me, he inquired who
I wished to see.   I informed him that I was bearer of dispatches from General Scott to General McDowell.   "I will
relieve you of them," was his reply; but seeing me hesitate to
deliver them, he added, "I am Major Wadsworth of General
McDowell's staff."   While I had hoped from ambitious pride
to have an opportunity to deliver the dispatches in person to
General McDowell, I could not decline longer, so placed the
documents in Major Wadsworth's hands, who took them to a
tent a few paces distant, where, through its half-open folds, I

saw him hand them to a large, portly officer, whom I at once rightly conceived to be General McDowell. Then, returning to where I still sat on my horse, Major Wadsworth (afterward General Wadsworth) asked of me the latest news in the capital, and when I replied that every person at Washington was looking to the army for news, he added, " Well, I guess they will not have to wait much longer. The entire army is under arms, and moving to attack the enemy to-day."

After inquiring at what hour I left Washington, and remarking that I must be tired, Major Wadsworth asked me to dismount and have some breakfast, as it would be difficult to say when another opportunity would occur. I was very hungry, and rest would not have been unacceptable, but in my inexperience I partly imagined, particularly while in the presence of the white-haired officer who gave the invitation, that hunger and fatigue were conditions of feeling which a soldier, especially a young one, should not acknowledge. Therefore, with an appetite almost craving, I declined the kind proffer of the Major. But when he suggested that I dismount and allow my horse to be fed, I gladly assented. While Major Wadsworth was kindly interesting himself in the welfare of my horse, I had the good fortune to discover in an officer at headquarters, one of my recent West Point friends, Lieutenant Kingsbury, aide-de-camp to General McDowell. He repeated the invitation just given by Major Wadsworth in regard to breakfast, and I did not have the perseverance to again refuse. Near the log-fire already mentioned, were some servants busily engaged in removing the remains of breakfast. A word from Kingsbury, and they soon prepared for me a cup of coffee, a steak, and some Virginia corn bread, to which I did ample justice. Had I known, however, that I was not to have an opportunity to taste food during the next thirty hours, I should have appreciated the opportunity I then enjoyed even more highly.

As I sat on the ground sipping my coffee, and heartily enjoying my first breakfast in the field, Kingsbury (afterward

Colonel Kingsbury, killed at the battle of Antietam) informed me of the general movement then begun by the army, and of the attack which was to be made on Beauregard's forces that day. Three days before I had quitted school at West Point. I was about to witness the first grand struggle in open battle between the Union and secession armies ; a struggle in which, fortunately for the nation, the Union forces were to suffer defeat, while the cause for which they fought was to derive from it renewed strength and encouragement.

So closes the record of the young officer's first tour of duty. As long as we can let us follow him, for no one else can tell his story so well as himself.

In the whole of his story of this period there is great freshness, and its only fault in the eyes of the general public, is that it tells so little of Lieutenant Custer, the real point of interest. In this, as all through his published memoirs, noticeably so in his " Life on the Plains," written at a later period of his life, when he was a public character, Custer always exhibits this modesty of self-reference, a characteristic of the true knightly soldier. Whenever he mentions Custer, it is only to make the story realistic, and never to boast of his own deeds. He never seems to have got over the fear that a personal story must be a bore to the general public. In a general sense he was quite right, for personal stories of adventure from commonplace people are very apt to be uninteresting. In the case of men like Custer, centres of popular favor, and of whom little is certainly known, the more particulars given us the better, and the more complete our knowledge of them, the more we are satisfied.

Very luckily for the success of his biographer, young Custer soon after became quite a constant and voluminous correspondent with his family at home, and did not make the same mistake with them. *There*, he was quite sure where the interest lay. The gentle loving women at home did not care a pin for de-

tails of battles and campaigns, which they hardly comprehend-
ed, but they *did* care *very much* for what Lieutenant Custer,
or rather their *dear boy Armstrong* was doing, and in his letters he tells them this freely, without any mock modesty. At
a little later period we shall see a good deal of these letters:
for the present it is thought better to go no further in our re-
searches than Custer himself has indicated that he wishes us to
go. We shall therefore follow him to Bull Run and to the
Peninsula, taking up the parable ourselves only when he stops.

The personal interest of these letters is great, and their reading is much more racy than the published narratives of Custer
himself. They reveal the real natural Custer, full of life and
spirits, generous and ardent, so clearly, that it is like talking
with a famous actor off the stage, far more interesting than seeing him act. Unlike most actors, however, Custer is better
company off the stage than on it, and we hope that these letters, when they come, will aid in undeceiving the world as to
his character, and free him from one very unjust charge, that
of *vanity*. From this vice no man was freer, and his most private letters show as much real modesty as his most studied
published memoirs.

CHAPTER II.

BULL RUN.

THE battle of Bull Run has been often discussed, and was once the occasion of the fiercest controversies. At the time it was fought, and for at least a year thereafter, it was almost impossible to form a clear idea of anything, except for a general impression that a great panic had taken place, that Mr. Russell, of the *London Times*, had abused the great Yankee nation in the most outrageous way, and that *some one* was to blame—it was hard to say who. McDowell and Scott went down at once under the popular storm, and the former has perhaps never entirely recovered from the hasty verdict then passed on him.

The preliminary reflections of General Custer on this remarkable battle, the first in which he was engaged, are so apposite that they well deserve quotation. He says truly that no battle of the war startled and convulsed the entire country, North and South, as did the first battle of Bull Run, although many succeeding it, both in the East and in the West, were more notable from the fact that greatly superior numbers were engaged, more prominent or experienced chieftains arrayed upon either side, and greater results obtained upon the battle-field. Nor is this difficult to explain. The country, after the enjoyment of long years of peace and prosperity, was unused to the conditions and chances of war. The people of neither section had fully realized as yet the huge proportions of the struggle into which they had been plunged. This is shown not only by the opinions of the people as shadowed forth in the press, but by the authoritative acts and utterances of the highest officials of the land ; for example, the proclamation of President Lincoln as late as April 15, 1861, after Fort Sumter had been fired upon and had been surrendered.   In this procla- mation, calling for 75,000 troops, or rather in the call sent to the loyal Governors of the States, the period of service was limited to three months.   To this can be added Mr. Seward's well-known " ninety days " prediction, all tending to incline the people to believe the war was destined to be brief, perhaps to be terminated by a single engagement.   Then again, war was not regarded by the masses as a dreadful alternative, to be avoided to the last, but rather as an enterprise offering some pleasure and some excitement, with perhaps a little danger and suffer- ing.   Last of all, the people of the two contending sections had, through the false teachings of their leaders, formed such unjust and incorrect notions in regard to the military prowess and resolution of their opponents, that it required the wager of actual battle to dispel these erroneous ideas.

How true these sayings of Custer are, we can remember. The awakening from delusion was marked by much of the same unpractical extravagance of feeling which dictated the previous blind confidence.   It was the childish and passionate resentment of those who knew nothing of war save from unprofessional books.   The United States had seen no real serious war from its foundation, the influence of the brief invasion of 1812–14 being so partial and slight that the distresses of campaigning were practically unknown.   The Mexican War was but a brilliant memory of a holiday excursion to the vast masses of the country, and its veterans were even then fast dropping off the list into superannuation.   In the first flush of bitter mortifica- tion and anger at the unexpected reverse, the general run of northern people were as feverishly unreasonable as the French Republicans of the year '93, and every man turned at once into a volunteer spy on his neighbor, if the latter were suspected of sympathy for the victorious South.

A somewhat ludicrous instance of this occurred within the knowledge of the writer, having been witnessed by a personal friend. It will give a very fair idea of the state of gloom and acrimony of feeling engendered in the North by the news of Bull Run. It took place, moreover, close to New York city, then and thereafter the place in the whole Union where Southern sympathizers were most common and outspoken, a place not to be compared in ardor of sectional feeling to the country towns.

Crossing on the Brooklyn ferry boat, the day after the news of Bull Run had electrified the country, the passengers seemed gloomy and preoccupied. A single exception was found in a foreign gentleman who was conversing with a friend, and who finally broke into a loud laugh where he sat. Instantly a man on the other side of the cabin, who had been regarding him with great disfavor since his entrance, rose, stalked over to him, and struck him a violent blow on the face, crying, " How *dare* you laugh, sir, when the country is in danger ? "

It seems hardly credible now, and yet the fact is undoubted, and it appears that the action attracted no sympathy for the sufferer, who had run counter to the intensity of popular feeling. At that time, it must be remembered that the sympathy of most foreigners was, actively or passively, for the South ; and the news of the Southern victory determined many waverers against the General Government. Looking back now, after the practical test of actual warfare, in which success depends so little on ardor of feeling, so much on dogged determination, these outbursts of feeling appear in their true light, as childish ebullitions, unworthy of earnest men, conscious of their strength. The real trouble then was, that the people were *not* conscious of their strength, but exaggerated their temporary weakness as they had their primary resources.

Such as it was, the battle of Bull Run had several curious points about it, which we will endeavor to elucidate for the general reader, assisted partly by General Custer himself, and

partly by the narrative of the Confederate commander, General
Joseph E. Johnston.

The Confederate forces were thus disposed, according to the
first: "Beauregard's headquarters were at or near Manassas,
distant from Centreville, where General McDowell was located
in the midst of his army, about seven miles. The stream which
gave its name to the battle runs in a south-east direction between Centreville and Manassas, somewhat nearer to the former
place than to the latter. The Confederate army was posted in
position along the right bank of Bull Run, their right resting
near Union Mill, the point at which the Orange and Alexandria
railroad crosses the stream, their centre at Blackburn's Ford,
while their left was opposite the Stone bridge, or crossing of
the Warrenton pike, at the same time holding a small ford
about one mile above the Stone bridge."

It consisted, according to the order of General Beauregard
prescribing the march to the battle field, (quoted in full in the
Appendix to Johnston's Narrative) of seven brigades of the
"Army of the Potomac," Beauregard's force proper, with forty-
two guns and twelve companies of cavalry. These brigades
were those of Ewell, D. R. Jones, Longstreet and Bonham in
the first line, stretching in the order named from Union Mills
on the right to Mitchell's Ford on the left, facing northeast.
Supporting them in the second line were those of Holmes and
Early. The last brigade, Colonel Cock's, was four miles further
to the left, guarding the fords. The cavalry was split up into
squadrons of two companies, one to each of the first four divisions, which were composed of two brigades each or one with
some additional forces. They were commanded respectively by
Ewell, Jones, Longstreet and Bonham. Jackson's brigade, of the
Army of the Shenandoah, with two regiments of another brigade, were also present from Johnston's forces in the valley, and
later in the day, Elzey's brigade of that army arrived just in time
to turn defeat into victory. The two extra regiments from the
valley were hastily consolidated with two others of Beauregard's

army, early in the day, and constituted Bee's brigade, which suffered worst of all. All the troops from the valley came *from the left*, and were put in *on the left*.

It had been Beauregard's intention before Johnston arrived, to strengthen his right, and attack the Federal left, so as to turn it and push it towards the valley, into the clutches of Johnston, who would take it in rear. This disposition was changed by the arrival of Johnston, about noon. It was then found that McDowell's plan was exactly the reverse of Beauregard's. He intended to attack with *his* right, under the impression that Johnston would be detained in the valley. If he succeeded, he would drive Beauregard into the sea, but his plan was entirely predicated on the absence of Johnston. If the latter came in during the battle, he was certain to strike the Federal right wing square in the rear. As it happened, that is just what Johnston's last brigade did.

McDowell's forces were otherwise disposed. They were organized into four divisions, led by Brig. General Tyler, (Connecticut Volunteers) and Colonels Hunter, Heintzelman, and Miles, of the Regular Army. Tyler's division was to threaten Cocke's brigade on the Confederate left, while Hunter and Heintzelman were to move still further up, and cross the stream above, so as to turn the Confederates. Miles was to be in reserve near Centreville, to frustrate any attempt made by Beauregard to attack on that side. One of Tyler's brigades was to assist Miles, and keep the enemy amused by cannonading his centre at Blackburn's Ford. McDowell had a fifth division, Runyon's, back on the Orange and Alexandria Railroad, guarding communications. It was not engaged.

Thus it will be seen that Hunter's and Heintzelman's divisions were to do all the fighting. Tyler and Miles were to keep the enemy amused. The only fault of the disposition, outside of the Johnston possibility, was that Bull Run separated half the army from the other half. From henceforth, let us permit the story to be taken up by Custer himself. It is so freshly, graphically and clearly told by him that it cannot be improved. He takes up the description from where we left him, eating his hasty breakfast at McDowell's headquarters, in the grey morning, and continues :—

In the preceding chapter I described my night ride from Washington to the camp of General McDowell's army, at and about Centreville. After delivering my dispatches and concluding my business at headquarters, I remounted my horse, and having been directed in the darkness the way to the ground occupied by Palmer's seven companies of cavalry, I set out to find my company for the first time, and report to the commanding officer for duty before the column should begin the march to the battle-ground. As previously informed by a staff officer at headquarters, I found it only necessary to ride a few hundred yards, when suddenly I came upon a column of cavalry already mounted, and in readiness to move. It was still so dark that I could see but a few lengths of my horse in any direction. I accosted one of the troopers nearest to me, and inquired, " What cavalry is this?" " Major Palmer's," was the brief reply. I followed up my interrogations by asking, " Can you tell me where Company G, Second Cavalry, is ? " the company to which I had been assigned, but as yet had not seen. " At the head of the column," came in response. Making my way along the column in the darkness, I soon reached the head, where I found several horsemen seated upon their horses, but not formed regularly in the column. There was not sufficient light to distinguish emblems of rank, or to recognize the officer from the private soldier. With some hesitation I addressed the group, numbering perhaps a half-dozen or more individuals, and asked if the commanding officer of my company, giving its designation by letter and regiment, was present. " Here he is," promptly answered a voice, as one of the mounted figures rode toward me, expecting no doubt I was a staff officer, bearing orders requiring his attention.

I introduced myself by saying, " I am Lieutenant Custer,

and in accordance with orders from the War Department, I report for duty with my company, sir." "Ah, glad to meet you, Mr. Custer. We have been expecting you, as we saw in the list of assignments of the graduating class from West Point, that you had been marked down to us. I am Lieutenant Drummond. Allow me to introduce you to some of your brother officers." Then turning his horse toward the group of officers, he added, " Gentlemen, permit me to introduce to you Lieutenant Custer, who has just reported for duty with his company." We bowed to each other, although we could see but little more than the dim outlines of horses and riders as we chatted and awaited the order to move " forward." This was my introduction to service, and my first greeting from officers and comrades with whom the future fortune of war was to cast me. Lieutenant Drummond, afterward captain, to whom I had just made myself known, fell mortally wounded, and died gallantly on the field, at the battle of Five Forks, nearly four years afterward.

The cavalry, on the Federal side, consisting of only seven companies of regulars under Major Palmer, were not employed to any considerable extent during the battle, except as supports to batteries of artillery. One charge was made in the early part of the battle, near the Warrenton turnpike, by Colburn's squadron. In advancing to the attack in the morning, Palmer's companies accompanied Hunter's division in the long and tedious movement through an immense forest by which Bull Run was crossed at one of the upper fords, and the left flank of the Confederates successfully turned.

After arriving at Sudley Springs, the cavalry halted for half an hour or more. We could hear the battle raging a short distance in our front. Soon a staff officer of General McDowell's came galloping down to where the cavalry was waiting, saying that the General desired us to move across the stream and up the ridge beyond, where we were to support a battery. The order was promptly obeyed, and as we ascended the crest I saw

5

Griffin with his battery galloping into position. The enemy had discovered him, and their artillery had opened fire upon him, but the shots were aimed so high the balls passed overhead. Following the battery, we also marched within plain hearing of each shot as it passed over Griffin's men. I remember well the strange hissing and exceedingly vicious sound of the first cannon shot I heard as it whirled through the air. Of course I had often heard the sound made by cannon balls while passing through the air during my artillery practice at West Point, but a man listens with changed interest when the direction of the balls is toward instead of away from him. They seemed to utter a different language when fired in angry battle from that put forth in the tamer practice of drill. The battery whose support we were, having reached its position on an advanced crest near the right of the line, the cavalry was massed near the foot of the crest, and sheltered by it from the enemy's fire. Once the report came that the enemy was moving to the attack of the battery which we were specially sent to guard. The order was at once given for the cavalry to advance from the base to the crest of the hill and repel the enemy's assault. We were formed in column of companies, and were given to under-stand that upon reaching the crest of the hill we would probably be ordered to charge the enemy. When it is remembered that but three days before I had quitted West Point as a school-boy, and as yet had never ridden at anything more dangerous or ter-rible than a three-foot hurdle, or tried my sabre upon anything more animated or combative than a leather-head stuffed with tan bark, it may be imagined that my mind was more or less given to anxious thoughts as we ascended the slope of the hill in front of us. At the same time I realized that I was in front of a company of old and experienced soldiers, all of whom would have an eye upon their new lieutenant to see how he comported himself when under fire. My pride received an additional incentive from the fact that while I was on duty with troops for the first time in my life, and was the junior officer of all present with the cavalry, there was temporarily assigned to duty with my company another officer of the same rank, who was senior to me by a few days, and who, having been appointed from civil life, was totally without military experience except such as he had acquired during the past few days. My brief acquaintance with him showed me that he was disposed to attach no little importance to the fact that I was fresh from West Point and supposed to know all that was valuable or worth knowing in regard to the art of war. In this common delusion I was not disposed to disturb him. I soon found that he was inclined to defer to me in opinion, and I recall now, as I have often done when in his company during later years of the war, the difficulty we had in deciding exactly what weapon we would use in the charge to which we believed ourselves advancing. As we rode forward from the foot of the hill, he in front of his platoon and I abreast of him, in front of mine, Walker (afterward captain) inquired in the most solemn tones, " Custer, what weapon are you going to use in the charge?" From my earliest notions of the true cavalryman I had always pictured him in the charge bearing aloft his curved sabre, and cleaving the skulls of all with whom he came in contact. We had but two weapons to choose from : each of us carried a sabre and one revolver in our belt. I promptly replied, "The sabre;" and suiting the action to the word, I flashed my bright new blade from its scabbard, and rode forward as if totally unconcerned. Walker, yielding no doubt to what he believed was " the way we do it at West Point," imitated my motion, and forth came his sabre. I may have seemed to him unconcerned, because I aimed at this, but I was far from enjoying that feeling. As we rode at a deliberate walk up the hill, I began arguing in my own mind as to the comparative merits of the sabre and revolver as a weapon of attack. If I remember correctly, I reasoned *pro* and *con* about as follows: " Now the sabre is a beautiful weapon; it produces an ugly wound; the term ' sabre charge' sounds well; and above all the sabre is sure;

it never misses fire. It has this drawback, however: in order
to be made effective, it is indispensable that you approach very
close to your adversary—so close that if you do not unhorse or
disable him, he will most likely render that service to you. So
much for the sabre. Now as to the revolver, it has this advantage over the sabre: one is not compelled to range himself
alongside his adversary before beginning his attack, but may
select his own time and distance. To be sure one may miss his
aim, but there are six chambers to empty, and if one, two, or
three miss, there are still three shots left to fire at close quarters.
As this is my first battle, had I not better defer the use of the
sabre until after I have acquired a little more experience?"
The result was that I returned my sabre to its scabbard, and
without uttering a word drew my revolver and poised it opposite my shoulder. Walker, as if following me in my mental discussion, no sooner observed my change of weapon than he did
likewise. With my revolver in my hand I put it upon trial
mentally. First, I realized that in the rush and excitement of
the charge it would be difficult to take anything like accurate
aim. Then, might not every shot be fired, and without result?
by which time in all probability we would be in the midst of
our enemies, and slashing right and left at each other; in which
case a sabre would be of much greater value and service than an
empty revolver. This seemed convincing; so much so that my
revolver found its way again to its holster, and the sabre was
again at my shoulder. Again did Walker, as if in pantomime,
follow my example. How often these changes of purpose and
weapons might have been made I know not, had the cavalry
not reached the crest meanwhile, and after being exposed to a
hot artillery fire, and finding that no direct attack upon our
battery was meditated by the enemy, returned to a sheltered
piece of ground.

A little incident occurred as we were about to move forward to the expected charge, which is perhaps worth recording.
Next to the company with which I was serving was one which

I noticed as being in most excellent order and equipment. The officer in command of it was of striking appearance, tall, well formed, and handsome, and possessing withal a most soldierly air. I did not then know his name; but being so near to him and to his command, I could not but observe him. When the order came for us to move forward up the hill, and to be prepared to charge the moment the crest was reached, I saw the officer referred to ride gallantly in front of his command, and just as the signal forward was given, I heard him say, "Now, men, do your duty." I was attracted by his soldierly words and bearing; and yet within a few days after the battle he tendered his resignation, and in a short time was serving under the Confederate flag as a general officer.

With the exception of a little tardiness in execution, something to be expected perhaps in raw troops, the plan of battle marked out by General McDowell was carried out with remarkable precision up till about half past three P. M. The Confederate left wing had been gradually forced back from Bull Run until the Federals gained entire possession of the Warrenton turnpike leading from the Stone bridge. It is known now that Beauregard's army had become broken and routed, and that both himself and General Johnston felt called upon to place themselves at the head of their defeated commands, including their last reserves, in their effort to restore confidence and order; General Johnston at one critical moment charging to the front with the colors of the Fourth Alabama. Had the fate of the battle been left to the decision of those who were present and fought up till half-past three in the afternoon, the Union troops would have been entitled to score a victory with scarcely a serious reverse. But at this critical moment, with their enemies in front giving way in disorder and flight, a new and to the Federals an unexpected force appeared suddenly upon the scene. From a piece of timber almost directly in rear of McDowell's right a column of several thousand fresh troops of the enemy burst almost upon the backs of the half victorious

Federals. I was standing with a friend and classmate at that moment on a high ridge near our advancing line. We were congratulating ourselves upon the glorious victory which already seemed to have been won, as the Confederates were everywhere giving way, when our attention was attracted by a long line of troops suddenly appearing behind us upon the edge of the timber already mentioned. It never occurred to either of us that the troops we then saw could be any but some of our reinforcements making their way to the front. Before doubts could arise we saw the Confederate flag floating over a portion of the line just emerging from the timber; the next moment the entire line levelled their muskets and poured a volley into the backs of our advancing regiments on the right. At the same time a battery which had also arrived unseen opened fire, and with a cry of "We're flanked! We're flanked!" passed from rank to rank, the Union lines, but a moment before so successful and triumphant, threw down their arms, were seized by a panic, and began a most disordered flight. All this occurred almost in an instant of time. No pen or description can give anything like a correct idea of the rout and demoralization that followed. Officers and men joined in one vast crowd, abandoning, except in isolated instances, all attempts to preserve their organizations. A moderate force of good cavalry at that moment could have secured to the Confederates nearly every man and gun that crossed Bull Run in the early morning. Fortunately the Confederate army was so badly demoralized by its earlier reverses, that it was in no mood or condition to make pursuit, and reap the full fruits of victory. The troops that had arrived upon the battle-field so unexpectedly to the Federals, and which had wrought such disaster upon the Union arms, were Elzey's brigade of infantry and Beckham's battery of artillery, the whole under command of Brigadier-General E. Kirby Smith, being a detachment belonging to Johnston's army of the Shenandoah, just arrived from the valley. Had this command reached the battle-field a few minutes later, the rout of Beauregard's army would have been assured, as his forces seemed powerless to check the advance of the Union troops.

General McDowell and his staff, as did many of the higher officers, exerted themselves to the utmost to stay the retreating Federals, but all appeals to the courage and patriotism of the latter fell as upon dumb animals. One who has never witnessed the conduct of large numbers of men when seized by a panic such as that was, cannot realize how utterly senseless and without apparent reason men will act. And yet the same men may have exhibited great gallantry and intelligence but a moment before.

The value of discipline was clearly shown in this crisis by observing the manner of the few regular troops, as contrasted with the raw and undisciplined three months' men. The regular soldiers never for a moment ceased to look to their officers for orders and instructions, and in retiring from the field, even amid the greatest disorder and confusion of the organizations near them, they preserved their formation, and marched only as they were directed to do.

The long lines of Union soldiery, which a few minutes before had been bravely confronting and driving the enemy, suddenly lost their cohesion and became one immense mass of fleeing, frightened creatures. Artillery horses were cut from their traces, and it was no unusual sight to see three men, perhaps belonging to different regiments, riding the same horse, and making their way to the rear as fast as the dense mass of men moving with them would permit. The direction of the retreat was toward Centreville, by way of the Stone bridge crossing, and other fords above that point. An occasional shot from the enemy's artillery, or the cry that the Black Horse cavalry, so dreaded in the first months of the war in Virginia, were coming, kept the fleeing crowd of soldiers at their best speed. Arms were thrown away as being no longer of service in warding off the enemy. Here and there the State colors of a regiment, or perhaps the national standard, would be seen lying on the ground along the line of retreat, no one venturing to reclaim or preserve them, while more than one full set of band instruments could be observed, dropped under the shade of some tree in rear of the line of battle, and where their late owners had probably been resting from the fatigues of the fight when the panic seized them and forced them to join their comrades in flight. One good steady regiment composed of such sterling material as made up the regiments of either side at the termination of the war, could have checked the pursuit before reaching Bull Run, and could have saved much of the artillery and many of the prisoners that as it was fell into the enemy's hands simply for want of owners. The rout continued until Centreville was reached; then the reserves posted under Mills gave some little confidence to the retreating masses, and after the latter had passed the reserves, comparative order began in a slight degree to be restored. General McDowell at first decided to halt and make a stand on the heights near Centreville, but this was soon discovered to be unadvisable, if not impracticable, so large a portion of the army having continued their flight toward Washington. Orders were then given the various commanders to conduct their forces back to their former camps near Arlington, opposite Washington, where they arrived the following day.

When the retreat began my company and one other of cavalry, and a section of artillery, commanded by Captain Arnold, came under the personal direction and control of Colonel Heintzleman, with whom we moved toward Centreville. Colonel Heintzleman, although suffering from a painful wound, continued to exercise command, and maintained his seat in the saddle. The two companies of cavalry and the section of Arnold's battery moved off the battle-field in good order, and were the last organized bodies of Union troops to retire across Bull Run. When within about two miles of Centreville, at the bridge across Cub Run, the crossing was found to be completely blocked up by broken wagons and ambulances. There being no other crossing available, and the enemy having opened with artillery from a position a short distance below the bridge, and commanding the latter, Captain Arnold was forced to abandon his guns. The cavalry found a passable ford for their purpose, and from this point no further molestation was encountered from the enemy. After halting a few hours in some old camps near Centreville, it now being dark, the march was resumed, and kept up until Arlington was reached, during the forenoon of the 22d. I little imagined when making my night ride from Washington to Centreville, the night of the 20th, that the following night would find me returning with a defeated and demoralized army. It was with the greatest difficulty that many of the regiments could be halted on the Arlington side of Long bridge, so determined were they to seek safety and rest under the very walls of the capitol. Some of the regiments lost more men after the battle and retreat had ended, than had been killed, wounded, and captured by the enemy. Three-fourths of one regiment, known as the Zouaves, disappeared in this way. Many of the soldiers continued their flight until they reached New York.

Here ends the vivid personal narrative of the young officer, placed so suddenly in the midst of the first great battle of the war. The reader will have noticed ere this, the frank and candid *naiveté* of his style, and the real modesty which pervades the account, the way in which he tells a story against himself, as to his first charge, and the perfect greenness to which he confesses, in spite of his West Point education. The reflections with which he closes his story of Bull Run, are as just and sober, as the narrative is fresh and picturesque, and equally worthy of quotation. Besides this, they have the further advantage of being true to the letter.

He says :—

While the result of the battle of Bull Run startled and aroused the entire country, from the St. Lawrence to the Rio

Grande, the effect upon the people of the North, and that upon those of the revolted States was widely different.

The press and people of the South accepted the result of the battle as forecasting if not already assuring the ultimate success of their cause, and marking, as they expressed it, the birth of a nation ; and while this temporary advantage may have excited and inspired their enthusiasm, and increased their faith as well as their numbers, by drawing or driving into their ranks the lukewarm, and those inclined to remain loyal, yet it was a source of weakness as well, from the fact that the people of the South were in a measure confirmed in the very prevalent belief which had long existed in the Southern States regarding the great superiority in battle of the Southron over his fellow-countryman of colder climes. This impression maintained its hold upon the minds of the people of the South, and upon the Southern soldiery, until eradicated by months and years of determined battle. The loyal North accepted its defeat in the most commendable manner, and this remark is true, whether applied to the high officials of the States and General Government or to the people at large. There was no indulging in vain or idle regrets ; there was no flinching from the support and defence of the Union ; there was least of all hesitation as to the proper course to pursue. If the idea of compromise had been vainly cherished by any portion of the people, it had vanished, and but one sentiment, one purpose actuated the men of the North, as if acting under a single will. Men were hurried forward from all the loyal States ; more offered their services than the government was prepared to accept. The defeat of the Union arms forced the North to coolly calculate the immense task before it in attempting to overthrow the military strength of the insurgent States. Had Bull Run resulted otherwise than it did, had the North instead of the South been the victor, there would have been danger of a feeling of false security pervading the minds of the people of the North. Their patriotism would not have been awakened

by success as it was by disaster; they would not have felt called
upon to abandon the farm, the workshop, the counting-room,
and the pulpit, in order to save a government tottering almost
upon the brink of destruction.

It only remains to follow the soldier-author in his analysis
of the subsequent careers of the officers present on both sides
in this famous fight, and the story of Bull Run will be
complete.

It is interesting, says Custer, to note the names of officers
of both contending armies who were present at the battle
of Bull Run, and who afterward achieved more or less distinction, and exercised important commands in later years of the
war. On the Union side there were McDowell, Hunter, Heintzelman, Burnside, Howard, Keyes, Franklin, Schenck, Wilcox,
Gorman, Blenker, Ward, Richardson, Andrew Porter, Terry,
Slocum, Wadsworth, Sykes, Barry, Hunt, Fry, Averill, Innes
Palmer, Wheaton, Barnard, Abbot, Webb, Griffin, Ricketts,
Ayres, Baird, Wright, Whipple, and Richard Arnold.

Of those officers who were present at the battle of Bull
Run, McDowell was the only one who held a rank above that of
field officer, he being a brigadier-general. Sixteen held the
rank of colonel, one that of lieutenant-colonel, six that of major,
five that of captain, and eight the rank of lieutenant. Nearly
all were advanced in time to the rank of major-general; more
than half the number were appointed subsequently to the command of armies, corps, or departments, while but few held
positions below that of division commander. Among the colonels of regiments at Bull Run was W. T. Sherman, now General of the Army of the United States. Of the present three
major-generals of the regular army, one was the commander of
the Union forces on that day; and of the six brigadier-generals
now in the line of the regular army, two, Howard and Terry,
were colonels of voluntere regiments at the battle of July 21.

" Upon the side of the Confederates there was Johnston,
Beauregard, Jackson (who obtained at this battle the *sobriquet* of

Stonewall), E. Kirby Smith, Longstreet, J. E. B. Stuart, Hampton, D. R Jones, A. P. Hill, Ewell, Early, Kershaw, Elzey, Echolls, Hunton, Cooke, Pendleton, Holmes, S. Jones, Barksdale, Jordan, and Evans. The great majority of these became prominent generals, and as commanders of armies or of large bodies of troops in several of the decisive battles and campaigns of the war, displayed great ability and gallantry, and won lasting renown by their prowess and military skill."

CHAPTER III.

ORGANIZING AN ARMY.

FOLLOWING our original design, we shall utilize, in describing the period immediately following the battle of Bull Run, the scanty memoirs left by General Custer, wherever they relate to personal adventures. We are convinced that they possess an interest and value to the public, especially since the early death of their author, to which a more elaborate narrative from another hand could not aspire. The matter most to be deplored is that they are so very short that we shall soon be compelled to drop them, and that the last part was written in such exceeding haste, in the midst of camp life and even on the march against the Indians, as not fairly to represent the author. Had General Custer been spared another year, enjoying the advantages of leisure under which he wrote his " Life on the Plains," his contributions to the early history of the war must have proved of exceeding value. As it is, let us continue with him on his journey as far as he goes with us.

In selecting from his memoirs, we consider it due to the public, however, to omit those purely personal estimates of the character of the various officers who at an early period of the war, fell, justly or unjustly, under popular or political censure, with which the early chapters of the memoirs abound. The proper place for such estimates is to be found in the future history of the war so often dreamed about, and some day, possibly, to be written. In the personal history of a single officer, other than that of the commander-in-chief, such estimates are only provocative of controversy, and needless for the eluci-

dation of truth. Where they affect only the private character of
the illustrious dead, whose peculiarities are matter of public
interest, as in the case of Kearny, we quote them in full,
especially where they illustrate the keen eye for character possessed by Custer himself. Accordingly we will let him take
up the narrative of events immediately following the battle of
Bull Run in his own language.

When McDowell saw the victory which he had planned so
ably to achieve swept from his grasp almost at the moment
when he deemed it secure, and beheld his forces, which but
a moment before were driving their adversaries in disorder
before them, now turn and abandon the field they had fought
so gallantly to win, his first idea was to retire his army behind
its reserves at Centreville, re-form the disordered regiments, and
renew the advance from that point. But when he reached
Centreville he saw that all efforts to stop or rally the flying
Federals must prove unavailing, many of the regiments having
without instructions continued their flight in the direction
of Washington. Orders were therefore given for the entire
army to fall back to its old camps near Arlington, opposite the
capital. The retreat was continued all night, and by noon
of the following day the Federal army could be said to be
safely back in its old camps near the capital. While the losses
in the battle had been severe, they would have been almost
unprecedented had all the absentees from the Union regiments,
upon the arrival of the latter at Arlington, been chargeable
to the legitimate losses of battle. The truth was that hundreds
of men belonging to some of the regiments had not pretended
to halt at their old camps, but had rushed across the Long bridge
over the Potomac, which separated their camps from the capital,
and, continuing their flight, made no halt until they had placed
hundreds of miles between themselves and the scene of their
late disaster. Hundreds of these fugitives, including among
their numbers a few officers, were seen in the streets of New
York within forty-eight hours after the arrival of the routed

army at Arlington. One regiment, the Second New York militia, reported one hundred and forty men missing after the battle, yet the regiment had not crossed Bull Run during the engagement.

The company of cavalry to which I belonged, and one other, with a section of Arnold's battery, as already stated, were the last organized bodies of troops to leave the battle-field, which they did under the immediate command of Colonel Heintzelman. The guns had to be abandoned upon our arrival at Cub Run, owing to the passageway becoming blocked with broken vehicles. I had ridden nearly all the night preceding the battle, to enable me to join the army and participate in the struggle. When the battle reached its disastrous termination, and night spread its mantle over our defeated and demoralized troops, I found myself hastening with the fleeing, frightened soldiery back toward that capital which I had left but a few hours before. To add to the discomforts and delays of the retreat, the rain fell in torrents, rendering the road almost impassable. Reaching Arlington Heights early in the forenoon, I scarcely waited for my company to be assigned to its camp, before I was stretched at full length under a tree, where, from fatigue, hunger, and exhaustion, I soon fell asleep, despite the rain and mud, and slept for hours without awakening. When I finally awoke, and attempted to take a retrospect of my late introduction to actual service, I could find but little to console or flatter me, and still less to encourage a hopeful view of the success of the Union cause in the future; and yet while I do not now recall, even among the many dark and trying days passed through at later periods of the war, any event which brought with it more despondency and discouragement than the defeat at Bull Run, neither then nor at any subsequent period did I ever lose or lessen my faith, my firm belief and conviction, that the cause of the Union was destined in the end to triumph over all obstacles and opposition.

General McDowell at once set himself to the immense work

of restoring order and establishing discipline among his badly-
shattered columns.   The President himself drove in an open
carriage through the camps of the volunteers, occasionally
halting and addressing a few words of comfort and encouragement to the groups of dispirited soldiery, as the latter formed
about his carriage.   But something more substantial than
speech-making was speedily resolved upon.   As the firing upon
Sumter had been immediately followed by a call from the President for 75,000 men to serve for a period of three months, so
was the disaster at Bull Run made the occasion for issuing a
second call for a much greater number of men to serve for
three years, or during the war.

The harsh and unjust criticisms which were showered from
all parts of the land upon General McDowell for the unfortunate termination of the battle of Bull Run, decided the government to call to the active command of the forces then
assembled, and about to assemble at Washington, a new chief.
In making the selection for this important position, the opinion
of the government officials charged with this duty, and that
of the people as indicated by the public press, seemed to centre
upon a single personage as the one best fitted to restore confidence to the troops, and to inspire the country with hopes of
success in the future.   General McClellan, on the breaking
out of the war, had been appointed by Governor Dennison,
of Ohio, to the grade of major-general of the State troops,
and charged with the duty of organizing and equipping the
immense force of volunteers furnished by that State, under
the call for three months' men.   Afterward assigned to the
command of the military department of West Virginia, containing at that time a considerable number of troops in the
field, opposed to which was a Confederate army under command
of educated leaders, McClellan devised and put in execution a
plan of operation which, after a series of rapid and most brilliant victories, resulted in the capture or overthrow of all the
forces of the enemy operating in his department.   So decisive

and gratifying were these victories, coming as they did almost simultaneously with the disaster and disappointment of Bull Run, and the operations of the Shenandoah, that all eyes had singled out the youthful victor in the West Virginia battles as the one destined to lead the armies of the republic to future victory.

On the 25th of July, four days after the defeat at Bull Run, McClellan, having turned over his command in West Virginia to General Rosecrans, the next in rank, was assigned to the command of a geographical division, which included the departments of Washington and Northeastern Virginia, with headquarters at Washington. No appointment to high command during the war received higher commendation or more universal approval from the people and the army, not even excepting that of General Grant in 1864. It can also be truthfully said, that no officer of either side ever developed or gave evidence of the possession of that high order of military ability which at that peculiar and particular time was so greatly demanded in the Federal commander, and which General McClellan brought to the discharge of his duties as the reörganizer and commander of a defeated and demoralized force, and to the formation of a new army composed almost entirely of new levies fresh from the counting-house, the farm, and the workshop. Subsequent events and results of the war, did much to detract from, and cover up, the real merit and worth of McClellan's achievements in this respect, but to him alone belongs the credit of that system of organization, discipline, and supply by which the Army of the Potomac was created, and owing to which that army was unlike as well as superior to any other army of the republic, in all the acquired elements which tend to make a powerful and efficient force."

After some personal estimates of the causes of McClellan's failure, Custer proceeds :

After remaining at Arlington a few days, the company to which I belonged was ordered to Alexandria, at which point it

6

only remained a brief period, being moved still further to the front, thus twice going beyond the Alexandria Seminary, where we were destined to remain some weeks. While at this point General Philip Kearny, who had just been appointed Brigadier-general U. S. Volunteers, arrived and assumed command of a brigade of volunteers composed of four regiments of New Jersey troops, afterward known and distinguished as the Jersey Brigade. To this brigade my company was temporarily attached, thus bringing us under the command of Kearny. When he arrived from Washington with his commission as Brigadier-general, and with orders to organize the Jersey Brigade, he was not provided with a single staff officer, and, being unacquainted with the younger officers of the brigade, was unable to select the necessary officers for his staff. In this dilemma he asked the officer commanding my company (Lieutenant Drummond) if, having three officers present for duty, he could not dispense with my services, I being the junior, to enable me to do duty upon the brigade staff. To this proposition Drummond assented; whereupon Kearny, by a formal order, detailed me first as aide-de-camp, afterward as assistant adjutant-general, I being the first staff officer detailed by Kearny. I found the change from subaltern in a company to a responsible position on the staff of a most active and enterprising officer both agreeable and beneficial.

Kearny was a very peculiar, withal a very gallant leader. Formerly an officer of the regular service, he had enjoyed rare and unusual opportunities for perfecting his knowledge and experience in all matters relating to the military profession. He had while an officer of the army been detailed by the government as one of three officers to be sent to Europe, particularly to France, to study the military art and customs of service as prevailing in that country. While abroad on this mission he had opportunities to see the French army in actual service; and as results of his observation, made some interesting and valuable reports to the government at Washington. He participated in our war with Mexico as a cavalry officer, losing an arm while leading a charge of cavalry which was characterized by its great boldness, if not by its success. After the war with Mexico Kearny resigned his commission in the regular army, and being possessed of great wealth and a love for foreign travel and adventure, he spent several years abroad, during a portion of which he entered the French service under Napoleon III., and by his gallantry and conspicuous conduct won the marked commendation of the French military authorities. He returned to his native country as soon as he learned of the threatened outbreak between the North and South, and promptly sought to obtain a command which would enable him to fight in defence of the Union. In this he was at first unsuccessful, and was forced to see other and inferior men appointed to commands which he would gladly have accepted. Finally successful in obtaining a commission, he at once formed his brigade, and began devoting himself to the discipline and organization of that splendid body of men afterward destined to become so famous as Kearny's or the Jersey Brigade.

Of the many officers of high rank with whom I have served, Kearny was the strictest disciplinarian. So strict was he in this respect that were it not for the grander qualities he subsequently displayed he might well have been considered as simply a military martinet. His severity of discipline was usually visited upon the higher officers, the colonels and field-officers, rather than upon the subaltern and enlisted men. Once aroused by some departure, however slight, from the established regulation or order, and the unfortunate victim of Kearny's displeasure became the object and recipient of such a torrent of violent invectives, such varied and expressive epithets, that the limit of language seemed for once to have been reached; and luckless offenders have more than once tendered their resignations rather than subject themselves a second time to such an ordeal.

Kearny was a man of violent passions, quick and determined

impulses, haughty demeanor, largely the result of his military training and life, brave as the bravest of men can be, possessed of unusually great activity, both mental and physical, patriotic as well as ambitious, impatient under all delay, extremely sensitive in regard to the claims of his command as well as his own. Distrustful of all those who differed with him in opinion or action, capable as a leader of men, and possessed of that necessary attribute which endeared him to his followers despite his severity, he presented a combination which is rarely encountered. He constantly chafed under the restraint and inactivity of camp life, and was never so contented and happy as when moving to the attack. And whether it was the attack of a picket-post or the storming of the enemy's breastworks, Kearny was always to be found where the danger was greatest. Notwithstanding the fame he achieved as an infantry commander, he never felt that he was in his proper place, but always longed to command immense bodies of cavalry, believing that with that arm he would find service more in keeping with his restless, impulsive temperament. Brave in battle, imperious in command, and at times domineering toward those beneath him, no one could wear a more courtly manner than Kearny, unless he willed to do otherwise.

During my brief but agreeable tour of duty with Kearny as a staff officer, I found him ever engaged in some scheme either looking to the improvement of his command or the discomfiture of his enemy. The pickets of the Confederates were stationed along a line but four or five miles distant from Kearny's headquarters. He determined, with the approval of higher authority, to organize a small expedition and effect the capture of what was believed to be one of the principal picket posts of the Confederates. In fact it was believed that on a particular night there were to be assembled at the house near which the picket reserve was located several Confederate officers of importance, who were reported to be reconnoitering the ground between the two hostile forces. Kearny fixed the

night in question as the one upon which the attempt to effect
the capture should be made. Three hundred picked men from
the Jersey Brigade were named for this duty. Lieutenant-
Colonel Buck was assigned to the command. Kearny directed
me to accompany the expedition as a representative from headquarters. It must be remembered that officers and men were
at that time totally lacking in the actual experience of war.
Those who fought at Bull Run had been discharged, and raw,
inexperienced regiments had taken their places.

The night chosen for the undertaking proved to be a
lovely moonlight one. The troops assembled near Kearny's
headquarters about nine o'clock in the evening, and leaving all
impediments in the way of blankets, overcoats, and unnecessary
accoutrements behind, we soon began our silent march to the
front. It was known that the Confederate pickets were posted
four or five miles in advance, but before marching half that
distance a halt was ordered, and additional precautions adopted
to preserve secrecy in our movements. From that point we
pursued our way as quietly as possible, no one being allowed
to speak above a whisper. Sometimes, instead of following the
road, we made our way through paths in the forest, feeling our
way as cautiously as if masked batteries, then the *bete noire* of
the average volunteer, were bristling from beyond every bush.
The cracking of a twig in the distance, or the stumbling of one
of the leading files over a concealed log, was sufficient to cause
the entire column to halt, and with bated breath peer into the
darkness of the forest in vain endeavor to discover a foe whose
presence at that particular time and place was not desired.

In this manner we continued our course, at each step the
tension on our nerves, to describe it by no other name, becoming greater and greater, until we resembled in enlarged form
some ludicrous stage picture in which the alarmed family,
aroused from their beds by noise of imaginary burglars, come
stealthily, timidly into the room, staring in all directions to discover the disturber of the household, and ready to drop all

weapons of defence and seek safety in flight at the first real cause of alarm. So it was with us. Inexperienced, magnifying the strength and terrible character of our unseen foes, dreading surprise, we had worked ourselves up to so excitable a condition, that all that was necessary to terminate our anxiety as well as the expedition, was to confront us with an undoubted enemy. We were not to undergo much longer delay. The house about which the picket was posted, and which was to be the object of our attack—a surprise if possible—was located at one end of a long lane, at the foot of which we now found ourselves. A brief halt was made, final instructions from our leaders were whispered from ear to ear, and again we moved forward. Owing to clouds we could only receive partial benefit from the moon ; sufficient, however, to discern in the distance at the head of the lane a clump of trees within which the house was said to be located.

As we silently made our way up the lane, moving in column of fours, with not a skirmisher or advance guard thrown to the front, every isolated tree or even the farmer's herd grazing in the fields near by, were sufficient to make us halt and determine whether or not we were being 'flanked.' Frequent discoveries of our errors in this respect might have inspired us with some little confidence, but at that moment we surely heard human voices up the lane in the vicinity of the house. Of course we halted. It did not impress me that we were engaged in a military undertaking ; on the contrary, it struck me as resembling upon a large scale some boyhood scheme involving a movement upon a neighboring orchard or a melon patch, and the time had arrived just before crossing the fence, when the impression prevails that the owner of the orchard and his dog are on the lookout. Halting to listen and distinguish the voices again, a few moments' silence ensued, during which the clouds cleared away, permitting the moon to shine forth and light up the whole scene, and enabling the enemy's pickets to take in at a glance who and what we were.

'Who comes there?' rang out on the still night air, and without waiting for an answer, bang, bang, bang, went three muskets. It was a sorrowful waste of ammunition to fire three muskets when one would have answered as well. I am sure that while we may all have been facing toward the house when the first shot was fired, we were not only facing but moving in the opposite direction before the sound of the last one reached our ears. I presume too that the fellows who fired the shots ran in the opposite direction, faster than we did; that is, if they were disposed to be active. But all chance to effect a surprise having been lost, our party did not propose to expend either time or ammunition in furtherance of the object of the expedition. We beat a hasty if not precipitate retreat, and returned to our camp in less than half the time it had required to march from there. The same officers and men who participated in this little affair, if charged with the same duty one year later, at a time when they had become more familiar with the operations of war, would have in all probability succeeded in capturing and bringing away as prisoners the entire picket guard and its immediate reserves.

I remained on Kearny's staff as aide until an order was issued prohibiting officers of the regular army from serving on the staffs of officers holding commissions as volunteers. Early in the fall of 1861 the principal portion of the cavalry, both regular and volunteer, was formed into one organization and collected near Washington, under the command of Brigadier-General Philip St. George Cooke, an officer who had rendered valuable service as a cavalry officer on the plains, and who had more recently attracted attention in military circles as the author of a system of cavalry tactics based upon the single rank formation, the principles of which, under another name, have been largely adopted by the government for all arms of its service. Brigadier-General Stoneman, another cavalry officer, was announced as chief of cavalry on the staff of General McClellan. To Stoneman was assigned the task of organizing and equipping the cavalry forces which were to operate in the field with the Army of the Potomac. The concentration of the cavalry near Washington transferred my company from its camp with Kearny's Brigade, below Alexandria, to Cliffburn, about two miles east of the capital. The fall and winter were passed in perfecting, as far as possible, the preparations for the spring campaign.

During the fall of 1861 Lieutenant Custer was ordered home on sick leave in October, and remained there till February, 1862, when he rejoined the Army of the Potomac, being assigned to the Fifth Cavalry.

This period of leave brings us to a time in Custer's career, which witnessed the final formation of his moral character, and changed him in many respects from a wild and reckless boy into a self-respecting man. In regarding his character as testified to by others, we have hitherto found everything to admire and little to censure, his uncommon *goodness* in youth being remarkable. This, his first army leave, was distinguished by his solitary lapse from exemplary life, but it was marked also by his sudden and permanent reform and awakening to principle.

We have said in an early chapter that Custer never at any time drank intoxicating liquors, nor smoked. This statement must now be qualified. In his early life, and while at West Point, he never did. The influence of a pure and virtuous home life, of a family of exemplary piety, saved him from all such dangers. It was not till he entered the army, and lived around Washington, that he learned what temptation was, and then it came on him with resistless force. It must be remembered that at that time the Army of the Potomac had gathered to itself, along with many good men, many worthless, dissipated scamps, even among the highest officers. The amount of hard drinking that was done by all, from general to lieutenant, was frightful, and the language in common use was of the vilest description. While all this at first made a pure-minded country boy disgusted and ashamed, he found, like all others, that familiarity blunted his senses, and finally he yielded to the prevailing habits. Poor lad, how could he help it! He saw his general, Kearny, whom he admired and respected as a model soldier, given over to both, swearing with an elaboration of blasphemy that shocked him at first, amused him later, and finally almost compelled his imitation, from unconscious habit. Every one drank deep, and there seemed to be no escape from the habit. Briefly, this period was the one little spot in Custer's career, the one fault in a perfect life. He fell in with the prevailing habits, drank as deep and swore as hard as any man in the army. With these habits he went home, and paid a long visit to Monroe. While there, he at once became somewhat of a pet. In those days every soldier was a favorite, and Lieutenant Custer "of the Regular Army" was a very different person from the schoolboy "Armstrong," who used to wrestle with the boys and run the streets in old times. He was becoming a man of mark, and was one of those who were "making history."

The public characters of the little town began to notice him, and among others Judge Bacon recognized him publicly and praised his conduct. The Judge was an original Old Line Whig, and therefore almost of necessity an ardent Republican and firm supporter of the Union under Lincoln. He was an enthusiastic admirer of the soldiers, and during the early part of the war lived much in public, frequently addressed Union meetings, and used all of his great influence to forward the cause he loved. It was quite natural therefore that he should look on the rising young officer, who had been on Kearny's staff, with great favor, and he did so. The Judge, however, was one of those men of firm and unbending rectitude and fastidious social sense, who make a great distinction between public and private life. While his acquaintance with young Custer in public life was quite cordial, he never (at that time) offered to introduce him into his private family. There was a certain gulf still existing between the chief personage of Monroe and the young officer, which might have been overlooked elsewhere, but not in a place where the distinctions of circles are so marked as in a small country town like Monroe. Still, the Judge was much interested in young Custer, and frequently spoke of him to his daughter, now a young lady of sixteen, and approaching her graduation at the Seminary. But with the natural perversity of the female sex, the more the Judge spoke in praise of the young man, the less did the daughter seem inclined to like him. She remembered him as one of a crowd of "boys," and like almost every young girl brought up at home and under strict religious teachings, she looked on "boys" as a sort of wild beasts, with whom she could have no feelings in common.

Affairs were in this state, young Custer on a long visit to Mrs. Reed, when he fell in one day with a number of old school cronies, and started on a grand spree. Custer had always been of a peculiarly nervous and excitable temperament, and liquor made him a perfect maniac, no matter how little he took. The result was that, towards sunset, the young officer and one of his old schoolmates were seen coming up Monroe Street past the Judge's house, going towards Mrs. Reed's, and Custer was taking the whole sidewalk to himself, in a peculiarly free and easy state. As luck would have it, the Judge's daughter was at the window; she saw him, and her dislike was intensified at once. Custer went home to Mrs. Reed's, and there too his sister saw him, for the first time in his life, as far as she knew, plainly under the influence of liquor, if not decidedly drunk. That night was the turning point of young Custer's life, and the country is to-day indebted for all the beauty and nobility of his subsequent career to the earnest will, love, and piety of one of the best Christian women that ever breathed.

Mrs. Reed saw him. Surprised, shocked, and grieved as she was, that good creature never hesitated. She went straight to him, wild as he was in looks, and told him she wished to speak to him alone. His companion left, feeling somewhat ashamed of himself, Custer throwing him a gay promise to meet him down town. Then as the door closed, Lieutenant Custer of the army found himself undergoing a strange transformation back to quiet docile Armstrong, before the grieved and steady gaze of his sister. She led him to her room in silence, locked the door on both, and then asked him " what he had been doing." The proud young soldier sobered in a moment, crimsoned like a girl, and felt horribly ashamed of himself.

What passed at that interview between the anxious loving sister and the impulsive erring boy, already repenting of his degradation and error, will never be fully known till the last day. Far be it from us to strive to lift the veil. It was a season of tears, prayers, and earnest pleading on one side, overcoming all resistance on the other. The result was that George Armstrong Custer then and there, in the presence of God, gave his sister a solemn pledge that never henceforth to the day of his death should a drop of intoxicating liquor pass his lips. That pledge he kept in letter and spirit to the last. His first excess in Monroe was his last anywhere, and henceforth he was a free man.

It may be asked perhaps why we have related this incident of Custer's career, the only painful one that mars an otherwise perfect life. We have done so because it was really the turning point for Custer, and for the purpose of reimpressing on the world the nature of those home influences, so sweet and pure, which ended in moulding a character of perfect knighthood. Mother, sister, and finally wife, three noble women aided to mould that character. True, the material was noble and plastic, but at that early period how easy it would have been to have made thereof a fierce type of destroying power, devoid of moral beauty. From all the errors of such a sombre figure of valor and unhappiness, Custer was saved by the influence of a Christian sister. Honor to her for it !

His punishment for the brief lapse was yet to come, but it found him prepared with strength of purpose and principle to live down the past and conquer his future. His error was public, and the one woman of all others whose opinion he valued had seen him degraded. How should he ever now attain her love? The gulf widened to an almost immeasurable distance at once. To most men it would have seemed hopelessly wide. Was it to him? We shall see further on. For the present let us turn from his private to his public life.

CHAPTER IV.

THE PENINSULAR CAMPAIGN.

WHEN Custer returned to his post in February he found that a marvelous transformation of affairs had taken place. Washington was securely girdled with fortifications, and, what was of more importance, the Army of the Potomac was created. The question of the best method of advance was even then in progress of hot discussion between McClellan and the President; and this discussion consumed most of the month. Into the merits of the controversy it is not the purpose of General Custer's biographer to enter, further than to state its nature, and chronicle its result.

The President wished McClellan to advance on the Confederate forces at Manassas, and fight a second battle of Bull Run. McClellan wished to transfer the army by water to the Peninsula and operate on Richmond from thence. The difference of opinion caused a long correspondence between the two, which ended in McClellan gaining his point; and the transports were accordingly gathered in the Chesapeake, to transfer the army to Fortress Monroe. General Custer, in his last published papers, enters warmly into the controversy in favor of McClellan, for whom he entertained a most sincere admiration. Without following him into the vexed region, we shall again quote from him in all that pertains to the record of facts affecting himself. On the eighth of March, 1862, the President issued his "War Order No. 2," dividing the Army of the Potomac into four corps, under Generals McDowell, Sumner, Heintzelman and Keyes.

On the 9th of March, continues Custer, McClellan received information that the enemy was evacuating his position at Manassas, a move, as was afterward ascertained, decided upon when an idea was gained upon the part of the enemy in regard to the transfer of the Army of the Potomac to a new base. This was the effect foreseen by McClellan, but the bad condition of the roads between Washington and Manassas prevented him from embarrassing the enemy in his retirement.

As the transports could not be ready for some time to move the army to its new base, McClellan decided to march it to Manassas and back, in order to give the troops some preliminary experience in marching and the rigors of actual service. Orders were issued during the 9th for a general movement of the army the next morning toward Centreville and Manassas. At noon on the 10th, the cavalry advanced under Averill, reached the enemy's lines at Centreville, and found them abandoned, the enemy having burned a considerable amount of military stores and other valuable property.

On the 13th of March McClellan called a council of war at his headquarters in the field of Fairfax Court House, the council consisting of the four corps commanders, McDowell, Sumner, Keyes, and Heintzelman, at which it was decided 'that the enemy having retreated from Manassas to Gordonsville, behind the Rappahannock and Rapidan, it is the opinion of generals commanding corps that the operations to be carried on will be best undertaken from Old Point Comfort, between the York and James Rivers.

" Operating against Richmond from Fortress Monroe as a base, it would be desirable to use both the James and York Rivers as lines of communication and supply; but the appearance on the 8th of March, of the Confederate iron-clad Merrimac off Fortress Monroe, and the havoc created in the Federal fleet, imperilled the adoption of the peninsular plan of campaign; but on the 9th of March, the Monitor, as invented by Ericsson, engaged the Merrimac near Fortress Monroe, and so clearly established its superiority over the latter, as to remove considerable of the apprehension entertained in regard to the Merrimac's ability to embarrass operations. Even if the James River remained closed, the line of the York and its tributaries was open.

While the army was being marched toward Manassas, I obtained my first experience with cavalry advance guards. General Stoneman, chief of cavalry, was directed to push a large force of cavalry along the line of the Orange and Alexandria railroad to determine the position of the enemy, and if possible drive him across the Rappahannock. Upon arriving at Catlett's Station, near Cedar Run, the enemy's pickets were discerned in considerable force on a hill about one mile in our front. The Fifth United States Cavalry, to which I then belonged, was in advance. Upon discerning the pickets, a halt was ordered, and intelligence of the enemy's presence sent to General Stoneman. An order was soon received from that officer directing that the pickets of the enemy be driven back across Cedar Run. When this order reached us, the officers of the regiment were generally assembled in a group at the head of the column, Major Charles J. Whiting in command. I at once asked permission to take my company, the command of which I accidentally held, owing to the absence of the captain and first lieutenant, and perform the duty of driving in the pickets. Permission being accorded, I marched the company to the front, formed line, and advanced toward the pickets, then plainly in view, and interested observers of our movements.

Advancing without opposition to the base of the hill upon which the pickets were posted, when within convenient distance I gave the command 'Charge' for the first time. My company responded gallantly, and away we went. Our adversaries did not wait to receive us, but retreated hurriedly and crossed the bridge over Cedar Run, setting fire to it immediately after. We pursued them to the bank of the run, and then exchanged several shots with the enemy, now safely posted on the opposite side. Being unable to advance across the stream, and exposed to a serious fire from small arms, I ordered my command to retire, which it did in excellent order, but not until one man, private John W. Bryaud, had been shot in the head, fortunately not seriously, and one horse wounded. Battles and skirmishes at that time were unfamiliar events to the men composing the Army of the Potomac, and the little episode just recorded, furnished a topic for general discussion and comment. The company that had been engaged in the affair was praised by its companions, while it was a question whether private Bryaud suffered most from his wound or the numerous and inquiring visits of the enterprising representatives of the press, each anxious and determined to gather and record for his particular journal, all the details connected with the shedding of the first blood by the Army of the Potomac.

Such was the first introduction of the young officer to actual fighting, for at Bull Run he must be considered merely as a spectator. When the great enterprise and moral force of the rebel cavalry at that time is considered, it is interesting to note how, even then, they always shrunk from the cold steel of a charge. The only American cavalry at that date, capable of a mounted charge in real earnest, was the small force of regulars, and the superiority of that method of fighting cavalry over the " shooting business," indulged in by the enemy, was first illustrated in Virginia by Custer—it was symptomatic of the future of the young officer, for almost all his subsequent successes, were obtained in the same manner, by rapid mounted charges.

Continuing his narrative of facts, we quote now from the last paper ever furnished by Custer to his publishers. It was written while on his march toward the foe that slew him, and was not received till some days after the news of his death.

In endeavoring, says Custer, to quiet the anxious fears of President Lincoln in regard to a movement of the Confederate army at Manassas against Washington after the transfer to the Peninsula of the Army of the Potomac, McClellan assured him that the latter movement would of itself be the surest and

quickest method as well as the one involving the least loss of
life by which the enemy would be forced to abandon his fortified
positions at Centreville and Manassas, and thus free Washington
from the menace of attack.

This opinion was promptly verified by the course adopted
by the Confederate leader, General Joseph E. Johnston. No
sooner did he learn of the contemplated transfer of the Army
of the Potomac to the Lower Chesapeake, than he evacuated
every fortified position in front of Washington, and retired
toward Richmond; and McClellan truly remarked afterward
that at no former period was southern Virginia so completely
in our possession, and the vicinity of Washington free from the
presence of the enemy. The ground so gained was not lost,
nor Washington again put in danger until the enemy learned
that orders had been sent to the Army of the Potomac to evac-
uate the Peninsula, and thus leave them free to move directly
toward Washington, which they did at once, and again seriously
menaced the national capital.

Fort Monroe having been selected as the base of operations
of the Army of the Potomac by the council of war assembled
March 13, and that selection having been acquiesced in by the
President, the next step was to transfer the Army of the Potomac from Washington to the Peninsula.

The first plan for the transfer of the army to its new base
involved the embarkation of McDowell's corps first; the intention being to land it either at a point termed the Sandbox, on
the right bank of York River, about four miles below Yorktown,
and thus turn the works of the enemy supposed to be at Ship
Point, Howard's Bridge, and Big Bethel, or to land it on the
Gloucester side of York River, and move from there to West
Point. This plan was subsequently changed, and the most convenient divisions were embarked first, and moved direct to Fortress Monroe. McDowell's corps, by the new arrangement, was
to embark last, and as an entire corps moved to such point on
York River as might afterward be decided upon. The first

7

division to embark was that of General Hamilton, of Heintzelman's corps, which left Alexandria March 17. On the 22d of March Fitz John Porter's division of the same corps embarked from the same point accompanied by General Heintzelman, the corps commander. McClellan, with his entire headquarters, embarked on the steamer Commodore on the 1st of April, the day after he had been informed by the President that Blenker's division, ten thousand strong, was to be taken from his command. He arrived at Fortress Monroe the afternoon of the following day, and at once began giving his personal attention to the disposition of his troops as they arrived and disembarked. When the enemy's batteries controlled or threatened the navigation of the Potomac, it had been arranged to embark the troops from Annapolis, Maryland, but upon the abandonment of these batteries by the enemy, it was no longer convenient or desirable to embark from Annapolis. Alexandria, Virginia, was therefore, chosen as the point of embarkation, and orders given for the chartering and assembling of the necessary water transportation. Omitting the details of what in itself was a stupendous undertaking, the transfer to a new and distant base, of an immense army with all its material and accompaniments, it will be sufficient at present simply to record that in thirty-seven days from the time the order was given to secure the transportation necessary for so extensive a movement, the transfer of the Army of the Potomac was effected from Washington to Fort Monroe. This transfer involved the shipment of 121,500 men, 14,592 animals, 1,150 wagons, forty-four batteries, seventy-four ambulances, besides pontoon bridges, materials for telegraph lines, and other miscellaneous matter. No accident or loss occurred to mar the success of this achievement, save the loss of less than a score of mules.

The vessels required to effect this transfer were as follows:

One hundred and thirteen steamers, at two hundred and fifteen dollars and ten cents per day. One hundred and eighteen schooners, at twenty-four dollars and forty-five cents per day. Eighty-eight barges, at one thousand four hundred and twenty-seven dollars per day.

"Nine of the latter drifted ashore during a severe gale, but their cargoes were saved. The troops were ordered to take up the line of march from Fortress Monroe up the Peninsula, the second day succeeding McClellan's arrival. This was the 4th. The troops moved in two columns; that on the right, under Heintzelman, by the Big Bethel and Yorktown road, that on the left, under Keyes, by the James River and Warwick Court House road. On the afternoon of the 5th, both columns were brought to a halt. Heintzelman's on the right, found itself in front of the enemy's earthworks at Yorktown, that of Keyes, consisting of Baldy Smith's division, came unexpectedly upon a heavy force of the enemy intrenched near Lee's Mills, at the crossing of Warwick River. The enemy opened upon Smith's troops with artillery and musketry. The Warwick River is a diminutive stream, undeserving the name of river, and in itself does not constitute a military obstacle, but the Confederates, by a series of dams, constructed at convenient points, the latter, protected by batteries and rifle pits, had enlarged Warwick River until it had become an almost impassable barrier to the advance of troops, unless the fire from the protecting batteries and rifle pits could be silenced. So formidable were the defensive arrangements of the enemy that General Keyes found it impracticable to execute the order which McClellan had given him, which was to carry the enemy's position by assault. By this system of dams, with their protecting batteries and rifle pits, the Warwick River which heads within rifle shot of Yorktown, and flows across the narrow peninsula to the James, became an excellent line of defence for the enemy, and a most serious obstruction to the advance of the Union forces.

" On the 16th of April, however, it was determined to push a strong reconnoissance against what was supposed to be the weakest point in the enemy's line, intending, if successful, to support the movement and make it general. The point selected was a short distance above Lee's Mills, and opposite that portion of the Federal line held by Smith's division. General Smith directed the attack, the brunt of which was borne by the Vermont brigade. The attacking party reached the first line of the enemy's works after wading to the armpits across the marshy Warwick, but only to find their position commanded by other lines of intrenchments. The movement was a failure, except so far as it developed the strength of the enemy's position. The Union troops were driven back with heavy loss.

" The slow operations of the siege continued. Batteries of heavy guns were brought up and placed in position. Each day marked a step toward the completion of the preliminary preparations. It was about this time that I received an order which greatly changed the character of my duties. I had left Alexandria, Virginia, with my company of the Fifth U. S. Cavalry as second lieutenant of the company, and was among the first to arrive at Fortress Monroe. I served with my company during the march from Fortress Monroe to the Warwick. When it was decided to commence a siege there was a demand for young officers competent to serve as subordinates to the engineer officers in superintending working parties engaged in making fascines and gabions and in laying out and erecting field works, a practical knowledge of which was supposed to belong to all recent graduates. It was my good fortune to be one of the young officers selected for this duty, and I was ordered to report as assistant to Lieutenant Nicholas Bowen of the Topographical Engineers, at that time Chief Engineer on the staff of General W. F. Smith (Baldy). I served in this capacity— obtaining a most invaluable experience—until the army found its advance to Richmond obstructed by the treacherous and tortuous windings of the Chickahominy River, a stream which, however chargeable with some of the misfortunes of the Army of the Potomac, was almost literally a stepping-stone for my personal advancement."

Here ends the record of Custer's military life, as written by his own hand, and the closing sentence brings us to the first important event of his career, whereby he was brought to the notice of the commander of the army, and earned his promotion to the grade of a captain.

Note.—Since the publication of his last article, written while on his last expedition, and forwarded from his last camp, and since the writing of the above paragraph, another manuscript has come to light among General Custer's papers, which covers this period of his life up to the close of the battle of Williamsburg. This manuscript was written after a triumphant Indian campaign, and was one of the general's first efforts at authorship. It begins almost the same as his Galaxy "War Memoirs," and traverses the same ground, with similar peculiarities of style, but with much superior freshness and raciness of detail. At the end of the battle of Williamsburg, it stops abruptly, the author having been discouraged from its continuance by a notion that it was unequal to the subject, and feeling, more keenly than the world gives him credit for, his own deficiencies in that mechanical education of a writer on which so much stress is laid now-a-days. This last article was published in the Galaxy for November, 1876, but its contents do not add any very important information as to the life of Lieutenant Custer at the time, save those details which are always of interest as concerning *him*.

From this paper it appears that Custer, while at the siege of Yorktown, was engaged with a working party in throwing up by night a line of rifle pits, the nearest to the enemy of any pushed out during the siege, so near that the working party was compelled to shovel the sandy soil in stealthy silence, while they could hear all the conversation of their enemies, within a very short distance. Besides this duty, Custer was also detailed for a large part of the time on balloon reconnaissances, and he gives a graphic description of his first ascent, and of his subsequent observations of the enemy's line at different periods. He was one of the first, while up in the balloon, to detect the fact of Johnston's evacuation, and hastened to General " Baldy " Smith's headquarters, to report the fact. He was met there by the same information, come in from two different headquarters ; one of them a negro who had escaped through the lines ; and so the credit of being the first to announce the evacuation was evenly divided.

This paper also makes it clear how Custer came to be at the rifle pit, and afterwards at the battle of Williamsburg with Hancock's brigade. The rifle pit was in front of General "Baldy" Smith's command, to which Custer was attached as assistant engineer, and Hancock's brigade was part of the same division. Custer therefore had a sort of roving commission to go anywhere he could to acquire information, that would aid him in his maps and sketches, and his idea of the duties of an engineer officer as laid down in that paper are exacting enough to fill the role of a general officer. There were not many such engineers as Custer.

WADING THE CHICKAHOMINY.

CHAPTER V.

WINNING THE BARS.

ON the 3d of May, 1862, General Joseph E. Johnston, who had been appointed to the command of the Confederate forces in the Peninsula, found that his position before York-town was no longer tenable. McClellan had pushed his siege works close to Yorktown, his army was all landed and his breaching batteries were ready to open. The Federal gunboats in the York River were moreover ready to move up the river as soon as the fire of Yorktown should be overcome; and that place once passed, there was nothing to prevent the landing of a heavy force in Johnston's rear. His army, as we learn from the 'Narrative,' then amounted to 53,000 men, while McClellan's forces, as stated by his own morning report, were 112,000 men. By the aid of heavy works Johnston had held him back so far, just as Lee subsequently did to Grant at Petersburg, but there was this important difference in McClellan's favor against Johnston, that the latter's flanks were only covered by water, and that Federal gun-boats controlled that water. It was inevitable that Yorktown should be evacuated as soon as it was seriously attacked. Johnston had done all that could be hoped for, when he detained McClellan a whole month in front of his works.

On the night of Saturday, the Confederates stole away from the lines of Yorktown in the darkness, and moved up the Peninsula towards Richmond. Johnston's army consisted of four strong divisions of infantry, those of Magruder, Longstreet, D. H. Hill and G. W. Smith. Magruder and Smith took the lead, then came the baggage, and Longstreet and D. H. Hill followed, Longstreet forming the infantry rear guard. Stuart's cavalry brigade, then inconsiderable in numbers, staid at Yorktown to the last, and followed the infantry leisurely.

At 2 A. M. May 4th, McClellan's army discovered the fact of the evacuation, and began preparations for a move. The small cavalry force of the Army of the Potomac, with a battery, started out in the morning, and followed Stuart with excessive caution, under command of General Stoneman. They struck Stuart about 4 P. M. near Williamsburg, drove him in, and penetrated to a redoubt called Fort Magruder, one of the works prepared by the providence of the first Confederate commander, as a good point to stay the advance of the enemy.

Longstreet sent back Kershaw's and Semmes's brigades of foot to Stuart's help, drove off Stoneman, and took one of his guns, which was found abandoned. That night Longstreet's division halted near Williamsburg, and his rear-guard occupied Fort Magruder and six redoubts on a line with it. It began to rain before morning, and the mud was soon very heavy, a foretaste of future Virginia campaigning.

Next day the Federal advance, consisting of Hooker's division, struck Fort Magruder, and fought all the morning, so hard that Hill's division of Confederates had to be sent back to Longstreet's help. On the Federal side, four more divisions came up, but did not join Hooker, who was left to fight his battle almost alone till later in the day, when the pressure of the enemy compelled Peck's brigade and some of "Baldy" Smith's division to be put in. Finally, Kearney's division, in the same corps as Hooker's, came up from the rear, having been the last to leave Yorktown, and went in beside Hooker who had suffered severely. The assistance, however, did not come in time to prevent the loss of seventeen hundred men, in killed, wounded, and missing, from Hooker's division, with ten colors taken and five guns carried off, besides five more injured and abandoned. In the mean time, however, Hancock's brigade, on the Federal side, had crossed a little run to the right of Fort Magruder, and occupied two of the chain of redoubts on the line of the fort, thus turning Longstreet's left.

With this brigade, Lieutenant Custer made his appearance, and behaved with his usual dash and vigor. He does not seem to have had any particular business to call him there, but his restless nature took him always to the extreme advance, where there was any duty to be done, and he seems early to have discovered that with Hancock's command was about as good a place as could be found for that sort of service. Very frequently afterwards during the campaign, he found himself with the same brigade. It is noticeable too, that at Williamsburg, his military eye led him to prefer Hancock's position to Hooker's. There was much harder fighting in front of Hooker, but it was early evident that it was a perfectly hopeless struggle for that single division to attempt to carry the Confederate works in front. It was a mere useless slaughter of brave men. In Hancock's direction, a success promised something. It turned Longstreet's flank; and had it been supported by other of the numerous troops that lay idly looking on, might easily have resulted in the capture of the greater part of Johnston's rear guard.

As it was, Hancock's single brigade caused Longstreet the only serious alarm he suffered during the day, according to the admissions made in "Johnston's Narrative." It did all that so small a force could be expected to do, occupied the redoubts, driving out the enemy's skirmishers, held its own all day; and when Early's brigade, towards evening, advanced to dislodge it, went in on the charge, and thrashed Early's brigade most handsomely, the only decided success of the day.

The part taken by Custer in the affair is characteristic, and is thus mentioned in Hancock's report: "I now placed the artillery in battery on the crest of the hill in front of the enemy's work at short range, deployed skirmishers on the right and left of the road, and sent the Fifth Wisconsin, preceded by skirmishers under command of Major Larrabee, and followed by the Sixth Maine in column of assault across the dam and into the work, Lieutenant Custer, Fifth Regular Cavalry, volunteering and leading the way on horseback." The little run mentioned had been turned into a millpond in former times, and the troops crossed on the dam.

A queer figure Custer then was, according to the accounts of eye-witnesses. One officer took him for a dashing newspaper correspondent, out to see the fun. He wore an old slouch hat and a cavalry jacket, with no marks of rank, the jacket flying open, while his muddy boots did not look worth more than a dollar. His hair was beginning to grow long, and aided his careless dress to give him a slouchy appearance, but even then there was something peculiar about him that made people ask, "Who is that young fellow?" It was not for more than a year after, that he came out as a dandy.

In the charge on Early's brigade, which cost Early four hundred men, this careless looking young officer was around as usual, waving his shocking bad hat, and cheering on the men in the style afterwards so famous. Few knew him, but his cheery ways, and the habit he had of laughing and joking in action, helped on the green troops as nothing else would. In a first fight, the best drilled soldiers are always nervous. When they come on an enemy and deliver their own volley they are all right, but when the counter volley strikes them, and they see their friends cut down all along the line, the faint hearted begin to drop out, with the peculiar suddenness that distinguishes the "skulker." Then the bravest feel discouraged, as if they were being left all alone, and they too are ready to fall back. If at that moment up comes a mounted officer, laughing and cheery, with his "Stand fast, boys, we'll beat them! Give 'em another volley now!" it is wonderful how those men will cheer up and load and fire. It comes to a test of who can take most punishment, and at Williamsburg, Hancock's brigade showed they could, and ended by sweeping Early from the field.

At the close of the battle of Williamsburg, Johnston withdrew during the night, and the next month was occupied by McClellan's slow advance up the Peninsula, feeling his way to West Point, whence he turned to the left, and bore down on Richmond from the northeast, following the line of the railroad into Richmond. How slow and cautious was his advance, may be judged from the fact that it was not till the 22d of May, seventeen days after the battle of Williamsburg, that his advance reached the Chickahominy River.

In order to understand the subsequent movements, and what is called the "Seven Days Fight," a short account of the Virginia Peninsula, and the localities around Richmond is here necessary, for those readers not familiar with the ground.

The City of Richmond, the objective point of the campaign of 1862, lies at the very head of the Peninsula, on the north bank of the James River, a large, navigable stream there and below it. About sixteen miles north of Richmond, runs the Pamunkey River, a deep black stream, nearly parallel with the James. It is crossed by the West Point railroad at Whitehouse landing, where it is deep enough for gunboats and schooners. The railroad then goes on and takes a curve to the east, avoiding the seven bends which the Pamunkey there takes, inside of ten miles, and terminates at West Point, on the other bank of the Pamunkey. Here the river receives a tributary from the north, and becomes an estuary two miles wide, called the York River. Between the Pamunkey and James Rivers, lies the Peninsula. It stretches out to sea for some seventy miles, to Fortress Monroe. Yorktown is on the north side, more than half-way down. Williamsburg is in the middle of the Peninsula, some ten miles from Yorktown. All of the lower part was unoccupied by either side after Williamsburg. The subsequent fighting was up in the very neck of the Peninsula, to the north of Richmond. Here arises a collection of little streams, which join together and constitute the Chickahominy. It splits the Peninsula in half. The whole Peninsula is low ground, formed by the accumulated mud of the two rivers, stopped and deposited for ages by the ocean tides. The Chickahominy steals along through swamps, and it is hard to tell which is river and which is swamp.

On the 22d of May, McClellan's army had arrived at the banks of the Chickahominy, only six or eight miles north of Richmond. The different corps came on various roads, or across country on each side the West Point railroad, and stopped on the north side of the stream. It lay in the bottom, fringed with timber and swamp. On each side was a very gentle open slope, about a mile wide, the crest covered with timber. The Federal pickets were on the north side, the enemy on the opposite crest. No one knew anything of the depth of the river. Two country roads crossed it by bridges. One was a mile below the railroad; it was called Bottom Bridge; the other was about eight miles above the railroad; it was called New Bridge. Meadow Bridge was two miles further up still. All these were broken down, and left with the bare piles sticking up.

On the 22d May, McClellan established his headquarters at Coal Harbor, about a mile from the Chickahominy; and General Barnard, the chief engineer of the army, at once started off to reconnoitre. The previous day he had been down to Bottom Bridge, eight miles below, and found no enemy there, while the stream was fordable on horseback. Barnard judged that it must be even shallower in all probability higher up, and if it could be crossed there the position would be better to cover the railroad to West Point, by which the army drew its supplies from the seacoast.

Custer, being on staff duty, happened to be around, and Barnard beckoned him to come with him, not knowing who he was at the time. Both passed through the picket line, and went down to the river. The Federal outside pickets were in the clear ground, perhaps two hundred yards from the edge of the swampy bank. The general and the lieutenant went on

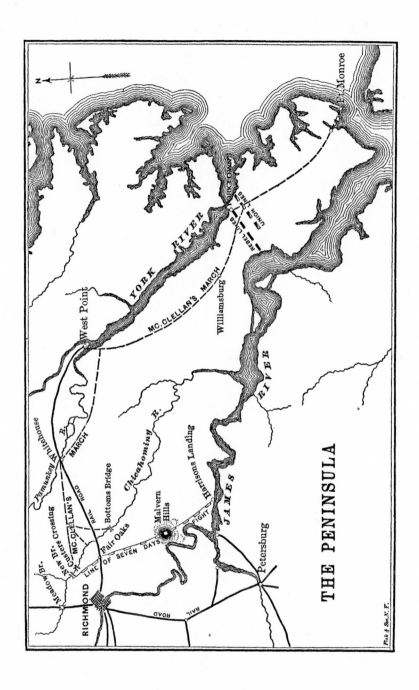

THE PENINSULA

past the pickets but were warned not to enter the timber, as it was full of the enemy's pickets. General Barnard heard them, but as no picket shooting had taken place from them, and as his own experience at Bottom's Bridge made him doubt it, he passed on with Custer, reached the swamp, penetrated it, and finally the two found themselves alone on the margin of the stream, the dark flow of which gave no revelation of its depths, nor of the nature of its bottom. Turning to his young subordinate, General Barnard said, "jump in." There might have been a passing look of surprise, but the order was instantly obeyed, and Custer forded the stream (finding firm bottom) and ascended the opposite bank. The young officer waded the stream, in the momentary expectation of being fired at by the enemy's pickets on the other bank. All around him was quite unknown. There was every reason to suppose that riflemen were in the bushes beyond, and Custer was in the open river, perfectly exposed. He had drawn his revolver, and held it up above the water, which rose to his armpits in the middle of the stream; and his feet sunk several inches into the soft, sticky, black mud of the bottom. General Parnard, in his report, calls it "firm bottom," but it will be noticed that the general did not wade it himself, and therefore his ideas of the bottom must be regarded as slightly formal and technical However, it was not a quicksand.

Arrived at the other side, Custer peered through the bushes and cautiously ascended the bank, being rewarded for his explorations by a distinct view of the enemy's picket fires, some distance off, and by the sight of their nearest sentry, lazily pacing his post, quite unconscious of the proximity of any foe. By this time, Barnard was becoming a little nervous for Custer's and his own safety, and began to make silent signals to him to come back, but the young fellow never heeded them till he had carefully examined the whole of the enemy's position, and had found that their main picket post was so situated in the midst of a bend of the river that it might be easily cut off by a bold

dash from a point either higher up or lower down. Not till he
had settled this in his mind did Custer return. Then he waded
his way back to Barnard, and briefly reported the stream as being "fordable." The old engineer was not much given to
compliments, but even he expressed a certain grim approval of
the deed, and told Custer to follow him back to General Mc-
Clellan.

At that time army headquarters were some half a mile from
the river, on the other side of the northern ridge of the valley,
at the Widow Gaines' house. The general and his young subordinate mounted and rode up to the house, where they found
McClellan about to ride out with his staff, to visit the different
positions. Here Custer fell back while Barnard went on. In
these army matters, the reader must remember the credit assigned
to an officer or soldier is almost always in proportion to his
rank. The soldiers fight the battle, and the officer gets the
credit. In this case, Custer had made the risky reconnoissance,
but as Barnard was the chief engineer, it would all go to Barnard's credit. So the boy thought, at least. He was yet
only a humble second lieutenant, and the riotous life he had led
at Washington the previous winter, with the sudden shock of
revelation and repentance produced by his sister's solemn warn-
ings and prayers, had tended to sober and subdue him greatly.
There are evidences at this time in his private correspondence
that he felt at times depressed in mind to some extent, and
thought that he had led an unusually wicked life. This ten-
derness of conscience was natural to him. Moreover, he had
spent most of his money, was hard up, shabby in his dress, and
at that moment was all covered with the black mud of the
Chickahominy. He felt very keenly the contrast between his
own forlorn appearance and that of the neat and handsome staff
of McClellan, where every officer was well brushed and shaved
and glittering with bright buttons. In short, Custer hung back
out of sight, and dropped to the rear of the staff as they rode
on. General Barnard rode by McClellan's side on the way to

the other positions, and made his report of the state of the river, so many feet of water, such a bottom, etc. The commander listened, asked a few questions, and finally it came out that the general had not gone himself, but had sent in some young officer, really could not say who—had seen him lounging near headquarters—guessed he was somewhere near—would the general like to see him?

Certainly the general would like to see him—wanted to see him at once—very important—where was he? Word was passed that "General McClellan wanted to see the officer who had been down to the river with General Barnard." It passed from a stately chief of staff, covered with buttons, through a still more gorgeous aid-de-camp, thence to another and another, till it reached the smart orderlies, and every body wanted to know where was "the officer that went with General Barnard." At last he was found, and brought up, dirty and muddy, with unkempt hair, coat not brushed, but all creased from being slept in, trousers far from guiltless of rags (fruit of hard riding), boots more russet than black, with red reflections, cap once blue, now purple from many rains and suns. Such was the figure that presented itself before McClellan—general, as always, neat as a pin—boy's face as red as fire with shame at his own carelessness.

But McClellan knew how to conquer *mauvaise honte* as few other men could. He pretended not to notice Custer's confusion, told the lad to ride with him, that he "wanted to hear all about this crossing of the river and what was on the other side."

By a few brief questions he set the boy at his ease, drew him on to talk, and, once talking, Custer was always a remarkably vivid and correct narrator. Before he knew how it happened, he found himself telling all about the position of the enemy's pickets, and how easily they might be attacked, forgetting all mention of himself, and treating his own exploit as nothing worthy of notice. The tables were turned now. Custer was

8

doing all the talking; McClellan listening. Suddenly the young officer recollected *himself* again, grew silent and bashful, touched his cap stiffly, and said, "That's all, sir."

Then it was that McClellan broke the silence abruptly. "Do you know, you're just the young man I've been looking for, Mr. Custer. How would you like to come on my staff?"

Custer made no answer. For a moment he *could* make none. He paled and flushed, perfectly overcome. He could not believe his good fortune.

" You don't—really—mean it—general?" was all he could stammer out.

" I do," said the general, kindly. "How say you? Will you accept?"

.   .   .   .

" How did you feel when the general spoke to you?" asked a friend of Custer's, long, long after.

His reply was brief, as his eyes filled with tears. " *I felt I could have died for him.*"

That was the commencement, for Custer, of a life-long adoration of McClellan, which nothing after ever served to weaken. McClellan was the first man whom he found to lend him a helping hand in his course through life, and he never forgot the fact. Hitherto he had been alone, helpless and friendless, all his gallant deeds apparently wasted. It was to no purpose that he had led the first charge in the Army of the Potomac, and piloted the way to victory for Hancock's brigade at Williamsburg. He was still a mere second lieutenant of cavalry, while other subalterns of the regular army, all round him, were entering the volunteer service as captains, majors, colonels, according to the strength of their friends and influence. He had no friends but humble ones, no influence at all. Now on a sudden, to find himself offered a conspicuous position, which almost certainly promised further advancement, seemed to the young officer like a gift from heaven, and he fell down and worshipped the giver forthwith. The feeling with which Custer, then and after, regarded McClellan, was such as he never gave to any subsequent general, not even Sheridan. It was a compound of respect, gratitude, and love amounting to adoration, which remained with him to the last. While his cooler military sense must have recognized, later in life, the undoubted faults of McClellan as a commander, he never would admit them, even to himself. He seemed to feel it a point of honor with him to defend his old commander and first friend against all assaults. When he commenced his War Memoirs in the "Galaxy," fourteen years after the events in which he then took a part, McClellan's reputation was regarded as settled by the fact of his ill success, and his apologists occupied a decidedly weak position, as well as an unpopular one. It is a characteristic of Custer's loyalty of heart and gratitude for benefits received, that he should have deliberately embraced the unpopular side of McClellan's defence, and have worked so hard and faithfully as he did. He never forgot his early friend, and no one else ever held the same place in his heart.

Custer, having gratefully accepted the offer, took leave of the general and returned to his quarters, where he soon received the following missive:

WAR DEPARTMENT, Washington, June 5th, 1862.

SIR—You are hereby informed that the President of the United States has appointed you Additional aide-de-camp on the staff of Major-General George B. McClellan with the rank of captain in the service of the United States, to rank as such from the fifth day of June, 1862.

Immediately on receipt hereof, please to communicate to this department, through the Adjutant-General's Office, your acceptance or non-acceptance of said appointment; and with your letter of acceptance, return to the Adjutant-General of the Army the oath herewith enclosed, properly filled up, subscribed and attested, reporting at the same time your age, residence, when appointed, and the State in which you were born.

Should you accept, you will at once report in person, for

orders, to Major-General George B. McClellan, U. S. Vols. This appointment to continue in force during the pleasure of the President of the United States.

EDWIN M. STANTON, *Secretary of War.*
CAPTAIN GEORGE A. CUSTER, *Addl. Aide-de-Camp.*

It is needless to say that the young officer filled out the oath and sent it back post haste, while he reported at McClellan's headquarters. The appointment he sent by mail to his sister Mrs. Reed, for safe keeping, and she retains it to-day. Even before this appointment came, however, Custer had justified McClellan's faith in his dash and energy. He had begged to be permitted to take over some troops and capture the picket post on the other side of the river. McClellan consented, and a detail was ordered to report to " Captain Custer," (as he was already called, before his appointment,) for detached service. The detail consisted of two companies of cavalry and one of infantry, and the attack was to be made at dawn. In the meantime Custer had taken the pains to wade the middle of the river, for nearly a mile up and down, finding it favorable everywhere. At the appointed time, in the grey of the morning, he found his detail waiting, and rode down to the river. The cavalry was to follow the infantry as a support, in the wrong-headed fashion of those days.

The young officer was absorbed in thought and anxiety about this, his first serious expedition, and consequently did not take much notice of the troops with him, till they came to the ford. Then, as the light was growing stronger, he heard a voice say " I want to know ! If that ain't Armstrong ! " Custer started and looked at the dingy blue-grey crowd of soldiers, and was greeted in a moment by animated cries. " Why, it's Armstrong." " How are ye, Armstrong." " Give us your fist, Armstrong."

He had, by a strange chance, fallen into the midst of Company A., Fourth Michigan Infantry, a company raised in Monroe, and composed almost entirely of his old school friends and playmates. With the peculiarly refreshing republicanism of the western and all American country volunteers, the boys recognized no barrier of rank between them and their old playmate. Here Custer's tact and knowledge of human nature enabled him to maintain discipline where another might have failed.

Instead of putting on cold and distant airs, he hastily grasped the proffered hands nearest, laughing, and said:

"Well, boys, I'm glad to see you, you don't know how glad; but I tell you I'm very busy now, too busy to talk, except to say this—All Monroe boys, follow me; stick to me, and I'll stick to you! Come!"

And he rode into the water, followed by cries of "That's us, Armstrong." "You bet we'll follow."

And they did. To make a long story short, they forded the river, and came down in rear of the enemy's pickets entirely unperceived, exactly as Custer had planned. Just before sunrise they opened fire on the surprised post of the enemy, part of the Louisiana tigers, shot several and stampeded the rest, driving them down toward the river, and taking arms, prisoners, and one color, the first ever taken by the Army of the Potomac, captured by Custer himself.

Well had he justified the choice of his chief.

In this fight Custer was associated with Lieutenant Bowen, who was still his nominal chief. Had they been supported by the cavalry that was with them, they intended to have charged much further. Custer came raging back to the river bank, waving a rebel sabre which he had captured, and urging, entreating, storming at the cavalry commander to come over, that a grand chance awaited them. The officer refused to be persuaded. He could see that the firing had drawn out a whole brigade of the enemy, and that if he went over a general engagement must follow. For this the army was not then prepared, so that Custer, alone and unsupported, with his Monroe boys, had the undivided credit of this affair.

NOTE.—From information received since the above was written
it appears that the whole of the Fourth Michigan regiment was
detailed for this service, but that the greater part was kept in
reserve with the cavalry, so that the brunt of the fighting fell on
Custer.   One great reason for the hesitation of the commander
was the black and formidable looking stream, which he hesitated
to cross for fear of entangling his horses in some hidden quicksand.   His conduct was decidedly prudent, but it must be remembered that in those early days of the war, dash was frowned down
and prudence extolled.   The Bull Run disaster had ended in exag-
gerating the caution natural to all beginners, and every one
seemed to be afraid to do anything dashing, for fear of an ambush
or a masked battery.

THIRD BOOK.—THE CAPTAIN.

CHAPTER I.

FROM RICHMOND TO MALVERN HILL.

CUSTER'S new won rank was not yet fairly settled, when the prestige of McClellan received a sudden check. After lying behind the Chickahominy for nearly a week, he had pushed out his left wing far in advance of the rest, Casey's division being at Fairoaks Station, on the railroad, while the rest of the army was nearly four miles away. Casey was in full view of Richmond, and his troops were the nearest of any force of infantry that reached there, for three long years after.

More than half of McClellan's army remained on the other bank of the Chickahominy, and Johnston saw that he had a good chance to annihilate that part which was so imprudently advanced. By this time he had accumulated 76,000 men, and felt able to move. He made his plans to strike Casey on the 31st June, and was much assisted by the fact that a heavy rain on the 30th had so swelled the Chickahominy that it became for the moment unfordable.

On the 31st Johnston struck Casey, nearly surrounded him, and drove him in confusion, beat back Kearny, who came to his support, and completely defeated that wing of the Federal Army. It was only saved from ruin by the coming of Sumner's corps over the trestle bridges that had been placed on the Chickahominy; Sumner partially restored the fight, but McClellan's advance was checked.

He experienced, however, a slight benefit of fortune in spite of the defeat. Johnston was so severely wounded as to be taken from the field, and this circumstance paralyzed the attack at nightfall. Next day G. W. Smith, who was next in Confederate command, proved totally unable to carry on the battle, and a lull ensued for some weeks, till Lee was appointed General-in-chief. The lull was a deceitful one for McClellan. It encouraged him in the belief that he could take Richmond by a regular siege, and he progressed slowly, just as he had done at Yorktown.

At last, just as he was ready to begin the bombardment, and had telegraphed the President to that effect, Lee, who had gathered together from all quarters an army of about 110,000 men, attacked him in flank and rear, on the side opposite to that which marked Johnston's attack, and at once broke his communications with West Point. Then followed the terrible slaughter of the "Seven Days Fight." The Army of the Potomac was driven from the railroad and the north side of the Peninsula, and compelled to take refuge on the south side, with a new base at Harrison's Landing on the James River, covered by gunboats.

In all these battles, Custer and Bowen, who seem to have been inseparable, were seen together, carrying orders from one part of the field to another, cheerful in spite of the disaster. One of the most remarkable features indeed of all the seven days' fight was this wonderful constancy of the whole army under misfortune. The first day's battle at Gaines' Mills, on the north bank of the Chickahominy, was a blow that would have paralyzed almost any army. Thirty-five thousand men, separated from their comrades by a river, were attacked by Lee with at least seventy thousand, surrounded, crushed, almost annihilated, the whole army found itself driven from its base, out-generaled and flanked; and yet fought on day by day, in fractions, covering the retreat of the rest, and repulsing every subsequent assault with terrible loss. The last battle at Malvern Hill, near Harrison's Landing, was the fiercest of all, and ended in the complete overthrow of Lee's army, which was mowed down by thousands as it urged its desperate assaults against a superior force of artillery, splendidly posted. A Confederate officer who afterwards wrote an account of the battle for the *Cologne Gazette*, which attracted great attention all over Europe, notices the fact that in the last battles, the Union troops advanced to meet them, attacked in their turn, and uttered loud cries of " On to Richmond."

Most of the corps and division commanders were indeed eager, after Malvern Hill, to advance once more on Richmond; but McClellan refused to move. He was too thoroughly convinced of the dangers of the way, and resolved to await reinforcements, as the safest, if not the most brilliant method of procedure.

It was at Malvern Hill that Custer and Bowen once more came to the front, in one of their gallant dashes. Always in the advance and reconnoitring, the pair of friends, accompanied by two orderlies, took a gallop outside of the lines, that morning, to explore a certain thicket in plain view of the army. Just as they came up to it, out dashed six or seven of the enemy's cavalry, and charged for them with loud yells and pistol shots. For a few moments, the two officers were demoralized, and fled towards their own army. Then, seeing by how few they were followed, for their pursuers had strung out considerably, Bowen called to their orderlies, who were regulars, turned, and charged the over impetuous foe, taking each man almost alone, and actually compelling the surrender of the whole party. The advancing enemy's lines were however so near that they could not bring back their prisoners, but they compelled them to give up their arms, and a great shout of laughter greeted the two mad-caps, as they returned, each carrying an armful of sabres, revolvers, carbines and belts, captured in fair sight of both armies. It was a foretaste of the future career of one of them.

Not very long after Malvern Hill, Custer alone enjoyed another dash of exceptional brilliancy into the enemy's lines.

In those days as a young officer he was not so reticent about himself in his letters home as he afterward became, and he thus tells the story of his adventure in a letter to his sister, Mrs. Reed, who was then his chief confidant:

HEADQUARTERS ARMY OF THE POTOMAC, Aug. 8th, 1862.

DEAR BROTHER AND SISTER :—I received your letter of the 30th in due time, and found it quite interesting. I received it in the evening about dark, and would have answered it at once, but my horse was saddled and standing in front of my tent ready for me to mount. I had returned the preceding day from a successful expedition across the river, and was about to start upon another. My regiment formed a part of the troops that were to go. As we were to start at two o'clock in the morning, I deemed it best to join the regiment in the evening, and be ready to accompany them in the morning. Our force was not a large one, consisting of about three hundred cavalry and four guns (horse artillery) under the command of Colonel Averill. Our object was to go about twenty miles to "White Oak Swamp" and surprise a regiment of cavalry stationed there. We arrived in sight of the enemy about eleven o'clock. I was the first to discover them. Our cavalry at once prepared to charge them, and away we went, whooping and yelling with all our might. The rebels broke and scattered in all directions, we following as fast as our horses could go. As soon as we came close enough, we began firing at them with our revolvers. Quite a number of them surrendered when they saw that their escape was cut off; others, who had good horses, were not of this way of thinking, but continued the race. I was mounted on my "black" who seemed to enjoy the sport as well as his master. During the chase I became separated from all the command except a bugler boy of my company, who was at a short distance from me, but concealed from my view by bushes. I heard him call out "Captain ! Captain !" I could not see him but called to him, asking what was the matter. He replied, "*here are two secesh after me.*" I put spurs to my horse and started in the direction of his voice. I found him with his carbine in his hand, trying to keep off two secesh cavalry who were trying to capture or kill him. I drew my revolver and dashed at one of them, telling the bugler to manage the other. They both clapped spurs to their horses as soon as they saw me. I followed one, the bugler the other, and away we went down the hill. My horse was the fastest. I kept gaining on him until I was within ten steps, when I called out for him to surrender. He paid no attention to me, so I fired twice at him with my revolver. This brought him to a halt. I again pointed my revolver at him, and told him if he did not "surrender at once, I would kill him." He had a short rifle in his hand, and hesitated a moment whether to surrender or fire at me. He chose the former, and handed me his gun. I then made him ride in front of me until I placed him in charge of a guard. Lieutenant Byrnes, of my regiment, myself and about ten men, then started out again. We had not gone far until we saw an officer and fifteen or twenty men riding toward us with the intention of cutting their way through and joining their main body. When they saw us coming toward them however, they wheeled suddenly to the left, and attempted to gallop around us. Byrnes called out, "Custer, you take the right hand and I'll take the left," which we did, and then followed the most exciting sport I ever engaged in. My pistol was fresh loaded. I recognized the rebel officer by his uniform. He rode in front of his men, and was mounted on a splendid horse. I selected him as my game, and gave my black the spur and rein. If I had been compelled to follow *behind* him I could never have overtaken him, but instead of doing so, I turned off with the intention of heading him. By this means I came very close to him. I could have fired at him then, but seeing a stout rail fence in front of him, I concluded to try him at it. I reasoned that he might attempt to leap it and be thrown, or if he could clear it so could I. The chase was now exciting in the extreme. I saw as he neared the fence that he was preparing for a leap, and what was more, I soon saw that the confidence he had in his horse was not misplaced, for he cleared the fence handsomely. Now came my turn. I saw him look around just as I reached the fence, but he certainly derived no satisfaction by so doing, as my black seemed determined not to be outdone by a rebel, and cleared the fence as well as I could wish. By avoiding some soft ground which I saw was retarding him, I was enabled to get close upon him when I called to him to surrender, or I would shoot him. He paid no attention and I fired, taking as good aim as was possible on horseback. If I struck him he gave no indication of it, but pushed on. I again called to him to surrender, but received no reply. I took deliberate aim at his body and fired. He sat for a moment in his saddle, reeled and fell to the ground, his horse ran on and mine also. I stopped as soon as possible, but by this time Byrnes and his party were around me firing right and left. I joined with them and captured another rebel who had leaped from his horse and endeavored to escape in the woods. We were now some distance from the main body; the colonel became alarmed for our safety, and caused the bugler to sound the "rally" when we were all compelled to join the main body. Before the "rally" was sounded, however, I saw the horse of the officer I had shot, but a short distance from me. I recognized him by a red morocco breast strap which I had noticed during the chase. Four other riderless horses were with him. I rode up to them, and selecting him from the rest, led him off, while the others were taken possession of by others of the party. He is a blooded horse, as is evident by his appearance. I have him yet and intend to keep him. The saddle, which I also retain, is a splendid one, covered with black morocco and ornamented with silver nails. The sword of the officer was fastened to the saddle, so that altogether it was a splendid trophy. Owing to the confusion and excitement of such an occurrence, I was not able to see the officer after he fell from his horse, but Lieutenant Byrnes told me that he saw him after he fell, and that he rose to his feet, turned around, threw up his hands and fell to the ground with a stream of blood gushing from his mouth. I had either shot him in the neck or body; in either case the wound must have been mortal. It was his own fault; I told him twice to surrender, but was compelled to shoot him. Our party then started to return home, as we were twenty miles from camp, and liable to be attacked at any moment. We did not lose a man of the party; two horses were killed by the rebels; we took about thirty prisoners, and killed and wounded quite a number besides. My horse is a perfect beauty, a bright bay, and as fleet as a deer. I also captured a splendid double barreled shot-gun, with which quite a number of the rebels are armed. I intend to send the shot-gun home to Bos.* You may expect to hear "something" from me before long, perhaps we will move our headquarters.

Write soon.   Your affectionate Brother,

ARMSTRONG.

---

* His brother, Boston Custer, then a young boy, afterwards killed along with Custer, at the Big Horn.

CHAPTER II.

McCLELLAN'S REMOVAL.

THE disasters of the Seven Days Fight were followed by a long period of repose, McClellan lying within his circle of entrenchments at Harrison's Landing, and Lee refitting his exhausted army for fresh work. At last Mr. Lincoln thought fit to recall the Army of the Potomac to Washington, and Lee started off across the interior of Virginia, found Banks and Pope, and beat them one after the other, the Army of the Potomac getting to the scene of action just in time to share in the defeat of the second Manassas.

Thence Lee pushed off toward Harper's Ferry, took it, and raided into Maryland. McClellan, who had been suspended from command pending Pope's battle, was reinstated after the latter's defeat, and commenced the Maryland campaign, ending in Antietam. During this campaign, as during the Seven Days, Captain Custer officiated as personal aide to McClellan, accompanying him wherever he went, and being dispatched to the front, whenever the advance struck the enemy.

There was not much work for him to do. It seems that he had an especially pleasant time, judging from what he wrote home about it. The letter was, as usual in those days, written to his old confidant, Mrs. Reed, and we quote it fully.

GENERAL McCLELLAN'S HEADQUARTERS,
Sharpsburg, Maryland, Sunday, Sept. 21st, 1862.

MY DARLING SISTER,—You are perhaps, in doubt whether I am still among the living or numbered with the dead. These few lines will show you that I belong to the former. I am well aware that I deserve severe punishment for my long silence and neglect in writing. I have really no excuse, although I have been unusually busy since I last wrote to you, yet I could have found time to drop you a few lines. I will candidly acknowledge my offence and ask your pardon. I was certainly not partial, as I have written to no one since I left Harrison's Landing, except two letters which I wrote to a person in Washington, since the first of the month. I have so many things to write about, that I am at a loss to know where to begin. I left Harrison's Landing with General McClellan and travelled by easy marches to Williamsburg. The General remained at this place one day and two nights. You remember that it was at the battle of Williamsburg that my classmate, L., was wounded and taken prisoner by our forces. I had heard that he had been allowed to go from Fortress Monroe to Williamsburg to visit some friends, he giving his parole of honor not to escape. As soon as we reached Williamsburg on our return, I began making inquiries of the citizens concerning L. I soon learned that he was in town staying at the house of a friend. I immediately visited him and was rejoiced to find him almost recovered from the effects of his wound. He was surprised and glad to meet me. I was covered with dust from travelling, but he insisted upon my entering the house of his friend and being introduced to his friends. I did so and met a cordial reception although the entire family were strong " secesh." After a few hours pleasantly spent in conversation, I left them to return to camp, but not until I had promised to return and spend the night at their house. I returned to camp, received permission from the General to be absent, changed my dress and again visited L. After partaking of a good supper we withdrew to the parlor where we listened to some very fine music (secesh). There were two beautiful young ladies in the house who I supposed were sisters. I soon learned that I was mistaken. L. called me to one side and in an undertone asked me what I thought of the two young ladies who were, then, sitting upon a sofa on the opposite side of the room. I remarked that they were very beautiful to say the least. He then informed me that he was engaged to the elder of the two and that they were to be married the coming week. I recongatulated him on the wisdom of his choice and wished him every imaginable success. He was anxious that I should be present at his marriage ; I replied that I would like to do so but feared I could not remain so long ; after consulting all the parties concerned, it was decided that the ceremony should be performed the next evening in order that I might be present. No strangers were to be there but myself. The other young lady, who I at first thought was a sister, but who proved to be a cousin from Richmond, was selected as bridesmaid, and I was to have the honor of "standing up" with her. I passed the night and most of the next day with L., going to camp just long enough to dress for the wedding, which was to take place at nine o'clock in the evening. I was at the residence of the bride long before the appointed time.

Both were dressed in pure white, with a simple wreath of flowers upon their heads. I never saw two prettier girls. L. was dressed in a bright new (rebel) uniform, which he had had made for the occasion. It was made of fine grey cloth trimmed with gold lace. I wore my full uniform of blue. It was a strange wedding. I certainly never heard of one like it. L. and I had met under strange circumstances after the battle of Williamsburg, he an officer in one army, and I in an opposing one. We had been warm friends at West Point, and now he was about to be married and I was to be present at the ceremony. We were both struck by the strange fortune which had thrown us together again, and under such remarkable circumstances. His marriage from beginning to end was certainly a romantic one. He was, as you know, badly wounded at the battle of Williamsburg. I had taken all the care I could of him while we remained near that place, but upon leaving, he and hundreds of others were left in barns and other outhouses. He had never met his destined wife until after the battle. She with her mother went one day in their carriage to carry nourishment to the wounded of both armies. In visiting the different places containing the wounded, *they for the first time met L.* She had him carried to her home, took care of him, etc., etc., and he fell in love with her, courted and married her. I never heard nor even read of a wedding so romantic throughout. The appointed hour was nearly at hand ; the young ladies were in their own room, L. and I were in the parlor. He seemed perfectly happy and *resigned to his fate.* The minister soon arrived, and at nine precisely we took our places upon the floor. The ceremony was performed according to the Episcopal form. L. made the responses in a clear and distinct tone. The bride made no response whatever except to the first question. She was evidently confused and excited, though she afterward said (laughing) that she neglected to respond purposely, so as to be free from any obligation. As soon as the ceremony was over we all wished them happiness, etc. I was the first person to address the bride by her new title of *Mrs. L.* Every one seemed happy except the young lady who had been my partner on the floor. She kissed the bride and sat down crying. L. observed this and said : " Why, Cousin Maggie, what are you crying for ; there is nothing to cry about. Oh I know. You are crying because you are not married ; well, here is the minister and here is Captain Custer, who I know would be glad to carry off such a pretty bride from the Southern Confederacy." She managed to reply, " Captain L. you are just as mean as you can be." After congratulations had all ceased supper was announced. *Mrs. L.* took her husband's arm, while I had the pleasure of escorting " Cousin Maggie." I told her that I could not see how so strong a secessionist as she could consent to take the arm of a Union officer." She replied *" you ought to be in our army."* I asked her what she would give me if I would resign in the Northern army and join the Southern. She said, " You are not in earnest, are you ? " The supper was excellent and passed off very pleasantly. The next morning I returned to camp, but found that the general had started for Yorktown. I afterwards sent a telegram to him, and obtained permission to remain in Williamsburg as long as I chose. I remained with L. or rather at his father-in-law's house for *nearly two weeks.* I would have staid even longer but the near approach of the rebels to Williamsburg and the departure of our own army rendered a longer stay dangerous (*in more senses than one*). I never had so pleasant a visit among strangers. L.'s friends did all in their power to render my visit pleasant. " Cousin Maggie " would regale me by singing and playing on the piano, " *My Maryland*" "Dixie" (Southern) " *For Southern rights hurrah,*" or " Bonnie Blue Flag," etc., etc. Every evening was spent in the parlor. We were all fond of cards and took great interest in playing. "Muggins" and " Independence " were the usual games, sometimes euchre. We would play for the Southern Confederacy. When doing so L. and I were the only players, while the ladies were spectators. He won every time when playing for the Confederacy, he representing the South, I the North.

L. has been exchanged, and is now in the rebel army, fighting for what *he supposes* is his right. I left Williamsburg for Yorktown at dark, and arrived at the latter place about one o'clock P. M. General McClellan was then at Alexandria. I took a boat from Yorktown for Fortress Monroe, at which place I spent one day. I then took a boat for Baltimore, having with me " Rose," (his dog. ED.) my two horses and servant. From Baltimore I went to Washington by railroad. Here I learned that General McClellan would establish his headquarters in Washington in three or four days, and concluded to await his arrival rather than to meet him at Alexandria. After staying in Washington about two weeks we set out upon the present campaign, which has lasted about fifteen days, during which time more has been accomplished than during any previous period of the same length. We have fought three battles, one of which was the greatest battle ever fought on this continent, and in all were victorious. General McClellan, after quietly submitting to the cowardly attacks of his enemies, has by his last campaign in Maryland, placed it beyond the power of his lying enemies to injure him, but what is remarkable, his enemies are all to be found among those who from lack of patriotism, or from cowardice, and in some cases from both causes combined, have remained at home instead of coming forward and fighting for their country. The New York —— is among the most prominent of the vile sheets that have assailed General McClellan. His enemies dwindle down in importance until they reach such insignificant and lying personages as the editor of the Monroe ——.* I do not at present remember his name, but I think he could devote the columns of his paper to a more worthy purpose than by defaming and basely slandering those of his fellow countrymen who have gone forth to battle in defence of a common country, while he, like a mean, cowardly liar, as he is, remains at home. If I could meet him I would horsewhip him.

Your Affectionate Brother,
ARMSTRONG.

It will be observed that Custer mentions no more fighting adventures in this campaign, for which indeed there was little opportunity. Pope's misfortune had proved McClellan's benefit, enabling him to have his own way at last and giving him command of an enormous army by the junction of his own to the forces of Pope, Banks and McDowell. The numerical superiority

---

* We could not resist inserting this letter entire, not to hurt the feelings of the brethren of the pastepot and scissors, but because it shows the generous, hot-headed boy so perfectly, as he wrote in a white heat of indignation, in defence of his beloved general. Both editors mentioned have gone to their long home, years ago.

of the Federals was indeed so great as to render the campaign really the most brilliant and successful that Lee ever fought, escaping annihilation as he did.

After the battle of Antietam, when McClellan had allowed his enemy to cross the river and get away safely, a long period of inaction followed, which was varied by Stuart's daring raid on Chambersburg, the Confederate cavalier marching all round his cautious foe, and getting off safely. The small Union cavalry force, under Pleasonton, started after Stuart just an hour too late, and had the pleasure of coming to the Potomac at the end of the chase, just the same time behind him.

At last, under the pressure of positive orders, the Union General started from Harper's Ferry, and taking the route east of the Blue Ridge, marched across country for Richmond once more, this time *via* Warrenton. On his way there, while at Warrenton, he was suddenly dismissed from his command, and General Burnside placed in his stead, November 7th, 1862.

Very few measures during the war provoked such strong controversy at the time, both at home and in the army, as the removal of McClellan. No commander who ever subsequently handled it, was able to acquire to so great a degree its love and affection, and the amount of ill-feeling and luke-warmness produced among the higher officers of the army by the removal of their beloved chief, afterward produced many disasters. Under McClellan the corps commanders always worked cheerfully, and generally did more than they were ordered. The only malcontents were the restless and ambitious ones, who thought their chief too slow. After McClellan's removal, all this was changed. Corps commanders not only did not exceed their orders, but got into the habit of disputing them, and from highest to lowest, the army was full of grumblers. The evil effects did not wear away till the battle of Gettysburg, after which more harmony was perceptible, but even then the habit of criticising orders continued, till the accession of the iron-willed Grant and Sheridan to the reins of practical power.

Without entering into the question of the rights and wrongs of
the McClellan matter, there is no question that the moral effect
of the removal, at the time it was made, was perfectly disastrous
to the Army of the Potomac, and very nearly excited a mutiny.
Nothing but the real and sober patriotism of the great mass of
rank and file, who in their hearts acknowledged that the law
must be obeyed, right or wrong, saved the country at that
moment from such a violent military revolution as used to take
place in the later days of the Roman republic, when the conquering generals dictated to the senate, and finally created out
of the simple name " Imperator," * a title that has been since
held to be superior to that of king.

The tumult at army headquarters was especially great, for
of course the first to hear the news were the officers of McClellan's staff. They were almost, without exception, furiously
excited. Had McClellan been removed at Harrison's Landing,
while the army was in the first despondency of defeat, it is
probable that little would have been said against the change.
An unfortunate general seldom has friends. But since that
time, Pope had suffered an equally crushing disaster, one
accompanied by more humiliations, and the government had
been compelled to place McClellan in command. Under his
orders, which were *cheerfully* obeyed, everything had gone on
smoothly, up to the battle of Antietam, and at that battle the
Federal forces had fought well. While actually a drawn battle, Lee's subsequent retreat had given it the prestige of a
Union victory, and no serious disaster had since taken place.
During the long period of idleness that elapsed after Antietam,
the contest between McClellan and the government as to further movements had endeared the General to his army. Revealed in all the newspapers, he appeared in the light of a wise,
humane chief, standing up for the interests of his men, who
needed clothes and shoes, against a clique of ignorant civilians,
who wished him to march on, regardless of the sufferings of

* General or Commander.

his army. Everything had tended to make him the soldier's idol, and—more than anything—their own real inexperience. In the Peninsula, up to the Seven Days, the Federals had only seen the soft side of war, such as prevailed in the days of Louis the Fourteenth of France, a system of slow movements, brilliant little picket fights, enormous armaments, imposing preparations, plenty of food and forage, and little danger. The brief fury of the Seven Days was now forgotten, or lingered only as a memory of tremendous and glorious fights, in which the army had finally beaten off its foes. The Maryland campaign had been pleasantly exciting, with the same characteristics of scientific warfare which distinguished the Peninsular operations. After a month's pleasant picnic life around Harper's Ferry, in glorious fall weather, when military life wore its brightest aspect, the march to the Rappahannock had commenced by easy stages; and now, in the midst of this movement, when every one was hoping for a triumph, McClellan was suddenly removed.

It was no wonder that the army was excited, and still less that the officers of McClellan's staff were furious. They especially idolized their chief for his kindness of heart, and verily believed that all the military knowledge of the army was gathered in his head. Under his command, a future full of glory was opened to their delighted imaginations, and now they found themselves suddenly discrowned, and sent back to rust in peace. No wonder they were excited. Especially was this the case with the personal and volunteer aids, of whom McClellan possessed such a number, amongst them young Custer.

An eye-witness who was present at headquarters on that night of sorrow, describes the excitement as intense. Some of the officers raved, and wanted McClellan to march to Washington, dispossess the government, proclaim himself dictator, and then return and beat the enemy. There was plenty of wild talk going on; and Custer, young and rash as he was, only a boy of twenty-two, adoring the commander who had given him such early distinction, joined in with the rest. Boy-like, he was wild with indignation. The presence of whiskey in large quantities accounted for much of the excitement of those around him, but in his case it was nothing but the natural, generous impetuosity of his character that put him off his balance, for he never smoked or drank. In the midst of all the turmoil, the deposed general walked out of his tent, and a hush fell on the scene.

There was the group of young officers, inflamed with passion and bad whiskey, grouped around Custer, whose fair curls were tossed back, his eyes bright with anger at the injustice his chief had suffered. McClellan's appearance produced immediate silence, and the narrator proceeds to describe how the fallen general began to speak to his unruly staff.

In a low and sad tone he commenced. He told them how surprised and grieved he was to hear such sentiments from men who had served with the Army of the Potomac. He reminded them that he and they were soldiers, alike with the private in the ranks, and bound to obey the nation they served, whatever its orders might be. He pointed out in a few words what would be the terrible consequence of such a course as they counselled, in the midst of a rebellion which threatened the nation's life; how it would result in certain anarchy; how every army and state would feel at liberty to repeat the operation; and how then indeed secession must triumph. He spoke to them, as described by this eye-witness, as a sensible and patriotic man should, and silenced them all. It is the last glimpse that we have during the war of the quiet figure of the unfortunate McClellan, and it is in keeping with his whole career.

Excellent and competent for almost any subordinate position, he had failed in the highest of all commands, partly from the lack of experience, and partly from the want of energy, induced in a naturally cautious nature by the slow methods of his early

training and his long practice as an engineer. A safe and
cautious commander generally, his only serious mistake was
made in the exposure of his right flank at Richmond, which
cost him the Seven Days Fight. He departed into private
life amid the regrets of his whole army; and with him went
Custer. It seemed perhaps to the boy captain, as if his work
was done, and he permanently laid on the shelf beside his commander. The personal staff of McClellan, by which is understood only his aide-de-camps, departed with their general. Their
appointments were not commissions, and only lasted during
" the pleasure of the President." McClellan was put on " waiting orders;" and as the status of his aides depended on him,
they also went home on "waiting orders." In the case of
Custer, his commander's recommendation had procured him
a more substantial benefit than the mere temporary appointment, in the shape of a promotion to First Lieutenant in the Fifth
U. S. Cavalry. At the time of his commission, all the cavalry
regiments were raised to twelve companies, and Custer was
assigned to an original vacancy in Company M. of the Fifth.
This was a substantial commission, and reached him one month
later than his appointment as an aide, namely, in July, 1862.
Until the staff appointment was revoked, however, Custer had
no work to do. He might go home, or stay with his general,
who was ordered to Trenton, New Jersey, his own home.
McClellan told him to go to Monroe and see his people, and
accordingly, to Monroe went Custer. It was to him a sad
return, and he felt very much embittered. The fact of his
father being a staunch old democrat, and he himself the same,
by imitation, prejudice and affection, added to the measure of his
bitterness against the President, who belonged to the opposite
party, who had humiliated his beloved general, and thrown him,
Custer, to all appearance, out of the path of success. He was,
as far as his military career went, thoroughly miserable that
winter. He felt like a fish out of water, and longed to be back
sharing the dangers of his comrades in the army.

A certain gloomy satisfaction of the " I told you so " kind assailed him, as it did all the strong " McClellan men," at the successive disasters of Burnside. In those days they did not wait to examine how much of those disasters were attributable to grumbling and mutinous corps commanders, but all joined in the chorus of the popular song, " Give us back our old commander,"—none so earnestly as Custer.

While his military life was so bitter during this winter, he yet enjoyed plenty of opportunity for fun in a civil capacity. Partly to drive away care, and partly from the natural physical buoyancy of youth, that would not be denied, he plunged into all the mild little dissipations of Monroe society with great zest that winter, sleighriding, flirting, dancing, enjoying all the pleasures of a holiday, during November and December, 1862, and part of January, 1863.

One more step in social life had been granted him, with many misgivings and much grudging, by the " upper ten " of Monroe. Cadet Custer had been a step above young " Armstrong;" Lieutenant Custer "of the Regulars " had been a little higher still ; but that last unfortunate spree, so small really, had been magnified by scandal into habitual orgies of alarming frequency, and Mrs. Grundy held up her hands in holy horror over the " dissipations of that young man, my dear." But Captain Custer "of General McClellan's staff," was a very different personage—the habitual associate on duty of two real live French princes, who were on the same staff. Mrs. Grundy smoothed the ruffled plumes of indignant virtue, and welcomed the rising sun, especially with a view to hearing something definite about " those princes."

Really, Monroe was beginning to think there was " something in that young Custer, after all, although we must allow, my dear, that his antecedents are not quite the thing, you know."

The said " antecedents " were that he had worked for his education, that his father before him had worked for his, that he had been compelled to climb the ladder from the bottom step, alone and unassisted. The world has always found the union of honesty and labor very hard to tolerate, but nothing succeeds with it like two or three successes. Monroe was beginning to forgive " Captain " Custer for not being born with a silver spoon in his mouth.

This winter witnessed the throwing of a single bridge, narrow and insecure, but still a tangible bridge, over a very wide gulf, which had hitherto parted Custer from one great object of his life. The little maid of his vision, she with the arch dark eyes and merry smile, had shot up into a full fledged young lady of seventeen, ready to " graduate," full of all sorts of knowledge, beginning to go into " society," and—he met her at last, that winter.

Yes, it was actually so, he was introduced to her, formally and fully, at last, by her most particular friend, a young lady who afterwards became the close confidant of the pair of lovers, during the whole of a long and romantic courtship. It was in this courtship that Custer first plainly showed the possession of that quality of invincible determination which was the real cause of all the success of his after life. Hitherto this had not shone out so conspicuously as it afterwards did. He had worked hard and faithfully, but had not been compelled so far to face active and obstinate opposition. Here, for the first time, he found it, found it in the most dangerous quarter, the young lady herself. She was not disposed to like him ; his war record went for nothing with her. Brought up in seclusion, she did not know the difference between a captain and a corporal. She only knew that she had heard of him as a dissipated young man, a desperate flirt, and that she had herself seen him, on one occasion, intoxicated. That was enough for her, bred up in the strictest kind of Presbyterian education. It had been more than enough for her father, to whom no young man seemed good enough for his darling. In short, the young lady received him with cold reserve, and tried to freeze the audacious youth. But Custer was not the man to yield to repulses in love or in war.

He totally routed the young lady's dignity before they had been five minutes together, by asserting that he had met her before, and that she had spoken to him first. A freezing suggestion that he " must be mistaken " was met by the bold response, " Oh no, I'm not. It was—let me see—seven—eight —nine years ago—you were swinging on a gate and you said to me, ' hello, you Custer boy.' "

What could an innocent young lady, fresh from boarding-school, do, but blush like fire at this brusque accusation, declare it was not possible, feel a guilty memory that it might have been so, feel half angry, half amused, half ashamed and wholly subdued by the audacity of this strange, abrupt, singular young man with the bright curls, the bold handsome face, and flashing blue eyes so full of fun! Custer had evidently, even in those early days, laid to heart the advice of the experienced Byron, that master of affairs of the heart. To overcome a lady's indifference, says Byron, " first pique, then soothe, soon pleasure crowns thy hopes." Custer had already attracted attention. The lady did him the honor to think him " a very impudent young man," for he had been in the habit of sending her messages through one of her friends, for some months before he was introduced to her. Somehow or other, though, the Judge never heard of these messages, which, to veterans in these affairs, is symptomatic. At all events that meeting proved the beginning of a certain amount of interest felt in the strange young man, and, as the winter wore on, he laid such fierce and audacious siege to the heart of the little Puritan maiden that no woman could resist him, nor did she.

Obstacle the first was soon safely surmounted, but the second proved more formidable. It was—the Judge. Now while the Judge was perfectly willing to take Captain Custer by the hand in public, and recognize him in his military capacity to the fullest extent, this was a very different matter to receiving him as a son-in-law, as the husband of an only daughter. The Judge was a man of the most rigid principles, and apt to believe that it was impossible for the wicked to reform permanently. At all events, he did not believe in the thoroughness of Custer's change, and especially distrusted his firmness and stability of character.

Under these circumstances, he positively forbade any engagement being entered into, and intimated that he should prefer the discontinuance of Captain Custer's visits.

It is under these circumstances that the real nobility of Custer's character first shines fully out. We have seen hitherto the virtues of courage, gratitude, fidelity, resolution to put down temptation; to these was now to be added that of the purest, most knightly and sensitive honor, exhibited under most trying circumstances. Nothing would have been easier than for the handsome, dashing, determined fellow to overcome the scruples of a tender, fond, trusting girl, and to have induced her to fly with him, or to marry him openly in defiance of her parents. Nine men out of ten, men in good repute in the world, would have done so, treating the father's scruples as mere trifles, not to be regarded in the settlement of the question. Not so Custer, not so did he treat his future wife.

Without a complaint, without a murmur, the lovers, now devoted lovers really, acquiesced in the fiat of the Judge that the intimacy should be discontinued. So scrupulous were they on this point, that they did not even correspond, although that had not been in terms forbidden. For the rest of the period during which Custer remained in Monroe (several weeks yet, for his wooing had been as short, sharp and decisive as his charges of cavalry), the lovers never conversed, in public or in private, though frequently meeting at parties. Custer apparently devoted himself with great ardor to flirting with other young ladies, and the Judge was fully convinced that the danger was over, and much relieved thereby.

But with all of his scrupulous honesty of obedience, Custer had by no means given up the idea of his marriage. He was only biding his time, trusting to that and his own exertions to overcome the opposition of the Judge. There is something, to me, particularly touching and noble in the spectacle of this fiery, impatient, young man, used to swift success, and hitherto always chafing under the least delay, now submitting himself to the requirements of a long and weary probation, ready to serve for his Rachel as long and patiently as Jacob of old. When we consider the ordinary morals of American society in the matter of filial obedience, and the ease with which marriage can be contracted by a pair of lovers desirous of evading parental injunctions, the contrast between the conduct of Custer and most young men is very marked. He was faithful to his love, and determined irrevocably that he would only receive his wife with the full approval of her father, if he had to wait ten years to gain that approval. He was too scrupulous to attempt in the faintest degree to shake the obedience of the Judge's daughter. He had learned from his own family experience the value of unhesitating filial obedience, of the overmastering claims of duty and honor, and now, in the first serious trial of his life, his character stood the test.

Fortunately for his own happiness, he was saved from the prolonged torture which must have attended his residence in Monroe in this state of affairs. In the middle of January he was summoned by letter to New Jersey to meet McClellan, and the rest of his period of absence from the army was passed in hard work with his chief, in the preparation of his voluminous report on the movements of the Army of the Potomac under his command.

The preparation of McClellan's report occupied a long time, during which Custer, very luckily for his peace of mind, was kept hard at work. All the work however could not blunt his feelings, nor dim the fervor of his love and his determination that the Judge's daughter and no one else should at last be his wife. He could not honorably write to her, but he kept up during the whole of that year a close correspondence with a mutual friend, which served to mitigate the severity of his banishment, as he heard in reply of the movements of the one woman he cared to hear about.

It was not till April that the report was finished, and at its close Custer was ordered to Washington, and finally to rejoin his company, then at the headquarters of Hooker's army near Falmouth, Va., opposite Fredericksburg. The order was one which put him back a step in rank. His staff position as captain lapsed and he became once more plain Lieutenant Custer. In that capacity he rejoined the army.

CHAPTER III.

THE CAVALRY CORPS.

THE winter of 1862-3 was a period of great gloom for the whole of the United States, and perhaps for none more than young Captain Custer, "awaiting orders" that did not come, and kept, like his chief, in forced retirement. At no period of the war were the national spirits so low, for the year had closed on the crowning disaster of Fredericksburg, where thousands of brave soldiers had been uselessly slaughtered. At that time too, the opposition party, in and out of Congress, was exceedingly strong, and this party at once took up McClellan as their representative, and exulted over every new disaster to the Army of the Potomac, as an evidence that no one but its first leader could ever conduct it to victory.

Every city of the north was full of deserters, who at that time numbered over a hundred thousand, and a very large proportion of these were from the Army of the Potomac. Numbers of officers who belonged to the McClellan faction resigned their commissions in disgust, and went home to spread dissatisfaction, so that, when Hooker was finally appointed third commander of the much abused army, he found it a jarring mass of discontented bodies, instead of the homogeneous whole it had once been, under McClellan.

It was, however, to the hard work and enthusiasm of this, its third commander, that the Army of the Potomac was yet to owe the first victory of a series that was never afterwards broken by positive disaster. Hooker reorganized it effectively. A very different army it was from that which triumphed at

Antietam, and even the severe repulse at Chancellorsville failed
to shake its spirit, for the reason that the meanest soldier could
see that the battle was a perfectly barren victory for Lee, in
which he lost more than he gained.

But the greatest change effected by Hooker was one which
affected Custer himself. It was the reorganization of the cavalry. Under McClellan and Burnside, the Union cavalry had been
scattered about at different headquarters, assigned to the command of infantry generals, used in small forces for outpost duty
and scouting, and seldom or never employed on the field of
battle. The few exceptions to the rule had been signally disastrous. At Gaines' Mills a single regiment of cavalry, the Sixth
Pennsylvania, then acting as McClellan's body guard, had been
sent to charge a whole hostile army, and had of course effected
nothing. One or two mounted charges, with equally poor
results, had taken place in Pope's campaign, but as a rule the
Federal cavalry was too green to be usefully employed. The
only portion kept in mass was a brigade under Pleasonton, and
this small force had been worked to death. Hooker gathered
together all the regiments, organized them into three divisions
under Pleasonton, Gregg and Averill, and kept them together,
where they remained ever after as the Cavalry Corps, Army
of the Potomac.

After a long winter's rest in huts before Fredericksburg, the
whole army commenced its move across the river at the end of
April. The design of the campaign was generally good, but
marred by one fault. The army was cut up into three parts.
It was nearly twice as numerous as Lee's forces, but the division
gave him the opportunity to strike and defeat each fraction in
detail, which he subsequently did, with much success. The
only part that escaped serious damage was the cavalry corps,
to which Custer had lately been attached, as an aide on the staff
of General Pleasonton.

Hooker retained with the main army, with which he fought
the battle of Chancellorsville, only a single brigade of cavalry,

that of Colonel Thomas C. Devin. With this brigade General Pleasonton himself was present, and, small as it was, it contributed materially to the repulse of Jackson's column at an early period of the fight, when the Eleventh Corps had given way, and a general Bull Run panic seemed impending. The rest of the division was off under Buford, with the rest of the cavalry on Stoneman's raid.

It is not our intention here to dwell on the battle of Chancellorsville, and the events of Stoneman's raid were so unimportant, compared to the means used, that they deserve no more than a brief account. The combination of circumstances under which the raid was made, was peculiarly favorable to success, owing to the foresight of Hooker. He had ascertained that most of Stuart's cavalry was absent in the back country, recruiting and procuring remounts. Only the brigade of Fitzhugh Lee was with the army, and that of W. H. F. Lee was at Brandy Station, some fifteen miles off. On the 29th of April, Stoneman crossed the Rappahannock on the right of Hooker's army, at Kelly's Ford, with the divisions of Buford, Gregg and Averill, eight brigades in all. On the 30th they marched from the Rappahannock to the Rapidan, taking matters very coolly. The force was there weeded of all poor horses and pack animals, and only the pick of it went forward. Next day, May 1st, they crossed the Rapidan with no more difficulty than the Rappahannock, driving off the few Confederate skirmishers, Averill pushing on to Brandy Station, in the direction of Culpepper, Buford turning towards Fredericksburg, Gregg moving on in the middle, straight for Columbia, on the James River. The only column that met with resistance was that of Averill, which found W. H. F. Lee's brigade at Brandy Station, fought him awhile, and then retired. The rest of the force continued on to Louisa Court House, northwest of Richmond, and half way between the Rapidan and James. There it was divided into a number of small columns, and roamed all over the country, burning bridges, cutting the banks of the

James River Canal, and destroying railroads, with perfect safety to itself and much discomfort to the enemy. The only force left in the whole country to oppose it was W. H. F. Lee's brigade of two regiments, which was utterly inadequate to resist effectively. The raid lasted till May 9th, the division of forces taking place May 3d. Kilpatrick, then a colonel, took his regiment to the very border of Richmond, found part of the Twelfth Illinois there, found also that he had roused the Home Guards, and that they were flocking out to catch him, and finally marched down the Peninsula, crossed the Pamunkey, and came out at Gloucester Point, opposite Yorktown, whence he was taken off by the Union gunboats, returning by way of Washington. The rest of the cavalry returned as they came, and recrossed the Rappahannock and Rapidan high up the river, finding Hooker's army after the defeat of Chancellorsville, back in its old quarters at Falmouth, watching Fredericksburg.

The results of the raid were thus stated at the time by an enthusiastic newspaper correspondent.

General Stoneman moved about at will for nine days within the enemy's lines; cut every railroad and canal; stopped traffic on the highways; kept ten counties in a turmoil; destroyed twenty-two bridges, seven culverts, five ferries, seven railroads (in spots), seven supply trains, one hundred and twenty-two wagons, two hundred horses (carried off), one hundred and four mules (same), three canals (in spots), five canal boats, three trains of cars, two storehouses, four telegraph stations, five telegraph lines (cut), three depots, (burned.) The cavalry visited twenty-five towns, and liberated one hundred and fifty slaves, who followed the column.

All this was very nice, but amounted to nothing, for the railroads were soon after repaired. The real weakness of the whole raid was that it only exasperated, without terrifying the enemy, and gave color to the accusations that the Federal cavalry were merely mounted robbers. Had Stoneman destroyed

W. H. F. Lee's brigade, which he might well have done, it would have been of far more value to the cause he represented than all the plunder and destruction that attended his path. As it was, it entirely failed to retrieve the disgrace of Chancellorsville, in public estimation, at the time, and the fact that Stoneman never attacked Richmond, which he might easily have done, as it was almost undefended, added to the unfavorable impression produced by his conduct of the raid.

He was shortly after relieved by Pleasonton, the First Division falling to General Buford, the senior brigadier; and on the staff of the former, Captain Custer found himself, in June, 1863, with the prospect of a career once more open to him. The success of the Stoneman raid, such as it was, had still a good effect on the cavalry of the army. It was the first success that had fallen on its banners since Antietam, and had fallen to the lot of the despised cavalry, which needed it.

At that time, and ever since the beginning of the war, a great jealousy existed between the horse and foot of the Army of the Potomac, and the former had been so badly handled that it had fallen into contempt with the infantry. Cut up into small detachments and placed under control of infantry generals, who disliked it, the few unfortunate charges it had made confirmed the general impression that was trumpeted through the press, that "the days of cavalry were over" as a fighting body, and that it was only to be used thereafter for picket and scouting duty, in other words to look at the enemy and run away. Hooker himself, while in command of the army, was currently reported to have heaped contempt on his cavalry, by starting the ironical question as to "who ever saw a dead cavalryman?" The plodding infantry soldier, weary with his long march, naturally feels jealous of the horseman riding by him, and if he is taught to despise him as a fighter, is only too glad so to do. Under these remarks, the cavalry officers, high and low, had long chafed, and longed for an opportunity to prove that they could fight, as well as the

10

"dough-boys" and "mud-mashers" whom they could not retort upon as yet. The time was however coming for these sneers to be silenced, and the young staff captain who now followed Pleasonton was destined to be a mighty instrument to change public opinion. Chancellorsville had hurt the infantry badly, while the small cavalry brigade that had shared in that fight had stood firm in the midst of a cloud of demoralized foot soldiers, whom they were detailed to drive back with their sabres in some instances. For the next two months, the infantry hardly fired an angry shot, while the cavalry under Pleasonton, covered itself with glory, beat back Stuart again and again, and finally won itself the fair right to be called the sword and shield of the Federal army.

The close of Stoneman's raid was followed by perfect inactivity in Hooker's army for a month. In the meantime, Lee was preparing for an offensive movement, behind Fredericksburg. He had fought Chancellorsville with less than sixty thousand men to Hooker's one hundred thousand; but by the end of June conditions were changed. Many of Hooker's regiments were broken, their time being out, and Lee had received reinforcements from all quarters. Stuart's cavalry remounted and recruited, was now at least ten thousand strong, and the Confederate infantry was increased till his army equalled if it did not exceed, Hooker's.

Screened behind the curtain of woods in the Wilderness, Lee prepared to start off up the valley, to repeat his Maryland campaign, and if possible raid into Pennsylvania. Hooker, deprived of all certain news, was still very uneasy, and at last did what he should have done earlier. He sent out his cavalry to the extreme right of the army, to cross the Rappahannock high up. They started under the lead of Pleasonton, and crossed at several points, Buford and Averill at Beverly Ford, Gregg several miles up, at Rappahannock Bridge.

Both columns met the enemy in heavy force, and drove him back past Brandy Station towards Culpepper. There reinforcements arrived, and the fight remained stationary during most of the morning. Several charges and counter-charges took place, and the enemy's force was found to consist of Stuart's cavalry, while country people reported that infantry had passed that way in heavy force towards Madison Court House, a day or two before.

In the evening, Pleasonton returned across the Rappahan-nock, followed at a distance by the enemy, but without suffer-ing loss. The cavalry had shown in their first general fight, that they were capable of holding their own against the much dreaded " Stuart's Cavalry," that caused the Army of the Potomac so much alarm, from the Peninsula to Maryland.

They had met and parted fairly, " broken a lance " as it were, found that all they needed was to put a bold face on matters; and so learned their first lesson under Pleasonton's command. In this fight, Custer was in attendance on his general most of the day, a great favorite of the latter. The time was coming and very near at hand, though he knew it not, for him to win his star, and emerge from the inconspicu-ous position of a staff officer to one in which he could com-mand public attention. The personal history of Custer during the time that intervened between joining the army and winning his star comes out so well in his animated and picturesque cor-respondence that we are sure our readers will be glad to see some of his letters. He still kept up his communications with his sister, but the letters to her are filled out and completed by some to another person, to whom he commenced to write early in April. From these letters it appears that after the comple-tion of the report he paid a short visit to Monroe, thence to New York city, where he met orders sending him to Washing-ton. Here he was put on nominal staff duty, which was really genteel idleness, and filled up his time by going to the theatres, and trying to forget his discontent. He was evidently, at the time, sore, dissatisfied, unsettled, but imbued with a strong notion that " Destiny " had something in store for him, which no power of his would be able to avert. In his letters to this second person he speaks very earnestly on this subject, and also of the earnest and enduring nature of his feelings towards " one of the parties most interested " to whom he never refers by name. It seems that this " party" had predicted that absence and time would change his feelings, but he earnestly assures his correspondent that this can never be, and warns her that time will only strengthen and deepen them.

On his first arrival in camp, General Pleasonton requested him to join his staff, but Custer expresses himself as doubtful whether he will go or not. He seems to have regarded it as a sort of possible slur on his former general, whom he speaks of in his first letter as " *the only man I ever loved,*" the words underscored. Writing after Chancellorsville, he is very bitter on Hooker, and says vindictively, " The whole army are speaking against him and asking for McClellan." This letter is dated May 6th, but a week later he writes in better spirits from General Pleasonton's headquarters, that he has accepted the position offered him and finds it very comfortable. The passion for dogs is already strong, " I have got another dog, a hound pup about two months old. One of my men got it from an old negro woman. I have named the handsomest of my two horses —the black—' Harry' after Aut." (His nephew Henry Armstrong Reed, born while he was a cadet.) He has picked up a little deserted waif of a boy called Johnny, who acts as his servant, and who always takes the pup to bed with him. Johnny was devoted to him. " I think he would rather starve than see me go hungry. I have dressed him in soldiers' clothes . . . he rides one of my horses on the march." Returning from a ride one day, " I found Johnny with his sleeves rolled up. He had washed all my dirty clothes and hung them on the bushes to dry. He did them very well."

Later comes a letter to the other correspondent, describing

a secret expedition full of romance, but unattended with fighting. This is too good to be lost.

HEADQUARTERS CAVALRY CORPS, ARMY OF THE POTOMAC,
Tuesday, May 26th, 1863.

DEAR FRIEND.—In accordance with my promise and my inclinations I now propose to hold a short and uninterrupted conversation with you. I will agree to do all the talking *to-night*. I was extremely glad to receive your letter and through you to hear of " one of the parties, etc." I will tell you about my expedition into Dixie. With my little party of seventy-five men (cavalry) I embarked at Aquia Creek on board the steamers Caleca and Manhattan, on the evening of the 21st, taking our departure down the Potomac as soon as it was dark. At 11 o'clock next day we arrived at our landing on the banks of the Yocomico river about five miles from its mouth. Mounting our horses we made a rapid march of forty miles, in but little over five hours, arriving in sight of the Rappahannock river near Urbana. To avoid discovery, our party remained concealed in the woods till next morning. Taking nine men and another officer in a small canoe, the only boat we could find, I started in pursuit of a small sailing vessel which was coming from the direction of Urbana. After a chase of ten miles down the river we compelled our *game* to run their boat aground on the south bank. The crew jumped overboard and reached the shore. We captured the boat and passengers. The latter proved to be a portion of the party which we desired to capture. They had only left Richmond the previous morning, and had quite a large sum of Confederate money in their possession. Six of the party composed a Jewish family. Do you remember what I said in case I captured a stage-coach full of young ladies. There were two young ladies in the party, Jewesses, who with the rest of the party I was compelled to make prisoners of. With four of my men I made my way on shore, leaving the remainder of the party to guard the prisoners and boats. The river at that point is over four miles wide, and so shallow near the land as to render it impossible for us to approach within three hundred yards of the shore in our boats, so that no course was left but to *wade*. After landing with the four men we went to the nearest house, which proved to be a fine country mansion. While at some distance from it I observed some one on the piazza lying down with a book in his hands ; his back was toward us so that we were not seen. As we neared the house I saw that whoever it was he wore the Confederate uniform. At first I thought we were in a trap, that others might be near, perhaps in the house, and with my little party of four men I could not hope to contend against a very large force.

Cautiously approaching, I was within four feet of the Confederate before he noticed us, it was then too late for him to escape or resist. I told him that he was my prisoner and must come with us. He replied very coolly, "I suppose so." On interrogating him, he informed me there were no other rebel soldiers within six miles of us. He was at *home* on a short visit. The volume he was so intently reading was a copy of Shakespeare, and he had just read the first few lines of that well-known soliloquy "To be or not to be." On our march back he and I had many a hearty laugh over his literary habits. His sisters were in the house, but heard nothing of what occurred until I entered and informed them that it was my painful but imperative duty to take their brother away with me. They were very sorry, of course, but tried to assume a very independent air at first. I could not but feel sorry that they were to be made unhappy through any act of mine. I imagined myself in their brother's stead, and thought how sorry my own dear sister would be if I were taken away under similar circumstances. Returning to our boats we took our prisoners to the north bank, leaving them in charge of the main party. Then with twenty men in three small boats, I rowed over to Urbana, on the opposite bank, where we burned two schooners and a bridge over Urbana bay, after which we drove the rebel pickets out of the town. We then returned to the north bank, where, after capturing twelve prisoners, thirty horses, two large boxes of Confederate boots and shoes, and *two barrels of whiskey which we destroyed*, our party remounted our horses, and with our captures set out on our return to the Yocomico, where the steamers were in waiting for us. To carry our *lady* prisoners, I pressed into the service a family carriage, horses and driver. We marched till two o'clock that night to avoid pursuit and capture, then camped till morning; resumed the march, reached our boats about noon on Saturday, and arrived here safely Sunday morning without having lost a man. Yesterday General Hooker sent for me and complimented me very highly on the success of my expedition, and the manner in which I had executed his orders. Now, I suppose I have wearied you with this long (interesting to me, but perhaps not to others) story. I will not apologize for it, however, as that would be breaking a rule which I have always laid down—never to regret anything after it is done. Yesterday I spent in visiting a number of my friends throughout the army. I saw the 4th Michigan and the Monroe members of the regiment. I took dinner with Lieutenant Yates, who you remember was in Monroe last winter. By the way, I have induced General Pleasonton to appoint Lieutenant Yates on his staff, so that I will have him with me hereafter. He was at our headquarters this evening, and will join us permanently in a few days.

ARMSTRONG.

A little later, in a letter to his sister under the date of June 6th, he writes that they are going to cross the river to Culpepper, but there is no account of Beverly Ford fight. The last letter accessible at this period of his life is dated June 25th, four days before his elevation to the dignity of a brigade commander, and the place for that will be more proper in the next chapter. Events were now beginning to crowd so fast, and the campaign was opening so actively, that home correspondence was practically impossible. Love and the softer side of his life was to be hidden for a while behind the murky clouds of war, and not till after Gettysburg was there a lull in the incessant activity.

Custer was still, as appears from these letters, nothing more immediately ambitious in feeling than a staff officer. There are no idle aspirations after high command in his wishes, and he seems, as always before and after, intensely practical in his notions of life. He is satisfied to do his duty in whatever position he is placed, only taking care to perform that duty thoroughly and completely, and better than any one else. The letter we have quoted, reveals the perfect officer of the staff, active and daring, on the watch for every little scrap of information, perfectly ready to hide and play the fox when the *rôle* of the lion is out of place, with that peculiar combination of qualities, very rarely found, which makes the model officer of *eclaireurs*.

These qualities are very rare, and no school can teach them.

Even experience totally fails if natural genius is not found in the man. The most pre-eminent attribute of the perfect *eclaireur* is *tact*, and this Custer developed in a remarkable degree. The sudden and rapid decision, the intuitive sense of the exact thing to do at the moment, and the energy that seizes the fleeting moment, are all present, and it is no wonder that Pleasonton treated him as the most useful officer of his staff. Custer could do what no one else could do. Nine men out of ten would have made a blunder of the secret expedition into the heart of the enemy's country, but Custer treats it almost as a joke and never falters a moment. What a wonderful contrast between this expedition and the one he so naively describes as occurring when he was on Kearny's staff, only eighteen months before. Truly Custer had graduated in the school of war. He was no longer a pupil, but a master in the duties of a staff officer. Even Hooker, far from being well disposed to any member of McClellan's staff, could not help complimenting Custer, and truly he deserved every word of praise he received.

CHAPTER IV.

WINNING HIS STAR.

THE spirited little fight at Beverly Ford, June 9, 1863, developed the intentions of the enemy. It showed that his cavalry was concentrated near Culpepper, and subsequent reports from signal officers and others showed that the concentration was only preparatory to a general movement of the Confederates round the Union right, by way of the valley, up towards Maryland and Pennsylvania. Hooker's army being then in front of Fredericksburg, two courses were open to it. One was to strike straight for Richmond, disregarding Lee, the other to fall back towards Washington, interposing before the enemy could do much damage. The first course was the boldest, and would undoubtedly have ended in the recall of Lee, and the fighting of a desperate battle to the northwest of Richmond, but it would have been in the nature of a gambler's last throw. The Union communications must have been left completely exposed by the line of the Orange and Alexandria Railroad, and would have certainly been cut unless changed to the seacoast bases, in later times occupied by Grant.

On the other hand, falling back toward Washington, Hooker would retain the advantage of interior lines, and his communications were secure. The second course was the safest, if not the most brilliant. At all events it was determined on, and the Union infantry started on the march which was to culminate in Gettysburg. For the next few weeks, the legs of the infantry of both armies were to do all the work, for they did not come in serious contact till they met at Gettysburg.

Beverly Ford fight checked Stuart in his first purpose, which was to cross the Rappahannock east of the mountains, followed by Lee, repeating the movements of 1862, and bringing on a third battle of Manassas. On the 6th of June he held his review at Culpepper, preparatory to his advance. Three days after, he concluded to go west of the mountains, take a longer trip, and trust to his heels to get to'Pennsylvania first.

The first week of the three that intervened between Beverly Ford and Gettysburg was passed by Hooker in feeling for the enemy with his cavalry, which scoured the country as far as the Blue Ridge. In the meantime Lee's columns were pushing on up the valley, Ewell's corps capturing Winchester on the 13th June. Lee's intentions being then fully developed, the Army of the Potomac started to catch him, and on the 14th was at Bull Run. On the 16th, Governor Curtin, of Pennsylvania, issued his proclamation, announcing the invasion of his State, and from thenceforward all was bustle and activity.

On the same day that Governor Curtin issued his proclamation, was fought the battle of Aldie in Virginia, in which battle Custer gained his star, and as it was the first cavalry action in which the Union forces met the enemy fairly and defeated him fairly, it is worthy of some special notice.

At the time, both armies were scattered over a considerable range of country. The head of Lee's column, preceded by Ewell and a small force of cavalry and mounted infantry, was in Pennsylvania, the rear still in Virginia. Stuart's cavalry was scattered along the flanks, and on the 16th a portion of it came through Snicker's Gap, hoping to take a short cut into Maryland and Pennsylvania. They were met by part of Gregg's division, consisting of Kilpatrick's brigade, and the First Maine Cavalry. With them was a young staff officer of Pleasonton, Captain George A. Custer. The rest of the Union cavalry was scattered through the country, the afterwards renowned Michigan brigade was not yet fully organized, but some of its component parts were in Maryland, fighting Jenkins'

raiders. Everything was in more or less confusion, especially
on Hooker's side, for Lee had undoubtedly stolen a march on
him, and got ahead.

On the 16th, General Gregg's advance reached Aldie, and
found a Confederate brigade, with which General Stuart was
present. It seems that Gregg must have struck the extreme advance of the Confederate cavalry. Colonel Kilpatrick's brigade
composed the Second and Fourth New York, First Massachusetts, and Sixth Ohio. The Second New York had the advance.
They ran into the enemy's picket outside Aldie, drove them
through the town, and found the Confederate line in position
near Middleburg, in front of the middle of Ashby's Gap. It
seems that Stuart was advancing through Ashby's Gap, and
this unexpected encounter checked him. When the exact position of the enemy was found by their fire, Kilpatrick deployed
his regiments and put them in the fight in the order following:
First Maine, Sixth Ohio, Second New York, Fourth New
York, First Massachusetts.

The enemy had four guns on a hill, in the centre of their
line. Their dismounted skirmishers held fences and ditches
enfilading the Middleburg road, on which the advance must
be made, and the position was strong. In front of the line of
battle were half-a-dozen haystacks, which concealed the ditch
and fence.

The Second New York was ordered to charge down the road
and take the haystacks. One squadron made the charge, and
passed the stacks, only to find themselves heavily punished by the
enemy in rear. The rest of the regiment galloped in on the left,
followed soon after by the Sixth Ohio, and the result was that
the Confederate line was broken; fences thrown down, and the
enemy were driven in confusion up the hill on their guns.
They made a short stand at a rail fence, halfway up, when a
squadron of the Fourth New York, that had been supporting
Kilpatrick's battery, dashed in and drove them over the hill,
Stuart's guns going to the rear full gallop.

The First Maine was then called in from the left, and placed beside the First Massachusetts, in support of the troops already engaged, and the line advanced again. This time Stuart was resolved on vengeance. His guns were in position further to the rear, and he now charged down the road, driving before him the remains of the Second New York, disordered and blown by previous charges. In a moment it seemed as if the tide were turned. Cavalry is always liable to sudden reverses of this sort, and Stuart's fresh reserves came yelling on, driving everything before them. Kilpatrick ordered in at once the Maine and Massachusetts regiments, as yet fresh, and that part of the Fourth New York which had not already charged.

Coming into action as a reserve to check the tide of defeat, is always the hardest task for young soldiers, and it must be remembered that this was the first serious action in which many of the Union regiments had been engaged. At all events, the reserves wavered and halted, confusion began to spread, horses were plunging and fighting, men turning pale, and shrinking back from the moral effect of the yelling line of Confederate cavalry coming on, wrapped in clouds of dust, and preceded by the scattered fugitives of the Second New York. Add to this, the shrieking of the enemy's shells, and the sharp crash of their explosions, the dead and wounded horses and men lying about, and the tremendous moral force at that day of the name of "Stuart's Cavalry," and it is not surprising that the green Northern men wavered, nor that their officers were yelling confusedly, instead of commanding coolly.

For a moment a rout seemed inevitable, when out of the press dashed Kilpatrick and Colonel Douty of the First Maine, the first shrieking out curses and wildly waving his sabre, the second beckoning his men to follow. So great was the turmoil that neither could be heard, when forth from the crowd rode a third figure, a young captain, wearing a broad plantation straw hat, from under which long bright curls flowed over his shoul-

CUSTER AT ALDIE.—"COME ON, BOYS!"

ders. His uniform was careless and shabby, but his bright curls attracted attention wherever he went. Out he rode beside Kilpatrick and Douty, waved his long blade in the air, and pointed to the enemy, then turned his horse and galloped alone towards them. An electric shock seemed to silence the line. He looked back and beckoned with his sword.

"Come on, boys," he shouted.

The next moment Kilpatrick and Douty were abreast of him, waving their swords and shouting "Come on." An involuntary yell burst from the men, and away they went. All fear and hesitation had vanished, and the long line, broken by its own impetuosity into little clumps of horsemen, went racing down to charge the enemy.

They were met by a tremendous fire. As usual, the Confederate cavalry shrank from the sabre and relied on fire-arms to repel the assault, and as usual they were worsted. The sabre was freely used for the first time during the war, and the enemy was driven in utter confusion, the Maine and Massachusetts men cutting and slashing right and left, the enemy fleeing in the direction of Ashby's Gap. In the foremost of the triumphant group was the young captain with the bright curls, and in all the confusion the men followed him as a guiding star. Kilpatrick went down, his horse shot under him, Douty was stricken dead, but the young captain with the floating curls seemed to bear a charmed life.

Away, with a thunder of cheers, a rapid rattling fusillade of shots, a cloud of dust, the clatter of innumerable horse shoes, the jingle of arms, bright flashes gleaming redly through the thin blue pall of smoke that hung over the field, the fierce hot smell of powder in the air, titillating the nostrils with a mad sense of intoxication, away went Custer and his men in that wild charge and pursuit! The faint hearts of a moment ago were turned to steel, and a frenzy of eager ferocity seized the mildest.

Were you ever in a charge, you who read this now, by the

winter fireside, long after the bones of the slain have turned to dust, when peace covers the land? If not, you have never known the fiercest pleasure of life. The chase is nothing to it, the most headlong hunt is tame in comparison. In the chase, the game flees and you shoot: here the game shoots back, and every leap of the charging steed is a peril escaped or dashed aside. The sense of power and audacity that possesses the cavalier, the unity with his steed, both are perfect. The horse is as wild as the man : with glaring eye-balls and red nostrils he rushes frantically forward at the very top of his speed, with huge bounds, as different from the rhythmic precision of the gallop as the sweep of the hurricane is from the rustle of the breeze. Horse and rider are drunk with excitement, feeling and seeing nothing but the cloud of dust, the scattered flying figures, conscious of only one mad desire, to reach them, to smite, smite, smite!

Far ahead of the Northern riders was the young captain with the floating curls. He rode his favorite black " Harry," named after the innocent child at home. In his hand gleamed the long straight blade he had captured from the Confederate, one year before, when he shot him and took his horse, down in front of Richmond. Custer wore that sword all through the war, a long straight Toledo blade, with the Spanish inscription, "*No mi tires sin razon, No mi envaines sin honra.*" " Draw me not without cause, sheathe me not without honor." Years after, men said that hardly an arm in the service could be found strong enough to wield that blade, save Custer's alone.

Far ahead of all his men he rode, outstripping the swiftest, and a moment later was in the midst of the enemy, and close to the left rear of one of their horsemen. The man heard him coming, turned in his saddle and fired his revolver at Custer, missing him. A moment later, the long Toledo flashed in the air, and his enemy fell from his horse, his left arm nearly cut off. A second man wheeled his horse and dashed at the daring officer, riding up alongside on the left, taking Custer at the same disadvantage he had taken the other man, and this fellow had a sabre. Then the two raced away in the midst of the flying cloud of dust, one cutting away at his foeman, the other parrying the blows, but unable to return them. The wild race lasted for several seconds, both horses at full speed, when they found themselves beyond all the fight, and in the quiet rear, out of the dust. Then Custer suddenly checked "Harry," and his enemy shot past him. Before his antagonist could stop, Custer was almost up to him, and as he wheeled round they met fairly, on the right front. The fight was short. Two or three mighty blows of the long sword, and the Confederate cavalier's guard was beaten down and himself knocked off his horse with a cloven skull.

Then Custer turned, and found himself all alone in the midst of the enemy, probably a good mile from the Union lines. He mentions this in a letter to his sister.

I was surrounded by rebels, and cut off from my own men, but I made my way out safely, and all owing to my *hat*, which is a large broad brim, exactly like that worn by the rebels. Every one tells me that I look like a rebel more than our own men. The rebels at first thought I was one of their own men, and did not attack me, except one, who rushed at me with his sabre, but I struck him across the face with my sabre, knocking him off his horse. I then put spurs to "Harry" and made my escape.

It was at this time that Mr. A. R. Waud of Harper's Weekly made a sketch of Custer, which is still in the possession of his sister, Mrs. Reed. It represents such a wild, careless, slouchy-looking figure, as the same artist has put in the illustration to the battle in the present book, "only a little more so." There are the long unkempt locks, the broad straw hat, a soldier's blouse and trousers, and a pair of captured boots. This picture accompanied the letter from which we quote, dated June 25th, 1863. We quote it especially for one reason. Only four days later, Custer was made a brigadier, and this letter would naturally be expected to show some inkling of knowledge on his part, of his coming promotion. So far from this, it is evident that he is quite unconscious of his coming honors. In one place he says, " General Pleasonton has been promoted to be a major-general. This will make me a captain again." The fact of his staff rank being relative to the rank of his commander, explains this passage, and shows that he had no higher aspirations at the time.

Thus ended Custer's connection with the battle of Aldie. After he cut down the last rider who tried to stop him, he got off in safety, and on his way back captured the first man whom he had cut. The poor fellow was glad to surrender and be taken in.

It turned out afterwards that the force with which Gregg's advance was thus engaged, was the extreme advance of Stuart's cavalry, pushing away from the rear of Lee's army to cross the Blue Ridge. Stuart's column was spread out and scattered over a large expanse of country, as also was Pleasonton's, and it took both of them four days more to concentrate their forces for the second and more decisive fight in the same vicinity, which took place at Upperville, some five miles from Aldie. At the time of the battle of Aldie, Colonel Duffié, a French officer on a two years' leave, who then commanded the First Rhode Island Cavalry, threw himself, with his regiment, two hundred and eighty strong, into the little town of Upperville, attacking the rear of the same brigade defeated by Kilpatrick, and putting more confusion into it. Unluckily, he found himself in the midst of all Stuart's advancing forces, and yet determined to hold on to the town, trusting to Pleasonton's advance to relieve him. He was ultimately completely surrounded, and cut his way out with only twenty-seven men, thus terminating that haphazard scrambling fight termed the battle of Aldie.

For his part in determining the principal success of the day, as well as for his past services, General Pleasonton sent in the name of Captain Custer, along with those of Colonel Kilpatrick, Captain Farnsworth, and Captain Merritt, to the President, for promotion to the rank of Brigadier General. Colonel Duffié was promoted at the same time.

The force with which Kilpatrick was engaged, consisted of the First, Third, Fourth and Fifth Virginia Cavalry, with four guns. A hundred prisoners were taken and one flag. Custer's promotion sent him to Maryland, where he joined the Michigan Brigade he was soon to render so famous, at Hanover, Md. From henceforth the young staff officer, so suddenly transformed into a general, instead of carrying others' orders, was to issue his own, and to fight more or less independently, in that confused series of cavalry actions that preceded and followed the battle of Gettysburg. Here begins that public career of Custer, which was so soon to eclipse that of all the other cavalry leaders of the army, and which, by a combination of audacity, ability, and good luck, was to carry him to Appomattox Court House.

We have previously said that Custer's promotion was entirely unexpected by himself: the way in which he received it, illustrates this. That he felt, from the very beginning of his career, a conviction that he should win distinction in the war, and become a general officer, is undoubted. His hopes and aspirations on this point were so well defined, that he did not hesitate to speak of it to his brother officers, in the course of their many firelight talks. As was inevitable in those early days, he encountered a great deal of sarcasm and merciless ridicule on this point from his comrades, far more so than would have occurred later in the war, when every man who staid at the front was in grim earnest. In the enormous staffs fashionable at that period, there were always to be found a few officers who did all the work, and a large residue of genteel idlers, whose highest ambition seemed to be to make the time pass pleasantly, and to do as little for their pay as they could. The same class of men, a few grades farther down, goes by the name of "malingerers" and "coffee-coolers," and indulges, when in camp, in the same general line of sarcasm towards those com-

11

rades who do duty cheerfully and aspire to win promotion by good conduct. At that early period of the war, the regular routine of promotion had not become so rapid and certain as it afterwards became, and many advances were still due to favor.

At all events, the incautious admission of Custer to some of his comrades, that he was "determined to be a general before the war was over," was received by many with ill-natured sneers, and was frequently made the occasion of severely sarcastic bantering.

One evening, eleven days after Aldie, when Custer returned to headquarters, after a long ride, in which he had been posting the pickets of the entire corps for the night, he was greeted in the large tent, where the staff was wont to gather at night, by the salutations, " Hallo, general." " How are you, general?" " Gentlemen, General Custer." " Why, general, I congratulate you." " You're looking well, general." The greetings came from all quarters of the tent, where staff officers were lounging, smoking, chatting, laughing, telling stories. They impressed Custer as being merely a continuation of the usual ill-natured banter on the subject of his aspirations, and, further, as being carried a little too far. However, he had always been noted for his remarkable control over a hot and hasty temper, and he was not going to allow his comrades to laugh him out of it on this occasion. Still, it was with some bitterness that he answered,

" You may laugh, boys. Laugh as long as you please, but I *will* be a general yet, for all your chaff. You see if I don't, that's all."

He was greeted by a universal shout of laughter in answer. It seemed as if his tormentors were determined to irritate him into an explosion; and they nearly succeeded; for his blue eyes began to flash, and he looked round as if seeking some one on whom to fix a quarrel. His old friend Yates,* whom he

---

* Afterwards brevet lieutenant colonel, and captain in the Seventh U. S. Cavalry, and one of the little band of heroes who fell with Custer. Yates

had been himself the means of putting on Pleasonton's staff, came to his relief with a few words.

"*Look on the table, old fellow. They're not chaffing.*" He pointed to the table in the tent, and there, in the midst, lay a large official envelope, and on it was written, " Brigadier General George A. Custer, U. S. Vols."

The reaction was instantaneous, and the young fellow was completely overcome. A moment later, and all his old comrades were gathered round him in real earnest, congratulating and shaking hands, while Custer, too much overpowered to speak, could only smile faintly, turn very pale, find his eyes full of tears, and sink down in a chair, feeling very much as if he was going to make a fool of himself and cry. However, he regained his self-control in a few moments, and was able to thank his comrades, who were really in earnest this time, and after a while was permitted to read the orders which accompanied his commission, and which directed him to report to General Pleasonton for instructions.

Of the interview between Pleasonton and himself it is unnecessary to speak. It was marked on the one side by great kindness and good sense. A few months later, Custer writes home about Pleasonton, " he has been more like a father to me than a general," and this was indeed the truth. There must, however, have been something peculiarly magnetic about Custer to have attracted to himself, as he did, the enthusiastic affection of three men of such very different characters as his three successive commanders. McClellan, the polished scientific soldier, kind-hearted to a fault, slow, methodical and cautious ; Pleasonton, acrid, sarcastic, exacting, an excellent cavalry chief, but generally failing to attract any affection from his subordinates, a martinet in his discipline ; Sheridan, fiery, impetuous, untiring, remorseless in the amount of work he exacted from his troops ; all these three men loved, admired, and trusted

was an old Monroe friend of Custer, and it was at Custer's request that Pleasonton appointed Yates on the staff, where he proved a valuable officer.

Custer entirely ; and it was nothing but the transcendent ability of his character that forced them to do so. Had McClellan remained in command and promoted Custer, it might have been said that favoritism and luck presided over his elevation. That a man like Pleasonton, who was notoriously hard to please, should have evinced so much trust in the abilities of a simple lieutenant, as to take the responsibility of urging his promotion to the command of a brigade, without even the intermediate experience of a colonelcy, was the proudest of tributes to Custer's real merit, for it must be remembered that he had not a single friend at court, and that his previous connection with McClellan's staff was at that time a positive disadvantage to him. It was the greatest misfortune of General McClellan that after his removal he was taken up, petted, and made a martyr of, for political purposes, by the party which at that time was, actively and passively, in sympathy with the rebellion, and *in the minority besides.* This fact rendered all his friends objects of political and partisan dislike—of all dislikes the most bitter and unreasoning—to the members of the party in power. The very strength of the McClellan party made it the object of the more bitter animosity, the instincts of self-preservation being enlisted against it in the minds of all ardent Republicans. It became impossible to secure fair play for a known " McClellan man," however brave and capable. The bad example of some of the less capable of McClellan's partisans in high places had rendered the government suspicious of them, down to their humblest ranks, and not without much reason.

Custer himself had experienced the evil effects of this feeling during the previous winter, when at Monroe, awaiting orders. During that period, backed by the earnest help of Judge Christiancy, now United States Senator from Michigan, and then a very influential member of the Union party, Custer applied to Governor Blair for the command of one of the cavalry regiments then being fitted out by the State of Michigan for the war. The last of these regiments, the Seventh Cavalry, was then only partly organized, two battalions leaving Grand Rapids, Michigan, in February, the rest in May. It was for this special regiment that Custer applied, without success, despite the influence of Judge Christiancy. The excuse made by Governor Blair was very plausible, and apparently convincing. It was that the commissions in the new regiments could only be given to those officers who were instrumental in raising them, and that it was not possible to depart from the rule, save in very exceptional cases. The governor promised, however, to remember Captain Custer's application, "the first vacancy that occurred," and with this promise Custer was obliged to be content, well aware that, like all politicians' promises, it was a mere delusion, and that the real obstacle behind all, was the fact of his being a "McClellan man."

This experience was one of those which occasioned the great bitterness of tone which marks his private letters about the time he first rejoined the Army of the Potomac. The man felt that he was unjustly treated, and that the holiest feelings of his nature, love and gratitude, had been made instrumental to his damage ; and he felt outraged. Only the advance of the season of hard work, and the activity which he enjoyed under Pleasonton, caused these feelings to fade away. It is probable too, that the creditable fight at Beverly Ford and the sharply fought action at Aldie, the latter culminating in victory, had aided to persuade him that there were as good generals left as McClellan, even if he would not admit it in public.

Now, his sudden elevation contributed to eradicate the last remains of bitterness from his mind, and Pleasonton put the final touch to the picture of happiness, when he announced that he had assigned the young general to the command of a brigade of troops from his adopted state, Michigan, comprising— *mirabile dictu*—the very regiment for the command of which Captain Custer had applied in vain, three months before, to Governor Blair. There let us leave him to join his command, all inexperienced and untried as he was.

It is rather curious in connection with what we have said before, that from the time of McClellan's fall to the end of his career, Custer always found himself directly opposed in politics to the party in power, he being a strong democrat.   He was even opposed to Pleasonton, who, then and since, has always been identified with the republicans, and it was solely on his military record, then and after, that he gained all his many honors. He never received favors, only work. When any work was to do which no one else could do, Pleasonton first, and Sheridan afterwards, always set Custer to do it. Months after he gained the star, when he had won many battles and had had four or five horses shot under him in action, it be-came a question whether his commission should be confirmed in the Senate on account of his being a " McClellan man."   Pleas-onton got him his promotion with the rest, because he wanted some one to do the work, and no one could do it so well as these young energetic officers. So it was all through the war and after. It seemed to be fated that he should always be an anti-administration man, getting all the hard knocks and little reward. What reward he had, he earned. The rest of his life will show how he earned it.

FOURTH BOOK.—THE MICHIGAN BRIGADE.

CHAPTER I.

THE GETTYSBURG CAMPAIGN.

THE first fight at Aldie on the 16th June was succeeded by four days of skirmishing and scouting, during which Pleasonton united his two divisions under Gregg and Buford, and Stuart brought up such of his forces as he could get together. On the 19th, the brigade of Colonel Gregg, a brother of General Gregg, and that of Kilpatrick, had a second fight near Aldie, in which they again drove the enemy, this time into Middleburg; and on the 21st, Pleasonton arriving, drove the enemy about eight miles further and took from them three guns and a lot of prisoners. So far as can be found, the Confederate forces in this last battle were inferior in number to the National forces, but the results were none the less inspiriting to the cavalry. Three victories under any circumstances were comforting, still more so to men who were depressed in spirit from the long succession of disasters that had followed the Army of the Potomac. In the meantime, the greater part of Stuart's forces were already over the border, and it became necessary to follow them. The battles at the gap had prevented Lee from crossing his army at Poolesville, below Harper's Ferry, and he was compelled to cross above the latter place, at Hagerstown. The Union army followed by way of Poolesville, and when it arrived at Frederick, Md., Hooker was replaced by Meade, and the two armies concentrated at Gettysburg.

The cavalry crossed the Potomac on the 25th June, and arrived at Frederick City next day. Here it was reorganized into the form in which it was afterwards to win such enduring fame, as the Cavalry Corps, Army of the Potomac. All the loose regiments were gathered up into brigades, forming the famous three divisions, which remained unaltered to the following spring. The First was commanded by John Buford, the Second by Gregg, while the Third, composed of the loose ends, was given to the just promoted hero of Aldie, General Kilpatrick. In his division appeared the Michigan brigade, assigned to Custer, who joined it on the 29th June at Hanover, Pennsylvania, as it went into camp.

The next day the Gettysburg campaign commenced in earnest, and the country was full of roaming bodies of Union and Confederate cavalry hunting for each other. On this day Kilpatrick himself, with Farnsworth's brigade, was attacked by Stuart, with Wade Hampton's division, in right and rear, and for some time was pretty roughly handled. Custer's brigade had marched to Abbottsville, but, hearing the firing, returned and aided in repelling the enemy, who lost fifty men and a flag. Here Custer made his first appearance on a battle-field as a general officer, and surprised and captivated every one by his peculiar and picturesque appearance, thereafter to be indelibly associated with his name.

When we remember the condition of the United States Army at that date with regard to uniform, it seems almost impossible to make out of such a dress anything handsome and showy. The fatigue uniform allowed was slouchy and untidy, the full regulation uniform the most hideous imaginable. The whole dress was the invention of John B. Floyd, a rebel general who, before the war, had been United States Secretary of War. Yet, keeping within the regulations, Custer managed to produce one of the most brilliant and showy dresses out of this hideous uniform, and to fashion it so that no one could mistake his rank.

The regulation hat was a soft felt abomination, redolent of reminiscences of Praise-God Barebones and the Rump Parliament. The crown cut down, the brim widened, it became, on Custer's head, the veritable headgear of Prince Rupert, a regular cavalier hat, exactly suited to the long fair curls of the wearer. The custom of the service allowed a cavalry officer to wear a tight jacket, instead of a coat. Custer wore a loose one. Velveteen was growing not uncommon for trousers, on account of its strength. Custer had both jacket and trousers made of it, to give richness of effect. Officers were permitted to wear on the sleeves of their overcoats, certain stripes of black braid to indicate their rank, when epaulettes and shoulder-straps were hidden. Custer put the braids in gold lace on his jacket sleeves, till they covered him nearly to the shoulder. A blue shirt with a broad falling collar, bore on its corner the silver star of a brigadier, and high boots, into which the loose trousers were thrust, completed the costume. He looked as if he had just stepped out of one of Vandyke's pictures, the image of the seventeenth century.

Such an appearance was exactly calculated to attract attention and wonder, comment and sneer, or else the most enthusiastic admiration. The boy general looked so pretty and effeminate, so unlike the stern realities of war, that he was certain to be quizzed and ridiculed unmercifully, unless he could compel the whole army to respect him. There was envy enough about his sudden elevation, as it was. There were men in the cavalry corps who had been colonels when he was only a second lieutenant, and who had commanded brigades when he was only a staff captain. Jumped over the heads of all these men as he was, they cordially disliked him, and none would have been sorry to see him come to grief with his fine feathers. The very assumption of his peculiar and fantastic uniform, was a challenge to all the world to notice him. He must do something brilliant, to justify the freak. Imitating as he did the splendor of appearance of Murat, he must equal him in deeds, if he did not wish to be set down for a carpet knight. Long after, in private life Custer used to describe his novel sensations, and those apparently controlling his regimental commanders, when he first took command of the Michigan brigade. He had not had time to go to Washington and procure the brilliant dress which he so soon assumed and rendered famous. He came to the brigade headquarters almost alone, and the first thing he had to do was to assume command and announce his staff. All he took with him was his personal baggage, his boy Johnny, and two buglers from his old regiment, the Fifth U. S. Cavalry. He looked so young and boyish when he came in, that it is no wonder if he felt awkward. He concealed all this feeling, however, as effectually as did Napoleon, sixty-two years before, when taking command of the Army of Italy, almost as boyish and untried. He assumed an abrupt and distant manner at first, was curt and decided in his orders, and made himself felt as master from the first hour. But he was distinctly conscious all the time, that his subordinates disliked, suspected, and distrusted him. Grey-headed colonels came in to salute him with outward respect, but the stiff dignity of their manners convinced him that they were inwardly boiling over with disgust and anger at having this "boy," this "popinjay," this "affected dandy," with his "girl's hair," his "swagger," and "West Point conceit" put "over *men*, sir, men who had left their farms and business, men who could make their own living, sir, and asked no government a penny for their support, men old enough to be his father, and who knew as much about real fighting, sir, as any epauletted government pensioner and West Point popinjay who was ever seen—too lazy to work for their living, and depending on government for support!—hired mercenaries, by heavens, good for nothing along side of the noble volunteers."

A good deal of this sort of thing was indulged in, that night, round the camp fires, and groups of irate officers poured forth their indignation in no measured terms. They were not aware that Pleasonton's recommendation of the three or four "boys" for high command was based on the fact that he found himself unable to get any sharp and effective work out of the elderly and over cautious colonels and generals in command of his divisions and brigades, in whom experience was the only military merit apparent to the eye, and who were so cautious and safe that there was no getting a hard fight out of them. In recommending Custer, Merritt, and Farnsworth for high station, Pleasonton imperiled his own future. All these three were young and untried officers, only known to himself. Kilpatrick and Duffié were different, both having commanded regiments and brigades. Strange to say, however, they were the very men who least justified their promotion in after days, both being excessively rash. Kilpatrick soon gained the unenviable sobriquet of "Kill cavalry," in spite of his really brilliant talents for getting out of scrapes as well as into them; and Duffié worked his division so hard and neglected its horses to such an extent, that Sheridan was obliged to break it up and dismount the men, the next year. Custer, Merritt, and Farnsworth did nobly. The career of the last named was cut short within a week by death, but he left behind him the memory of a gallant and perfect cavalry general. What Custer did we shall soon hear.

The first day, or rather night, (for he joined the brigade in the evening,) was passed in detailing a staff, which Custer did from the brigade itself, not going outside for a man. He selected his old Monroe acquaintances, where he could find them, and at once set them to work. He was compelled to be cold and distant in his manner to the colonels at first, as Napoleon was, and for the same reason, otherwise "I should soon have had them clapping me on the back and giving me advice." He could see that they envied him, and felt disposed to hate him, but he trusted confidently to the opportunity of the first battle to change all their opinions. That opportunity came very soon.

One thing that made the Michiganders dislike their boy general on his very first night, was the excessive severity of discipline, as they thought it, which he at once inaugurated. They came from the loosest of schools, that of volunteer regiments, scattered over a peaceful country, officers without any of those traditions of the service that are second nature to a regular. All those little vexatious rules, apparently so trifling, which are enforced in a regular cavalry regiment, as matters of habit, were unknown to them, and Custer enforced every one from the first. It was made a rigid rule from his first entrance that not a stable call should pass in a single company in the brigade, without the attendance of a commissioned officer to superintend the cleaning of the horses, and there is nothing the average cavalry officer abominates so utterly as stable duty. The sergeants were no longer left alone in their glory at reveillé roll-call, but the officers had to turn out. The baggage of regiments was curtailed, officers were brought up with a round turn for the slightest neglect of regulations, the salute was rigidly enforced, the new general went riding along from camp to camp, finding fault in his sharp quick way, and adding every moment to his unpopularity. All this on the very day after he assumed command, and when the brigade was still lying in camp. How the angry officers and men cursed these "newfangled West Point notions," and made up their minds to hate their boy general, when they received orders to start next morning toward Gettysburg. That day, however, witnessed a change in their relations.

It was the first of July, 1863. The infantry was already hard at work at Gettysburg, fighting Lee. The Third Cavalry division, Kilpatrick's, was moving from Hanover toward Gettysburg, Custer's brigade in the advance. Custer had already been an hour on the road, when Wade Hampton's rebel cavalry attacked Kilpatrick in the rear, just as Farnsworth's brigade was moving out, and charged him ferociously. For some time the fate of the battle was very doubtful, till Custer, hearing the firing, halted his column, faced it about and trotted up, putting in his own men with such judgment that the Michiganders were compelled to own that the boy understood his business. There was, however, no severe fighting that day after they arrived, and the grumblers were not yet silenced.

The next day, July 2d, Kilpatrick moved on a place called Hunterstown, near Gettysburg, on the prolongation of Meade's position. The battle of Gettysburg was now in full progress, and the cavalry on each side was feeling its way toward the flanks of its own army. The division arrived at Hunterstown at four in the afternoon, when the very fiercest battle was in progress a few miles off, between Sickles and Longstreet. Kilpatrick ordered in Custer's and Farnsworth's brigades, the first on the left, the second on the right of the road leading to Gettysburg, to attack Stuart's cavalry, (again Wade Hampton's division) which barred the way.

Now was Custer's time. He ordered out Co. A. Sixth Michigan for a mounted charge, and deployed two more companies of the same regiment on foot in a wheat field at the side of the road, so as to rake it with their fire. At the end of the road could be seen a party of the enemy, apparently a squadron. Capt. Thompson commanded Co. A. All was ready, and Thompson was preparing to charge, when to every one's surprise, the boy general flashed out his long Toledo blade, motioned his staff to keep back, and dashed out in front of Co. A. with the careless laughing remark,

" I'll lead you this time, boys. Come on ! "

Then away he went down the road at a gallop, his broad white hat on the back of his head, while the men raised a short yell of delight and followed him. Down the road in a perfect cloud of blinding dust went the boy general in front of that single company and the next moment they were into the midst of the enemy, only to find they had struck a very superior force. They were received with a rattling fire of carbines, more efficacious than common, and the next moment down went the general, horse and all, in the road, the animal shot stone dead.

The enemy raised a yell, and came rushing on. Thompson

was shot down, mortally wounded, and a man rode at Custer, who was struggling up from his dead horse. The Michiganders were demoralized and turned, all but one boy named Churchill, who was near the general. He shot down Custer's assailant, took up the general on his horse, and started back with him. They had not far to go, for the dismounted men were already nearly up to them, running and firing with the dash and vim peculiar to dismounted cavalry. Pennington's and Elder's batteries in the rear were both beginning to pitch shells into the rebels, and the end of the affair was that the exulting enemy was repulsed.

But the Michiganders had learned one lesson, that their "popinjay," their "boy general," was not afraid to fight like a private soldier, and they began to feel a little more in the humor to follow him, which they did that very night to join the main army at Two Taverns, on the right of Meade's position at Gettysburg.

At Two Taverns, Custer arrived with Kilpatrick, on the morning of July 3d; and from henceforth he shall tell his own story, as embodied in his report, made subsequent to the battle. Omitting the preamble, we come at once to the narrative, written in the same graphic and picturesque style which marks all his reports and orders, and which makes them such interesting reading. As, with his usual personal modesty, he omits mention of his own exploits, we shall supplement the report with the account of an eye-witness present at the time.

In his report of the battle General Custer says: At an early hour on the morning of the 3d, I received an order, through a staff-officer of the Brigadier-General commanding the division, to move at once my command, and follow the First brigade on the road leading from Two Taverns to Gettysburg. Agreeably to the above instructions, my column was formed and moved out on the road designated, when a staff officer of Brigadier-General Gregg, commanding Second division, ordered me to take my command and place it in position on the pike leading from York to Gettysburg, which position formed the extreme right of our battle on that day. Upon arriving at the point designated, I immediately placed my command in position, facing toward Gettysburg. At the same time I caused reconnoissances to be made on my front, right, and rear, but failed to discover any considerable force of the enemy. Everything remained quiet till 10 A. M., when the enemy appeared on my right flank and opened upon me with a battery of six guns. Leaving two guns and a regiment to hold my first position and cover the road leading to Gettysburg, I shifted the remaining portion of my command, forming a new line of battle at right angles to my former line. The enemy had obtained correct range of my new position, and were pouring solid shot and shell into my command with great accuracy. Placing two sections of Battery M, Second (regular) Artillery, in position, I ordered them to silence the enemy's battery, which order, notwithstanding the superiority of the enemy's position, was successfully accomplished in a very short space of time. My line, as it then existed, was shaped like the letter L, the shorter branch formed of the section of Battery M, supported by four squadrons of the Sixth Michigan cavalry, faced toward Gettysburg, covering Gettysburg pike; the long branch composed of the remaining two sections of Battery N, Second Artillery, supported by a portion of the Sixth Michigan cavalry on the right, while the Seventh Michigan cavalry, still further to the right and in advance, was held in readiness to repel any attack the enemy might make, coming on the Oxford road. The Fifth Michigan cavalry was dismounted, and ordered to take position in front of my centre and left. The First Michigan cavalry was held in column of squadrons to observe the movements of the enemy. I ordered fifty men to be sent one mile and a half on the Oxford road, while a detachment of equal size was sent one mile and a half on the road leading from Gettysburg to York, both detachments being under the command of the gallant Major Webber, who from time to time kept me so well informed of the movements of the enemy that I was enabled to make my dispositions with complete success. At 12 o'clock an order was transmitted to me from the Brigadier-General commanding the division, by one of his aids, directing me, upon being relieved by a brigade from the Second Division, to move with my command and form a junction with the First brigade on the extreme left. On the arrival of the brigade of the Second Division, commanded by Colonel McIntosh, I prepared to execute the order. Before I had left my position, Brigadier-General Gregg, commanding the Second Division, arrived with his entire command. Learning the true condition of affairs on my front, and rightly conjecturing that the enemy was making his dispositions for attacking our position, Brigadier-General Gregg ordered me to remain in the position I then occupied.

The enemy was soon after reported to be advancing on my front. The detachment of fifty men sent on the Oxford road were driven in, and at the same time the enemy's line of skirmishers, consisting of dismounted cavalry, appeared on the crest of the ridge of hills on my front. The line extended beyond my left. To repel their advance, I ordered the Fifth cavalry to a more advanced position, with instructions to maintain their ground at all hazards. Colonel Alger, commanding the Fifth, assisted by Majors Trowbridge and Ferry, of the same regiment, made such admirable disposition of their men behind fences and other defences, as enabled them to successfully repel the repeated advances of a greatly superior force. I attributed their success in a great measure to the fact that this regiment is armed with the Spencer repeating rifle, which, in the hands of brave, determined men, like those composing the Fifth Michigan cavalry, is in my estimation, the most effective firearm that our cavalry can adopt. Colonel Alger held his ground until his men had exhausted their ammunition, when he was compelled to fall back on the main body. The beginning of this movement was the signal for the enemy to charge, which they did with two regiments, mounted and dismounted. I at once ordered the Seventh Michigan cavalry, Colonel Mann, to charge the advancing column of the enemy. The ground over which we had to pass was very unfavorable for the manœuvering of cavalry, but despite all obstacles this regiment advanced boldly to the assault, which was executed in splendid style, the enemy being driven from field to field, until our advance reached a high and unbroken fence, behind which the enemy were strongly posted. Nothing daunted, Colonel Mann, followed by the main body of his regiment, bravely rode up to the fence, and discharged their revolvers in the very face of the foe. No troops could have maintained this position; the Seventh was, therefore, compelled to retire, followed by twice the number of the enemy.

By this time Colonel Alger of the Fifth Michigan cavalry had succeeded in mounting a considerable portion of his regiment, and gallantly advanced to the assistance of the Seventh, whose further pursuit by the enemy he checked. At the same time an entire brigade of the enemy's cavalry, consisting of four regiments, appeared just over the crest in our front. They were formed in columns of regiments. To meet this overwhelming force I had but one available regiment, the First Michigan cavalry, and the fire of Battery M. Second Regular Artillery. I at once ordered the First to charge, but learned at the same moment that similar orders had been given by Brigadier-General Gregg. As before stated, the First was formed in column of battalions. Upon receiving the order to charge, Colonel Town, placing himself at the head of his command, ordered the "trot" and sabres to be drawn. In this manner this gallant body of men advanced to the attack of a force outnumbering them five to one. In addition to this numerical superiority the enemy had the advantage of position, and were exultant over the repulse of the Seventh Michigan cavalry. All these facts considered would seem to render success on the part of the First impossible. Not so, however. Arriving within a few yards of the enemy's column, the charge was ordered, and with a yell that spread terror before them, the First Michigan cavalry, led by Colonel Town, rode upon the front rank of the enemy,

12

sabring all who came within reach. For a moment, but only a moment, that long, heavy column stood its ground; then, unable to withstand the impetuosity of our attack, it gave way in a disorderly rout, leaving vast numbers of dead and wounded in our possession, while the First, being masters of the field, had the proud satisfaction of seeing the much-vaunted chivalry, led by their favorite commander, seek safety in headlong flight. I cannot find language to express my high appreciation of the gallantry and daring displayed by the officers and men of the First Michigan cavalry. They advanced to the charge of a vastly superior force with as much order and precision as if going upon parade; and I challenge the annals of warfare to produce a more brilliant or successful charge of cavalry than the one just recounted. Nor must I forget to acknowledge the invaluable assistance rendered by Battery M, Second Regiment of Artillery, in this charge. Our success in driving the enemy from the field, is due, in a great measure, to the highly efficient manner in which the battery was handled by Lieutenant A. C. M. Pennington, assisted by Lieutenants Clark, Woodruff, and Hamilton. The enemy made but slight demonstrations against us during the remainder of the day, except in one instance he attempted to turn my left flank, which attempt was most gallantly met and successfully frustrated by Second Lieutenant J. H. Kellogg, with company H. Sixth Michigan cavalry. We held possession of the field until dark, during which time we collected our dead and wounded. At dark I returned with my command to Two Taverns, where I encamped for the night.

In this engagement my command lost in killed, wounded and missing, a total of five hundred and forty-two. Among the killed I regret to record the name of Major N. H. Ferry of the Fifth Michigan cavalry, who fell while heroically cheering on his men. It would be impossible for me to particularize those instances deserving especial mention; all, both men and officers, did their duty. There were many cases of personal heroism, but a list of their names would make my report too extended.

To Colonel Town, commanding the First Michigan cavalry, and to the officers and men of his regiment, for the gallant manner in which they drove the enemy from the field, great praise is due.

Colonel Mann of the Seventh Michigan cavalry, and Colonel Alger, of the Fifth Michigan cavalry, as well as the officers of their commands, are entitled to much credit for their united efforts in repelling the advance of the enemy. The Sixth Michigan cavalry rendered good service by guarding both my right and left flank; also by supporting Battery M, under a very hot fire from the enemy's battery. Colonel Gray, commanding the regiment, was constantly seen wherever his presence was most needed, and is deserving of special mention. I desire to commend to your favorable notice Lieutenants Pennington, Clark, Woodruff, and Hamilton of Battery M, Second Artillery, for the zeal and ability displayed by each on this occasion. My thanks are personally due to the following named members of my staff, who on many occasions exhibited remarkable gallantry in transmitting and executing my orders on the field: Captain G. A. Drew, Sixth Michigan cavalry, Assistant Inspector General, First Lieutenant R. Baylis, Fifth Michigan cavalry, Acting Assistant Adjutant-General, First Lieutenant William H. Wheeler, First Michigan cavalry, A. D. C. First Lieutenant William Colerick, First Michigan cavalry, A. D. C. I desire also to mention two of my buglers, Joseph Fought, company D, Fifth U. S. Cavalry, and Peter Boehn, company B, Fifth U. S. cavalry; also Orderlies Norval Churchill, company L. First Michigan cavalry, George L. Foster, company C, First Michigan cavalry, and Benjamin H. Butler, company M, First Michigan cavalry.

Respectfully submitted,
G. A. CUSTER,
Brigadier-General Commanding Second Brigade."

Jacob L. Greene,

Assistant Adjutant-General.

The charge of the First Michigan at Gettysburg is described by an eye-witness as something magnificent, and yet the one thing that gave it weight is not mentioned in Custer's report. We have seen how, the previous day, the general had charged at the head of a single company, solely for the purpose of encouraging his men and to win their respect and affection. At Gettysburg he completed his victory over the brigade by the manner in which he led the second charge in which he participated with his men. When that single regiment, in column of squadrons, moved forward to the attack, every man knew that it was the last reserve and had started on an almost hopeless task. Nothing but the sight of the young general at their head sharing their dangers could have inspired them to such an effort, and it was the magnificent spectacle of his gallant and knightly figure, far in the van, that nerved every arm in that column. Hating him at Hanover, they began to respect him at Hunterstown; after Gettysburg they adored him.

The result of this attack was that Hampton's cavalry was driven back, the infantry ordered up to support it, the whole ammunition train of Lee threatened, and much of the vigor of the assault on the Union right paralyzed. Meanwhile Buford, on the other flank of the army, had prevented an equally dangerous turning movement in that direction, and the battle of Gettysburg had been won.

CHAPTER II.

AFTER GETTYSBURG.

IN giving an account of the cavalry movements which followed the battle of Gettysburg, we are indebted largely to the spirited narrative of Mr. E. A. Paul, then correspondent of the *New York Times*, who accompanied Kilpatrick's division throughout the expedition. Those portions which relate to Custer are especially interesting. It must be remembered that the young general was then entirely unknown to the public, but these letters opened people's eyes. At the same time they marked the brilliant commencement of that career which henceforth never knew a serious disaster. At Gettysburg he began by charging whenever he had a ghost of a chance, and he continued in the same way.

Saturday morning, July 4th, according to Mr. Paul, it became known that the enemy was in full retreat, and General Kilpatrick moved on to destroy his train and harass his column. A heavy rain fell all day, and the travelling was anything but agreeable. The division arrived at Emmetsburg about midday, during a severe storm. After a short halt, the column moved forward again, and at Fountaindale, just at dark, commenced ascending the mountain. Imagine a long column of cavalry winding its way up a mountain, on a road dug out of the mountain side, which sloped at an angle of thirty degrees— just wide enough for four horses to walk abreast. On one side a deep abyss, and on the other an impassable barrier, in the shape of a steep embankment; the hour 10 o'clock at night, a drizzling rain falling, the sky overcast, and so dark as literally

not to be able to see one's own hand if placed within a foot of
the organs of vision. The whole command, both men and
animals, were worn out with fatigue and loss of sleep. Then
imagine that, just as the head of this tired, hungry and sleepy
column nears the crest of the mountain, a piece of cannon
belches forth fire and smoke and destructive missiles directly in
front. Imagine all this, and a little more, and the reader can
then form some idea of what occurred to General Kilpatrick's
command on Saturday night, July 4th, 1863, as it ascended
the mountain to the Monterey Gap, and so across to Waterloo
on the western slope. The column commenced to ascend at
about dark, and arrived at the Monterey House, at the top,
between nine and ten o'clock. The enemy had planted a piece
of artillery near this spot, so as to command the road, and also
had sharp-shooters on the flanks. It was intended to make a
strong defence here, as one half-mile beyond, Lee's train was
crossing the mountain on the Gettysburg and Hagerstown pike.
The Fifth Michigan Cavalry was in advance, and although on
the lookout for just such an occurrence, it startled the whole
column. A volley of musketry was fired by a concealed force
at the same time at the head of the column ; the first squadron
of the Fifth broke, fell back upon the second and broke that,
but there was no such thing as running back a great way on
that road. It was jammed with men and horses.

The broken squadron immediately rallied, skirmishers were
posted on the most available points, the First Virginia, Major
Copeland, was ordered to the front, and upon arriving there
was ordered to charge. Charge they did, at a rapid gait, down
the mountain side into the inky darkness before them, accompanied by a detachment of the First Ohio, Captain Jones.
As anticipated, the train was struck, in rear of the centre, at
the crossing, just one half mile west of the Monterey House.
A volley was fired just as the train was reached. "Do you
surrender?" "Yes," was the response, and on the First Virginia dashed to Ringgold, ordering the cowed and frightened

train-guard to surrender, as they swept along for eight miles, when the head of the train was reached. Here the two hundred men who started on the charge had been reduced to twenty-five, and seizing upon a good position, the rebels made a stand. As the force in front could not be seen, Major Copeland decided not to proceed further, but to await daylight and reinforcements. Both came, and the enemy fled. Arriving at Gettysburg pike, the Eighteenth Pennsylvania was placed here as a guard, and a barricade was hastily thrown up. No sooner was this done, than cavalry was heard charging down the road. "Who comes there!" calls the officer in charge at the barricade. "Tenth Virginia Cavalry," was the reply. To —— with your Tenth Virginia Cavalry, and the squadron fire a volley into the darkness. That was the last heard of the Tenth Virginia cavalry that night, until numbers of the regiment came straggling in and gave themselves up, prisoners of war. Other rebel cavalry moved up and down the road upon which the train was standing, and some most amusing scenes occurred. The train belonged to Ewell's division, and had in it also a large number of private carriages and teams, containing officers' baggage. Four regiments were doing guard duty, but as they judged of the future by the past, they supposed our army would rest two or three months after winning a battle, magnanimously permitting the defeated enemy to get away his stores and ordnance and have a little time to recruit. Therefore the attack was a complete surprise. A thunderstorm was prevailing at the time, and the attack was so entirely unexpected that there was a general panic among both guard and teamsters. The howling of the storm, the rushing of water down the mountain-side, and the roaring of wind, altogether were certainly enough in that wild spot, to test the nerves of the strongest. But when is added to this a volley of pistol and carbine shots occasionally, a slap on the back with the flat of a sword, and a hoarse voice giving the unfortunate wight the choice of surrendering or being shot, then add to this the fearful yells and imprecations of the men, wild with excitement, all made up a scene certainly never excelled before in the regions of fancy. Two rebel captains, two hours after the train had been captured, came up to one of the reserve commands and wanted to know "what regiment that was"—supposing it belonged to their own column. They discovered their mistake when Lieutenant Whittaker, of General Kilpatrick's staff, presented a pistol and advised them to give up their arms. Several other officers, who might easily have escaped, came in voluntarily and gave themselves up.

Under so good subjection were the enemy, that there was no necessity of making any change in teamsters or drivers, they voluntarily continuing right on in Uncle Sam's service, as they had been in the Confederate service, until it was convenient to relieve them. At first, the prisoners were corralled near the Monterey House. When the number had got to be large, they were driven down the mountain toward Waterloo. A gang started off in this direction about midnight. It was not prudent to wait until morning, for daylight might bring with it a retreating column of the enemy, and then all the prisoners would have been recaptured; finally, when near the Gettysburg road crossing, a band of straggling rebels happened to fire into the head of the party from a spur of the mountain overlooking the road. Here was another panic, which alike affected guards and prisoners. The rain was falling in torrents, and the whole party, neither one knowing who this or the other was, rushed under the friendly shelter of a clump of trees. All of those prisoners might have, at that time, escaped. Hundreds did escape before daylight dawned.   .   .   .

The head of the column reached Ringgold at about daylight—the whole command, horses as well as men, tired, hungry, sleepy, wet, and covered with mud. Men and animals yielded to the demands of exhausted nature, and the column had not been halted many minutes before all fell asleep where they stood. Under the friendly protection of the dripping eaves of a chapel, a gay and gallant brigadier could have been seen, enjoying in the mud one of those sound sleeps only obtained through fatigue, his long golden locks matted with the soil of Pennsylvania. Near him in the mud, lay a dandy-ish adjutant, equally oblivious of the toilet, upon which he generally bestowed so much attention. Under a fence near at hand is reclining a well-got-up major, whose stylish appearance and regular features have turned the heads of many fair dam-sels on Chestnut street; here a chaplain, there a trooper, a Commanding General, aids, orderlies, and servants, for the nonce, meet on a level. The faithful trooper lies by his horse, between whom and himself there seems to exist an indescribable community of feeling. Two hours are thus passed in sleep— the provost-guard only on duty—when word is passed that "the column has all closed up," which is the signal to move on again. The indefatigable Estes shakes himself, and proceeds to shake the Commanding General, to let him know that the object for which the halt was made had been accomplished; that it is time to move. Five minutes more, all are in the sad-dle again, and marching for Smithsburg. A body of armed men, mailed in mud! What a picture. Smithsburg was reached by 9 o'clock A. M. The reception met with there made all forget the trials of the night—made them forget even their fatigue. It was Sunday. The sun shone forth brightly, young girls lined the street-sides, singing patriotic songs; the General was showered with flowers, and the General and troops were cheered until reëchoed by the mountain side; young ladies and matrons assailed the column with words of welcome and large plates heaped up with pyramids of white bread, spread with jelly and butter, inviting all to partake. While the young sang, the old shed tears and wrung the hands of those nearest to them. The little town was overflowing with patriot-ism and thankfulness at the arrival of their preservers. While these things were detaining the column, the band struck up "Hail Columbia," followed by the "Star-Spangled Banner."

Many eyes, unused to tears, were wet then. The kind reception met with here did the command more good than a week's rest. Even the horses, faithful animals, seemed to be revived by the patriotic demonstration. No one who participated in the raid of Saturday night, July 4th, 1863, can ever forget the reception met with in Smithsburg. It was like an oasis in the desert—a green spot in the soldier's life.

Early on Monday, July 6th, General Kilpatrick, hearing that the enemy had a train near Hagerstown, moved upon that place. The enemy's pickets were met near the edge of the town.

It was 4 o'clock P. M., when General Kilpatrick, with the main column, reached the crest of the hill overlooking Williamsport, on the Boonsboro' pike. General Buford's command had been engaged with the enemy two or three miles to the left, for two or more hours; Major Medill, of the Eighth Illinois, had already fallen mortally wounded. Two pieces of Pennington's battery were placed on the brow of the hill to the right of the pike, and the other pieces to the left. A squadron of Fifth Michiganders had previously charged down the pike, driving in the enemy's pickets and a battalion which occupied an advanced position. The First Michigan, Colonel Town, was deployed as skirmishers to the right, and ordered to drive the enemy from a brick house a little in advance, and to the right of the artillery. Several unsuccessful attempts were made to obey this order; but before it could be done, the brisk firing of the rear-guard warned the commanding general that his force occupied a dangerous position. Never was a command in a more critical situation; never before was a man cooler, or did one display more real generalship than General Kilpatrick on this occasion. Tapping his boot with his whip, and peering in the direction of the rapidly approaching rear-guard, he saw it falling back, apparently in some disorder. Not a moment was to be lost; inaction or indecision would have proved fatal, and the moral effect of a successful campaign destroyed in an hour.

Fortunately, General Kilpatrick was cool and defiant, and felt
the responsibility resting upon him. This made him master of
the situation, and by a dashing movement, saved the cavalry
corps from disaster. Seeing his rear-guard falling back, he
bethought himself of what force could be withdrawn from the
front in safety. The enemy were pressing his front and rear—
the crisis had arrived; he ordered the Second New York
(Harris's Light) to charge upon the exultant foe, then coming
like an avalanche upon his rear. Nobly did this band of heroes
perform their task. They fell into the breach with a yell, and,
sword in hand, drove back the enemy, relieving the exhausted
rear-guard, and holding the enemy in check until the whole
command was disposed of, so as to fall back, which they did in
good order, fighting as they went. For three miles, over one
of the worst roads ever travelled by man, was this retreat conducted, when the enemy, dispirited at their want of success in
surrounding and capturing the whole command, halted, and
the cavalry corps went into camp, men and officers, exhausted
from the labors of the day, falling asleep on the spot where
they halted. Colonel Devin's brigade, of General Buford's
command, had relieved the rear-guard, and were harassed by
the enemy all night.

Tuesday morning, July 7th, the cavalry force moved back
to Boonsboro', the enemy following the rear-guard, and at
intervals there was brisk skirmishing between General Buford's
command and the enemy. The same was true of the night.
The Sixth Cavalry, (regulars,) under Captain Chafiant, made
a reconnoissance at night and had a brisk fight, in which they
lost eight or nine men. Wednesday morning there were indi-
cations that the enemy were present in large force, and by ten
o'clock the "fandango" opened in real earnest, in which both
Buford's and Kilpatrick's troops participated. The enemy
were forced back to Antietam Creek. Thursday the fight was
renewed, and again on Friday, when Funktown was occupied.
Saturday the enemy was again forced back, and on Saturday

General Kilpatrick's command again moved upon Hagerstown.

After fighting for an hour, the town was fully occupied, and the enemy fell back to the crest of the hill, one and a half miles west of the town.

The streets picketed by the enemy were barricaded, and the troops were disposed of outside the town so as to resist an attack. In clearing the outskirts of the town for skirmishers, the One Hundred and Fifty-seventh New York Infantry, of General Ames's brigade, (Eleventh corps,) rendered material assistance. Upon entering the town, the hearts of our troops were made glad by finding between thirty and forty Union soldiers, who had been missing since the Monday before, a majority of whom were supposed to be dead. A few were wounded; all had been concealed by citizens, and had been treated well. Captain Snyder, reported killed, was found wounded at the Franklin Hotel, carefully attended by a bevy of lovely damsels.

General Kilpatrick was much annoyed at the restraint he was under all day Monday and Tuesday; he desired to move on, believing that the enemy, while making a show of force, was crossing the river. This subsequently proved to be true. Had the army advanced on Tuesday morning, Lee's whole army would either have been captured or dispersed. When, on Wednesday morning, an advance was made without orders the fact was ascertained that the enemy had commenced falling back when the attack was made, the day before, the enemy believing that it was the initiatory movement of a general advance. Such was the panic among the rebel troops, that they abandoned wagons, ammunition, tents, arms, and even provisions. Hundreds of rebels, fearing Kilpatrick's men, fled to the right and left to avoid their charges, and subsequently surrendered themselves. One strapping fellow surrendered to a little bugler, who is attached to General Custer's brigade. As he passed down the line escorting his prisoner, a Colt's revolver in hand, he called out: "I say, boys, what do you think of this fellow?"

" This fellow " looked as if he felt very mean, and expected he
would be shot by his captor every moment for feeling so. All
along the road to Williamsport, prisoners were captured, and
their rear-guard was fairly driven into the river. The Fifth
Michigan charged into the town, and captured a large number
of soldiers, as they were attempting to ford the river. From
thirty to fifty of the rebels were drowned while attempting to
cross ; twenty-five or thirty wagons and a large number of
horses and mules were washed away. A regiment of cavalry
was drawn up on the opposite bank, but a few of " Pennington's
pills " caused them to skedaddle. They fired a few shells in return, but no harm was done.

Hearing that a force had marched toward Falling Waters,
General Kilpatrick ordered an advance to that place. Through
some mistake, only one brigade, that of General Custer, obeyed
the order. When within less than a mile of Falling Waters,
four brigades were found in line of battle, in a very strong
position, and behind half a dozen crescent-shaped earth-walls.
The Sixth Michigan Cavalry was in advance. They did not
wait for orders, but a squadron—companies D and C, under
Captain Royce (who was killed) and Captain Armstrong—were
deployed as skirmishers, while companies B and F, led by
Major Weaver, (who was killed) made the charge. The line
of skirmishers was forced back several times, but the men
rallied promptly, and finally drove the enemy behind the works.
A charge was then made, the squadron passing between the
earth-works. So sudden and spirited was the dash, and so demoralized were the enemy, that the First Brigade surrendered
without firing a shot. The charging squadron moved directly
on, and engaged the Second Brigade, when the brigade that had
surrendered seized their guns, and then commenced a fearful
struggle. Of the one hundred who made this charge, only
thirty escaped uninjured. Seven of their horses lay dead within
the enemy's works. Twelve hundred prisoners were here captured, and the ground was strewn with dead and wounded

rebels. Among the killed was Major-General Pettigrew, of South Carolina. A. P. Hill was seated, smoking a pipe, when the attack commenced; it came so suddenly that he threw the pipe away, mounted his horse, and crossed the river as speedily as possible.

Three battle-flags were captured, two of them covered with the names of battles in which the regiments owning them had been engaged. Prisoners were captured all along the road between Williamsport and Falling Waters, in which service the First Ohio squadron, under Captain Jones, acting as body-guard, as usual, took an active part. Sergeant Gillespie, of company A, being in advance, overtook a body of men trying to get off with a Napoleon gun; the horses balked, and the Sergeant politely requested the men to surrender, which order they cheerfully obeyed. Seven men and four horses were taken with the gun. The caissons were filled with ammunition, and Captain Hasbrouck of the General's staff, at once placed it in position, and used it upon the enemy—a whole brigade being then in sight. Another Napoleon gun was abandoned, and taken in charge by the Eighteenth Pennsylvania cavalry, Lieutenant-Colonel Brinton. Captain Royce, of the Sixth Michigan, was with the skirmishing party, and was shot twice; the first time through the leg, the second ball through his head. Company C, of the skirmishers, lost fifteen men, ten of whom were wounded.

Just at the close of the fight, General Buford's command came up, and pursued the flying foe to the river, capturing four hundred and fifty prisoners. The enemy succeeded in destroying their pontoon bridge, however, and thus effectually prevented immediate pursuit.

This closed the Gettysburg campaign. It was the last time that Lee crossed the Potomac. From henceforth he was compelled to defend Virginia. A detachment under Early tried the same operation next year, but his force proved insufficient to detach Grant's hold on Richmond, and the advent of Sheridan introduced a new phase—constant aggression and victories consummated—with the Union programme.

During the rest of July and August, the cavalry had but little work to do. Meade was moved down to Virginia, and occupying the same line on which McClellan had moved the previous fall, while Lee, behind the shelter of the Blue Ridge, was gathering up his forces, which he finally concentrated behind the Rapidan. The cavalry work did not begin till September.

The operations immediately after Gettysburg, in the case of Custer's brigade, first show clearly, in the handling of the command, a high order of military talent in the young general. Just as, when an aide-de-camp, he had placed his whole ambition on being the best and most active officer of all Pleasonton's staff, so now, as a brigade commander, he became indisputably the best in the cavalry corps, and his single brigade seemed to do more work and attract more notice than any other. This success was owing mainly to the same qualities conspicuous in the Urbana expedition—*tact*. What had been tact in the lieutenant became *coup d'œil* in the general. The basis of the faculty is found in most brilliant men, and still more so in brilliant women. In the arena of politics it makes the ready debater, in society the wit and the belle, in journalism the powerful writer whom every one fears to oppose, in business the bold and successful operator. It consists in doing (or saying) the right thing at the right time, the power of rapid decision.

The battle of Falling Waters illustrates this character in Custer, as also his superiority to the headlong rashness of Kilpatrick. Custer came up alone, saw his enemy wavering, and with the use of only four companies *put in at the right moment*, captured a whole Confederate brigade. Then he stopped: he knew when audacity had been pushed far enough. A moment later up comes Kilpatrick. Not satisfied with a single brigade, he must needs attempt to take *four*, with an inadequate force, and ordered the charge of the Sixth Michigan *continued*.

What was the result? Of the one hundred who made the charge only thirty escaped uninjured. The surrendered brigade, thinking no quarter was to be shown, resumed the struggle, and the victory, gained by Custer's tact, was nearly lost by Kilpatrick's foolhardy assault. It was not the last time, as we shall see further on. With the possession of plenty of physical courage, Kilpatrick mingled so much of besotted rashness and vanity during his career as a division commander, that his greatest successes were always marred by unnecessary slaughter, while he suffered more than one mortifying and humiliating defeat. In Custer was found that temper of discretion which made his courage tact. While under Kilpatrick, few believed he possessed it. His independent career demonstrated it, long after.

In his handling of cavalry as a tactician he seems always to have observed the just medium between exclusive charging work and that which degenerates into mere mounted infantry contests. No man knew better than he that the sole aggressive strength of cavalry is found in the charge, while dismounted skirmishers are the best weapon for defensive battles. This truth was very seldon observed by other brigade commanders, who grew altogether too fond of dismounted work. Custer, at Gettysburg and after, always used both kinds of lines together, just as Cæsar did at Pharsalia, when opposing an enemy of superior force, but when his foes were equal or inferior, as invariably availed himself of the moral influence of the mounted charge, as the most efficacious of all.

CHAPTER III.

TO THE RAPIDAN AND BACK.

A T the beginning of September, the Army of the Potomac had resumed on the upper Rappahannock the same lazy attitude, much resembling that of a siege, which it had occupied before Richmond under McClellan, and before Petersburg under Burnside and Hooker. The different infantry corps were grouped at points near the bank of the river, and comfortably settled in permanent camps, while the cavalry was drawn back on either wing, almost entirely out of danger, picketing the back country to prevent raids on Meade's line of supply, the Orange and Alexandria Railroad.

Lee's position was different, as his line of supply was different. His main force was drawn back to Gordonsville, at least forty miles off, and before him lay both the Rappahannock and Rapidan Rivers. The triangle of country between these streams was occupied by his cavalry, which served as a veil to his army, behind which it could move in perfect security. In a military point of view the whole position was far better than that of Meade. Lee knew all the latter was doing, and Meade was ignorant of his enemy's exact position.

At last, on the 13th September, a move was made to dissipate the uncertainty. The cavalry was taken from its camps in the rear, moved down to the Rappahannock, and on that day crossed the river, Buford in the centre, Gregg on the right, Kilpatrick on the left, and advanced toward Culpepper, midway between the two rivers.

The advance was made on the line of the railroad which

went straight to Culpepper, the country being quite open and level, with beautiful park-like clumps of huge trees dotting the green-sward around Brandy Station, the first house. From thence to Culpepper the whole place was beautifully adapted to cavalry fighting, fences being all destroyed and ditches few. A fringe of coppice hid the movements of the cavalry near the Rappahannock, while they were preparing for the advance.

In half an hour or so, all was ready. There were now nine brigades in the three divisions, and their method of fighting had become uniform. The advance on Culpepper will give a very good idea of its nature. Each brigade had an average of four regiments, with a regimental average of three hundred men. Thus the whole force was nearly 12,000 strong. In front of each brigade was a full regiment, deployed as skirmishers, each man riding some twenty feet from his fellows, carbine in hand. Behind the right and left of this open line of men, at a distance of some two hundred yards, were two regiments with drawn sabres, in line of battle, but moving at a walk. In rear of the centre, and retired some two or three hundred yards further, was the last regiment, in column of march. Before this was the brigade commander, and in front of him was his battery. Each brigade thus occupied more than half a mile, and the whole line was between five and six miles in length.

At last, at a given signal, this great line started on its way, and the word was passed to "trot on to Brandy Station." In a few minutes the sharp crack of carbines along the line, told that the enemy were found, and answering puffs told that they were resisting the advance. Then, from the summit of a gentle slope beyond Brandy Station, came broad bright flashes, and great clouds of white smoke, as the enemy's batteries opened on the advancing cavalry.

Their efforts were perfectly useless, for the rapidly trotting and wavy line of skirmishers offered nothing to fire at, and the length of the line threatened to curl round the flanks of the defenders every moment. There was no serious fight. Ere five minutes were over, Brandy Station was reached, a picket-post captured bodily, and the advance was resumed across the open country to Culpepper, without a check. As the cavalry swept on, the enemy gathered thicker in the front, and more guns came into action, but it was evident at all times that they were heavily overmatched, as they fell back from knoll to knoll, fighting all the time, but in vain. Some idea of the rapid and dashing nature of the fight may be gathered from the time it occupied. The advance left Rappahannock Bridge about 10 o'clock, and by half past twelve the enemy were driven through Culpepper, nine miles off.

Custer had the extreme left of the line, covering the flank of Kilpatrick's division. It was a race, and a matter of emulation between all the components of that long line, to keep abreast of each other, " dressed " in perfect order. Of course this was impossible sometimes, on account of the different nature of the ground in front of different brigades; but whenever the line assumed a wavy appearance, one could hear the officers shouting to the men to " dress up," and the poor horses would be spurred on to a more rapid pace, to make up for lost time. The whole advance resembled a fox hunt, animated and inspiriting to the highest degree, with just enough spice of danger to make it delightfully exciting. At Culpepper the enemy made a stand with all his artillery. General Stuart was there, getting ready to leave, fancying the whole of Meade's army was advancing. A locomotive and train of cars was ready, all steam up, when Custer's brigade came dashing on, only to find themselves stopped by a deep creek with a single ford. The enemy opened fire with three batteries, and Custer's guns tried to cripple the locomotive. In the hurry and confusion at the ford, however, the train got away. Custer himself was far ahead of his own skirmishers, who were bothered by the swamps at the border of the creek below, and he rode on with the skirmishers of the next brigade on the right, which happened to be the Second New York (Harris' Light). With them and a few of his own men he galloped into Culpepper, cut off two of the enemy's guns, and captured them. Ten minutes later Culpepper was ours, and the enemy hastily retreating towards the Rapidan.*

The advance had been so rapid that a halt was necessary at Culpepper to gather up the loose ends, and it was not till two hours later that the march was resumed. It was unaccompanied by serious resistance and by the next morning the whole triangle of country between the Rapidan and Rappahannock was in full possession of Meade's army.

Now was the real time for Meade to advance in force. At the time of the fight at Culpepper, Lee was seriously weakened, having sent away the whole of Longstreet's strong corps to help Bragg at Chattanooga. Had Meade struck hard at that time, when all the roads were dry, and at least two months active work was possible, the heroes of the war would have been differently named. But like all the commanders of the Army of the Potomac, he was paralyzed by the fear of Lee, and did not dare to undertake a rapid movement. The rest of September was passed in camp around Culpepper, the cavalry picketing the fords of the Rapidan; and it was not till the beginning of October that he ventured, in a hesitating manner, to move. When he did, Lee, by a simple feint at his flank, frightened him so much that he abandoned all his ground in haste, and fell back in confusion, without a battle, to Washington, leaving the cavalry to cover his retreat, alone and unassisted, in the face of the greater part of Lee's army.

Of this retreat of Meade's no one has ever spoken a good word. The only feature of its origin pleasant to contemplate, is in the light of a compliment to Lee. The latter, at the time

---

* It was on this occasion that Custer received his first and only wound from a piece of shell.

he made his flank movement, possessed less than two-thirds of Meade's force, but Meade occupied the exact position occupied by Pope and Banks, the previous year, when the disasters of Cedar Mountain and Manassas Second occurred. He was out at Culpepper, and Lee was moving round his flank by way of Thoro'fare Gap, threatening his communications, just as Jackson had done the year before.

True, he was in a very different position otherwise from Pope. Pope was numerically inferior to Lee, and depended for help on McClellan's army, which help came too late. Meade's force was all concentrated, his cavalry superior to that of his enemy, his men had the moral advantage of the recent victory of Gettysburg to inspirit them, and he had every reason to trust the issue to a desperate and decisive battle. Nevertheless, Lee's shadow scared him out of his wits.

On the ninth of October, Meade cautiously began his advance on Lee, by sending his cavalry over the Rapidan and its upper tributaries, one of which was called Robertson's River. Buford occupied the extreme left, Kilpatrick the centre, Gregg the extreme right, up at White Sulphur Springs. In narrating the part taken by Custer's Michiganders we shall quote the language of his report bodily.

On the night of October 9th, 1863, says Custer, my picket line, which extended along the north bank of Robertson River in the vicinity of James City, was attacked, and a portion of the line forced back upon the reserves ; at the same time my scouts informed me that the enemy was moving in heavy column toward my right ; this report was confirmed by deserters. In anticipation of an attack of the enemy at daybreak, I ordered my entire command to be saddled at 3 A. M. on the 10th. At daybreak, the enemy began by cautiously feeling my line; but seeing his inability to surprise us, he contented himself by obtaining possession of Cedar Mountain, which point he afterwards used as a signal station. At 1 P. M., I received orders from the General commanding the division, to report with my

command at James City. The head of my column arrived in
the vicinity of that point at 3 p. m. The enemy had already
obtained possession of the town, and had brought several guns
to bear on the position I was ordered to take. Battery M.,
Second United States Artillery, under command of Lieutenant
Pennington, was unlimbered, and succeeded in shelling the
enemy out of the woods on the right of the town. At the
same time Colonel Alger, of the Fifth Michigan Cavalry, who
held the extreme left of my line, moved forward with one
battalion of his regiment, under the gallant Major Clark, and
charged the enemy's battery. The charge, although daring in
the extreme, failed for want of sufficient support. It was successful so far, however, as to compel the enemy to shift the position of his battery to a more retired point. Night setting in,
prevented us from improving the advantages we had gained.
Most of my command rested on their arms during the night.
Early in the morning I retired on the road leading to Culpepper, which point I reached without molestation from the enemy.
It was not until the rear of my column was leaving the town
that the enemy made his appearance, and attempted, unsuccessfully, to harass my rear-guard. On the hills north of the town I
placed my command in position to receive an attack.

The enemy not feeling disposed to accept the invitation, I
retired on the road leading to Rappahannock Station. My
column had scarcely begun to march, before the officer commanding the rear-guard—Colonel Mann, of the Seventh Michigan Cavalry—reported the enemy to be pressing him closely.
At the same time a strong column was seen on my outer flank,
evidently attempting to intercept our line of march to the river.
The vigorous attacks now being made upon my rear-guard
compelled me to place my battery at the head of the column,
and to employ my entire force to keep the enemy from my
guns. My advance had reached the vicinity of Brandy Station,
when a courier hastened back with the information that a brigade of the enemy's cavalry was in position *directly in my*

front, thus cutting us completely off from the river. Upon examination, I learned the correctness of the report. The heavy masses of Confederate cavalry could be seen covering the heights in front of my advance. When it is remembered that my rear-guard was hotly engaged with a superior force, a heavy column enveloping each flank, and my advance confronted by more than double my own number, the perils of my situation can be estimated. Lieutenant Pennington at once placed his battery in position, and opened a brisk fire, which was responded to by the guns of the enemy. The Major-General commanding the cavalry corps at this moment rode to the advance. To him I proposed, with my command, to cut through the force in my front, and thus open the way for the entire command to the river. My proposition was approved, and I received orders to take my available force and push forward, leaving the Sixth and Seventh Michigan Cavalry to hold the force in rear in check. I formed the Fifth Michigan Cavalry on my right, in column of battalions; on my left, I formed the First Michigan in column of squadrons. After ordering them to draw their sabres, I informed them that we were surrounded, and all we had to do was to open a way with our sabres. They showed their determination and purpose by giving three hearty cheers. At this moment the band struck up the inspiring air, "Yankee Doodle," which excited the enthusiasm of the entire command to the highest pitch, and made each individual member feel as if he was a host in himself. Simultaneously, both regiments moved forward to the attack. It required but a glance at the countenances of the men to enable me to read the settled determination with which they undertook the work before them. The enemy, without waiting to receive the onset, broke in disorder and fled. After a series of brilliant charges, during which the enemy suffered heavily, we succeeded in reaching the river, which we crossed in good order.

So far Custer, but it seems necessary to explain how it was that he found himself thus surrounded. It all came of Meade's falling back. On the 8th he had thrown his cavalry over the Rapidan to scout up and down the river. Had he merely followed them, he must have marched right into Lee's camp, for only Stuart's cavalry was left in that vicinity. But on the 8th he heard that Lee's infantry was trying to get around his flank, and instead of cutting in on this flanking party, he fell back without any warning, leaving his three cavalry divisions spread out like a fan, each pressed by cavalry and infantry combined. Buford, who had crossed at Germania Ford, with the promise of the whole First Corps to support him, next day found himself driven back over Morton's Ford, and not an infantryman to be seen. He fell slowly back in the direction of Brandy Station, and as his road there was much shorter than that of Kilpatrick's division, found himself there before Kilpatrick. Custer's brigade was on the right of the Third division, and Pleasonton was with Kilpatrick. Therefore the position was now very curious. At Brandy Station, with his back to the river, was Buford, a force of cavalry and infantry, with several batteries, pressing all round him. Several mounted charges had been made to drive back the enemy, and in every instance they fell back. Suddenly the heavy fire in Buford's front ceased, and then recommenced with tenfold fury, but not a shot came near Buford's men. It increased to a perfect roar, while the yells of charging men were plainly audible over the firing. The next moment, out of the woods into the open fields, came tearing Kilpatrick's men, charging in column, dark masses of horsemen in considerable confusion, Pleasonton with the guns, in the middle of the column, all looking pretty well used up. Had it not been for the firm attitude of Buford's division, whose flanks were safe, and who had kept the enemy all in the front, Kilpatrick's men must have suffered as fearfully as they did, a few days later, at Buckland's Mills.

As it happened, Buford's stand gave them time to rest and get into decent order, and the rest of the afternoon the two divisions confronted the enemy without further disaster, till

nightfall. The most exasperating part of this battle at Brandy
Station was however yet to come. It was when the cavalry
after dark, rode down to the fords to cross the Rappahannock
and beheld the whole country on the further bank bright with
the camp-fires of their own infantry, who had been compelled
to lie idle all day, passive spectators of a fight which their
presence could have determined. The sight was a fair speci-
men of the pusillanimous policy of General Meade in this
celebrated retreat. It was a courting of disgrace.

To the cavalry, the battle at Brandy Station was creditable.
It was a gallant struggle against fearful odds. The figure
borne by Custer is evidenced in the following racy anecdote by
a member of the Fifth Michigan.*

"At 'Brandy' Station, Va., during Meade's fall back,
'Custer' and the cavalry brought up the rear, and all soldiers
know it is the worst place on God's footstool to cover a retreat.
To allow the infantry ample time to cross the Rappahannock
the cavalry kept *fooling* around with an average of 10,000
'Rebs' on *all* sides of them. Once when a lull had seemed to
come with an ominous stillness some one remarked, ' Helloa,
look ahead,' and sure enough about 5,000 'Rebs' were suddenly seen to be massed in our front and right in the *path
we must travel if we ever saw ' the girls we left behind us.'*
Custer was sitting on his horse at the head of our regiment, the
Fifth Cavalry. He took one look of about ten seconds, then
snatched off his hat, raised up in his stirrups and yelled out,
' Boys of Michigan, there are some people between *us* and
home; I'm going home, who else goes?' Suffice it to say we
all went. General Alger, then colonel of our regiment, can
vouch for our flying movements as we followed Custer, with
his bare head and golden locks, and long straight sabre, putting
the very devil into the old Fifth Cavalry, until a clear track
was before us. When ' out of the woods' up came Kilpatrick,
and sung out, ' Custer, what ails you?' His reply was, ' Oh,

* Mr. J. Allen Bigelow, of Detroit, published in *Detroit Evening News.*

nothing, only we want to cook coffee on the Yank side of the Rappahannock.' "

In narrating the further events of the campaign, Custer shall resume the story, in his report, made at the time.

From the eleventh to the fifteenth, my command was employed in picketing and guarding the flank and rear of the army. On the afternoon of the fifteenth, the brigade being posted on the Bull Run battle ground, I detailed Major Kidd with his regiment, the Sixth Michigan Cavalry, to reconnoitre the strength and position of the enemy in the vicinity of Gainsville. The reconnoissance was entirely satisfactory, and showed the enemy to be in considerable force at that point. Sunday, the 18th October, at 3 P. M., the entire division was ordered to move on the pike leading from Groveton to Warrenton. The First brigade moved on the pike, the Second moved on a road to the left of, and parallel to the pike, but soon encountered the enemy, and drove him as far as Gainsville, where the entire command bivouacked for the night. The First Vermont Cavalry, under Colonel Sawyer, deserves great credit for the rapidity with which they forced the enemy to retire. At daybreak on the morning of the 19th, my brigade took the advance and skirmished with the enemy's cavalry from Gainsville to Buckland; at the latter point I found him strongly posted upon the south bank of Broad Run. The position for his artillery was well chosen. After a fruitless attempt to effect a crossing in his front, I succeeded in turning his left flank so completely as to force him from his position. Having driven him more than a mile from the stream, I threw out my pickets, and ordered my men to prepare their dinner. From the inhabitants of Buckland I learned that the forces of the enemy, with whom we had been engaged, were commanded by General J. E. B. Stuart in person, who, at the time of our arrival at that point, was seated at the dinner-table eating; but owing to my successful advance, he was compelled to leave his dinner untouched—a circumstance not regretted by that portion of my command into whose hands it fell. The First brigade took the advance. At this point I was preparing to follow, when information reached me that the enemy was advancing on my left, from the direction of Greenwich. I had scarcely time to place my command in position to resist an attack from that direction, before the enemy's skirmishers appeared. Pennington's battery opened upon them, while the Sixth Michigan cavalry, under Major Kidd, was thrown forward and deployed as skirmishers. One gun of Pennington's battery, supported by the First Vermont cavalry, was placed on my extreme left. The First Michigan cavalry, under Major Brewer, acted as a reserve, and as a support for the remaining five guns of the battery. The Fifth Michigan cavalry, under Colonel Mann, were engaged in the woods on my right. At first I was under the impression that the skirmishers were composed of dismounted cavalry, but later developments convinced me that it was a very superior force of infantry that now confronted me. After completing his dispositions for an attack, the enemy advanced upon me. In doing so, he exposed a line of infantry of more than a mile in extent; at the same time he opened a heavy fire upon me from his artillery. Pennington's battery, aided by the Sixth Michigan cavalry, poured a destructive fire upon the enemy as he advanced, but failed to force him back. A desperate effort was made to capture my battery. Pennington continued to fire until the enemy was within twenty yards of his guns. He was then compelled to limber up and retire to the north bank of Broad Run. The First Michigan cavalry was intrusted with the duty of covering the movement—a task which was gallantly performed. My command being very much exhausted, I returned to the vicinity of Gainsville, where I encamped for the night. Major Clarke, Fifth Michigan cavalry, was detached from his regiment with one battalion. When the command retired to the north bank of Broad Run, he with a small portion of his battalion, became separated from the rest of the command, and was captured by the enemy

Computing my losses from the 9th October, I find them to be as follows :

							Officers.	Men.	Total.
Killed	.	.	.	.	.	.	0	9	9
Wounded	.	.	.	.	.	.	2	41	43
Missing	.	.	.	.	.	.	8	154	162
Aggregate	.	.	.	.	.	.			214

Before closing my report, I desire to make honorable mention of the highly creditable manner in which both officers and men of my command have discharged their duty during the long and arduous marches, as well as the hard-fought engagements of the past few days. Too much praise cannot be given to the officers and men of Battery M. Second Artillery, for the gallantry displayed on more than one occasion. For the untiring zeal and energy, added to the unflinching bravery displayed in transmitting and executing my orders upon the field, my acknowledgments are due to the following members of my staff: Captain R. F. Judson, A. D. C., Lieutenant R. Baylis, A. A. D. C., Lieutenant William Colerick, A. D. C., and to Lieutenant E. G. Granger, A. A. A. G. Lieutenant Granger, while leading a charge at Brandy Station, had his horse shot in two places. Surgeon Wooster of my staff, in addition to his professional duties, rendered me valuable assistance by aiding in transmitting my orders.

G. A. CUSTER,

Brig. Com. Second Brigade, Third Cavalry Corps.

It will be noticed in both of Custer's reports, during this summer and fall, how much stress he lays upon the doings of Pennington's battery. The commander of this force seems always to have been a fast friend and favorite of Custer, and he was subsequently promoted to the command of a volunteer cavalry regiment, and became senior officer and commandant of a brigade in Custer's division, in which capacity he served all through the Valley campaigns, and up to Appomattox surrender.

After the fight at Buckland's Mills, in which the division of Kilpatrick was so roughly handled, Meade's army resumed its advance, and finally took up winter quarters at Brandy Station, the cavalry picketing the front and flanks out toward Madison Court House.

It is time, now that the summer and fall campaigns of 1863 are concluded, to advert to the private life of the young general during this interval. During the first period of his career as a commander, his occupations and cares seem to have been too engrossing to permit of any home correspondence, and after the Michigan brigade entered Virginia he did not relax his work. Well as the brigade behaved at Gettysburg, it was far from satisfying Custer, who was determined to make it fully the equal of a regular cavalry command in drill and discipline. With that object, no sooner did the cavalry get a week's rest, than the indefatigable young general began to give them daily drills of great severity, and by constant inspections so harassed the souls of the honest volunteers that they began to hate him as badly as ever, or thought they did. Just as at Gettysburg, however, the first battle compelled them to forego all their bad language, and made them sorry they had ever uttered a word against him. This first battle was the advance on Culpepper, and in the action, it will be remembered, Custer was wounded.

A piece of shell killed his horse, and inflicted a painful wound on the inside of the rider's thigh, which, though not dangerous, compelled Custer to retire from the field. Inasmuch as the rest of the month was passed in perfect quiet, the general experienced no difficulty in obtaining, on the strength of this wound, a leave of absence for twenty days. He took it, hastened to Washington, and one day later was travelling due northwest, just as fast as the iron horse could carry him. To those who remember the state of mind in which he left home in the spring, it will not be surprising to learn that he made his way to Monroe, Michigan, with the utmost rapidity, nor that when there, he happened to meet " one of the parties most interested." He had, during the summer, many things to make him anxious and unhappy in regard to matters at Monroe, especially intimations that reached him that " one of the parties interested" was quite likely to meet some one else, while his own affair was still unsettled. He realized very keenly that the objections of the Judge to his engagement were not based altogether on his want of fortune, but on an apprehension of the fickleness and instability of his disposition, and that his sudden success in life had not altogether removed this. Only a week before the time of his wound, he received a letter from his kind-hearted confidant, warning him that his persistence was " not for the best," and that a time must at last come when he " must give her up utterly and forever." To this he replies, sadly but bravely :

That time may come, perhaps soon. When it does come, I hope it will find me the same soldier I now try to be, as capable of meeting the reverses of life as I am those of war. You no doubt know me well, perhaps better than any person in Monroe, except L., and yet you know little of my disposition. You, fearing that disappointment might render me unhappy, are doubtful as to whether it is best for me to cherish the remembrance of one who is now to me, all that she ever will be. I would think the same, were I the adviser instead of the person advised. Do not fear for me. . . What you have hinted as being probable in reference to L. *may* occur. My bosom friends may desert me : my own mother may disown me and turn me from my home ; I may lose my position among men, and be thrown solitary and alone among strangers, without the sympathy of a single friend ; and yet, with all this, there is a strange, indescribable *something* in me, that would enable me to shape my course through life, cheerful, if not contented. . . . Rest assured, that whatever fortune may have in store for me will be borne cheerfully. Now that you know this, you need not hesitate in future to tell me *all.* . . .

These are good brave words, but they are not quite brave enough to hide the sad heart beneath them, and when we remember the position of Custer at the time, we can see how strong must have been his feelings to force such a letter from the outwardly brilliant and successful general. No doubt he hailed with gratitude the piece of ragged iron that gave him the excuse, a week later, to return to Monroe, and see for himself how affairs stood.

He arrived there to find himself a lion. Captain Custer, the idle and discontented officer on waiting orders, sharing the sombre cloud which enshrouded his unfortunate chief, with the reputation of a reckless dissipated soldier in love with every fresh face, a desperate flirt, was a very different person from the " boy general with the golden locks," the pet of the papers, brilliant, successful, a rising man, a real live brigadier-general. On his previous visit, Monroe had begun to think that there might possibly " be something in that young Custer." Now, Monroe had " always prophecied that young Custer would do something," and the only trouble was, who should be the first to welcome him, ask him to his house, be able to say to his friends, " Ah, by the by, I had General Custer to dinner to-day."

Mrs. Grundy was ready and anxious to go down on her knees to arrange a soft pillow, " under his poor wounded limb, you know, my dear," and Miss Grundy was amiably anxious to sing the pathetic ballad of " When this cruel war is over" to the listening general, ogling him all the time, and ending with a languishing gaze of perfect love at the line, " Praying we may meet again," as she slowly left the piano. To a man with any sense of humor, and Custer had his share of this quality, what a spectacle Mrs. Grundy and the charming Miss Grundy presented, especially when he remembered their neglect in former days. However, he kept his counsel, and wore his honors meekly.

There was, however, one man on whom the brilliant success

of the young general had not yet operated as a complete blind. This man was Judge Bacon, stern, upright, and honorable, who had not yet got beyond the point of thinking that there might be "something in that young Custer, after all." The Judge knew a good deal more of the world than most Monrovians, and he had heard of the celebrated stone thrown by Orpheus C. Kerr, which struck so many brigadier-generals. He knew moreover, that the commission was subject to confirmation by the senate, which might be refused, a piece of knowledge not common to all Monroe. In a worldly point of view, therefore, the Judge was quite right in being cautious as to receiving the brilliant young warrior as a conqueror. In a moral point of view, a matter which weighed far more with Judge Bacon, his objections to Custer remained unaltered, and were even strengthened. He was forever mentally referring to his intemperance, and especially distrusted his fickleness. The latter was Custer's own fault. In order to calm the Judge's uneasiness, the previous spring, Custer had entered into a violent flirtation with a young lady of the place, and the result had been to disgust the Judge. However objectionable as a suitor for your daughter a man may be, still you do not like to see him, as soon as rejected, off with the daughter of some one else, as if nothing had happened. The rapid consolation is decidedly uncomplimentary to your own family, which is of course always the best in the country.

With all these objections, in a private capacity, to Custer, even coming back as a general, the Judge yet welcomed him cordially as a public character, and permitted him to resume his visits at the house, ostensibly in the guise of ordinary friendship. He was apparently completely deceived as to the strength and duration of Custer's affection for his daughter, and imagined that the affair was safely over. On the contrary, it was only just really beginning, and Custer was already laying his plans to gain the consent of the father of his lady love, as his leave progressed. Whether absence might in time have caused him to be forgotten is uncertain, but certain it is that his second visit was just in time to settle the affair in his favor, and to secure a perfect understanding, conditional on the Judge's consent, it is true, but none the less an implied engagement. This was towards the close of Custer's visit, and he made up his mind to ask the Judge before he went.

In this instance, however, resolution and action were not the same with Custer. Days passed on, opportunities were rare, and possibly courage was lacking. At all events, the time came for his departure, the lovers were compelled to leave each other and still the Judge *had not been asked.* Brave as Custer was, he actually seems to have trembled before the Judge, and it is no wonder when we reflect on what he was about to request from him—an only daughter.

He was finally compelled to leave Monroe, and return to the front, with the question unasked, the matter to be finally decided by letter. The sensitive conscientiousness and strict honor of the two lovers is shown in the fact that they both still declined to avail themselves of a clandestine correspondence to evade the Judge's notice.

Nothing would have been easier than for this to have happened, and the fact of its still being steadfastly refused by both is an honor to both. They cannot be blamed for their love, that being a matter beyond the control of any human being. It comes and goes like the wind, and it is hard to assign a cause for it. That Custer, young, brilliant, successful in everything else, knowing himself secure in the most vital point of all—the feelings of the " party most interested "—should have been willing to wait as he did, patiently and uncomplainingly, for the consent of one whom he knew to be prejudiced against him, shows a devotion to duty remarkable in these days, and especially in this country, where filial obedience is subject to so many drawbacks. The sequel proved that he did wisely, and duty met its reward.

To console himself for his self-enforced abstinence from

14

correspondence with " the party most interested," Custer threw himself with fresh ardor into letters to his kind and sympathizing confidant. From this time forth, these letters are frequent; beginning even while on his journey to the east. The first is dated on board the lake steamer "Morning Star," October 6th, 1863, the very day of his departure. In its course he refers, as he frequently did in those days, to the motto which he had adopted and wore engraved on his seal ring, " *Per augusta ad augusta.*"

ON BOARD THE " MORNING STAR,"
9 P. M. Monday, Oct. 6, 1863.

KIND FRIEND :—I feel so sad and lonely, so sick at heart, that to kill time and "drive dull care away," I have determined to occupy a few moments in writing to you. We are just getting under full headway, and will soon be bounding o'er the billows of Erie. I have been sitting on deck watching the motion of the vessel as it speeds through the crested waves, and while intently watching wave after wave, as they roll along in their ceaseless motion, I cannot but be reminded of the great ocean of life on whose stormy bosom each of us is engaged, steering our little barks over, each acting under a separate impulse, yet all tending to the same harbor. When I look back on the track passed over by mine, I cannot but feel unbounded gratitude to that power which thus far has carried me safely through so many storms. Hour after hour have I seen wave after wave rolling down on my little bark, threatening to swallow it with all it contained, and yet that unseen power would interfere, and either avert the coming danger, or cause it to strike harmlessly. If I look around me now, I see evidences of danger in all directions, but buoyed up with hope and guided by duty, I trust for the best, confident that my motto " Through trials to triumphs " will still hold good. How I wish I could be with my little girl to-night, and yet I cannot complain. I saw the Judge at the depot, who spoke very encouragingly of my prospects in my profession and of the bright future he pictured for me ; said he would be disappointed if he did not hear such and such things of me soon. I had no opportunity to speak of that which was nearest my heart. I only said just before leaving that I had desired to speak to him, but being prevented from doing so, I would write to him, to which he replied, " Very well." Good bye,

ARMSTRONG."

Only twenty-four hours later, and he writes from Baltimore as follows :

COLEMAN'S EUTAW HOUSE, BALTIMORE,
Wed., Oct. 7th, 1863, 2.30 P. M.

DEAR FRIEND :—Do not be alarmed. I am not going to write to you again to-day. I have taken a stroll and a drive around the Monumental City, and it is yet an hour till car time. I know of no more pleasant mode of occupying that time, than by writing to you. In every city I pass through, I see something to admire, something which gives rise to pleasant thoughts, and often I am struck with wonder at the extent to which man's art and ingenuity have improved what nature has already rendered beautiful. But after all, my heart turns longingly to one quiet little town far away on the banks of the Raisin, and I find infinitely more enjoyment, more real pleasure from the memories and associations of that unassuming little spot, than in contemplating all the world beside. I need not tell you why this is so. I do not think a single half hour has passed since I bade adieu to Monroe, during which I did not think of the place, or more particularly perhaps, of those whom it contains. I have also thought much of my intended letter to L.'s father. My mind has been alternating between hope and fear, hope that my letter will be well received ; that now, when all else appears bright and encouraging, no obstacle will be interposed to darken or cloud our happiness. And yet I cannot rid myself of the fear that I may suffer from some unfounded prejudice. Oh, I wish some guardian angel would tell me what course to pursue, to insure her happiness and mine. I feel that her father, valuing her happiness and welfare as he does, will not refuse if he learns from her lips, our real relation to each other. I regret that I was unable to have a personal interview with him, and yet it may be better as it is ; I will hope. I will write you to-morrow, or next day from camp. Tell my little girl I am so lonely without her. Kiss her for me, and tell her I have been real good since I left her. Good bye,

ARMSTRONG.

We have inserted these letters to show the state of anxiety and uneasiness that still oppressed Custer when he returned to his command, where he was received with the most rapturous demonstrations of delight.

HEADQUARTERS SECOND BRIGADE, THIRD DIV.,
Oct. 9th, 1863, 8 P. M.

DEAR FRIEND :—I promised to write you soon after my return to " camp." I arrived here last evening about dusk, and was welcomed in a style that was both flattering and gratifying. I wish you could have seen how rejoiced my men seemed to be at my return. Whatever may be the real sentiments entertained by the world at large, I feel assured that here, surrounded by my noble little band of heroes, I am loved and respected. There is such a feeling of mutual trust and confidence existing between us, as renders our intercourse one of pleasure. Often, in my meditations, I think of the vast responsibility resting upon me; of the many, many lives entrusted to my keeping ; and consequently, of the happiness of so many households depending upon my discretion and judgment. And to think that I am just leaving my boyhood, makes the responsibility appear greater. And yet I have no fears, nor do I think that this latter fact is due to any self-conceit or egotism on my part. I try to make no unjust pretensions. I assume nothing that I know not to be true. It requires no extensive knowledge to inform me what is my duty both to my country and to my command. Knowing my duty, all that is then requisite to insure success, is honesty of purpose, and fixed intentions, or, to express the same meaning in different language, I have only to adopt the well-known motto, " First, be sure you're right, then go ahead." To this simple rule, framed though it be in humble language, I can attribute, more than to any other, my success in life. When deciding upon any course to pursue, I have asked myself, is it right ? Satisfied that it is, I allow nothing to swerve me from my purpose. Few persons have disregarded public opinion so much as I. Not but that I think a proper regard should be shown for that which the " world might say," but one who adopts public opinion as his guide, cannot entertain one purpose long. He will find that what pleases one, displeases another.

Why have I written all this ? Surely I do not know. You did not say it was not so.

I have been very busily engaged all day. I found time, or

rather stole time to write. I would have written *that* letter to *her* father to-day, but that I knew I should be interrupted, which I do not wish to be, when writing so important a document. I can scarcely realize its importance. How much depends upon the result it obtains. All my future *destiny* hangs on the answer my letter shall bring. I will not despond, nor will I take trouble before it is upon me, but I cannot but be anxious. I shall probably defer the writing of that letter until I have heard at least once from you and of her. I had hoped to be left free and undisturbed this evening, and thus permitted to write you a long letter. But several applicants are waiting my pleasure, and I must defer my anticipated pleasure. Do write me soon. Tell me all about my little girl. Is she well, etc., etc. Kiss her for me, and tell her I had a dream last night concerning somebody in Monroe, who I think very much of, " But I'll not tell you who."

Ever your friend,
ARMSTRONG.

Please give these flowers to L. They were plucked in front of my headquarters, not far from the " Rapidan."

Luckily for Custer's peace of mind he was soon at work, for within forty-eight hours of his return he started on the expedition which ended in the Brandy Station fight, of which he gives, in a letter of October 12th, a short account, much the same as in his report. Three days later he writes a hasty pencil scrawl from the Bull Run battle-field.

I dreamed of my little girl last night, and was so disappointed to wake and find it but a dream. How often I think of her. Last Sunday, while in front of my men, and just as we were about to charge the enemy, I unclasped my locket, and took what I thought might be my last look at her likeness. Even in the thickest of the fight I can always find time to think of her.

Five days later he writes, evidently under great mental depression, just after the disaster at Buckland's Mills, an interesting letter, which shows that his was not the rashness which brought on that defeat. In its course, after telling of his first victory over Stuart, he tells of Kilpatrick coming up and congratulating him on his success, and adds :

All would have been well had General K. been content to let well enough alone. My scouts had informed me of heavy columns of infantry moving around on both my flanks, their intention evidently being to cut me off. I informed General K. of this, and advised him to guard against it ; but no—he did not believe it, and ordered me to halt till the First Brigade passed me and then to follow on the road to Warrenton. The First Brigade had scarcely passed, and I was preparing to follow, when the enemy made a vigorous attack from the direction I had prophecied they would . . . My consolation is that I am in no way responsible for the mishap, but on the contrary urged General K. not to take the step which brought it upon us, and the only success gained by us was gained by me.

He refers at the close of this letter to the one which he had written to Judge Bacon soon after Brandy Station fight, in which he formally asks the Judge for his child. That letter is a model in its way of quiet dignity and self respect, mingled with a modesty peculiarly touching from a man in Custer's position. Were it not for those private details which are too sacred for publication, it would be the pride of Custer's biographer to lay it before the world, exhibiting as it does in the truest and most unconscious manner the real nobility of the writer's character. In making his request he refers, fully and frankly, to the objections to himself existing in the Judge's mind, especially those of dissipation and fickleness. In regard to the first he tells him how two years before he had made a solemn pledge to his sister Mrs. Reed, in the presence of Almighty God, never to taste another drop of intoxicating liquor, which promise he had strictly kept ever since. With regard to the second, he referred the Judge to his own daughter for an explanation of the apparent fickleness of his conduct. Of his success in life and his ability to maintain a wife he speaks briefly, with modest pride, and adverts to the fact that he had not ventured to correspond with the object of his love till he should obtain her father's consent.

The Judge's reply is exactly in character with the whole of this stately and Quixotically honorable correspondence. He speaks of his intense love for his only child, left motherless so early, of his anxious fears for her future, and the care he must exercise over the character of the man to whom he can entrust her happiness. He owns that "it may be weeks, perhaps months, before he can make up his mind to give a decided answer," but expresses his intention of conversing with his daughter on the subject, the result of which interview "she is at full liberty to communicate to you." It appeared, moreover, from the letter, that the Judge and his daughter had already had a full confidence with each other on the same evening on which poor Custer, gloomy and dispirited, had left Monroe. It was clear that the Judge had virtually yielded, though the fond idolizing father still hesitated to perform that irrevocable act of consent which would forever separate him from the child who had so long been the very core of his heart. Most young men think little of this feeling, but to Custer it seems to have been peculiarly sacred. There is something touching in the correspondence between these two noble, high-minded men, both sensitive to a fault, both idolizing this one delicate girl in their different ways, both anxious only for her happiness, both respecting each other as highly as men could, and yet jealous and stiff at first. So punctilious was Custer, that he refused in a second letter to take the implied permission to correspond contained in the expression "which she is at liberty to communicate to you," without a clear understanding and an explicit answer, one way or the other.

Pressed in this manner, and having learned from his daughter how much her happiness was really interested in Custer, the father yielded at last, and consented to the engagement, the consent reaching Custer late in November. During this interval the punctuality and frequency of his correspondence with his kind-hearted confidant are alike exemplary, but that correspondence comes to an abrupt close December 4th, with the satisfactory information, "Your kind favor of the 26th was received last evening *along with two from my little girl*."

We cannot suppose that any one would desire this love-making by proxy to continue any longer. We have brought our hero through his love troubles, as interesting as those of a novel hero, in safety. Henceforth, he was formally engaged. The close of this last letter, is however very symptomatic of the curious fact well known to ladies of all time that there is "no satisfying these men." A little while ago, his only aspiration was for an open engagement and permission to correspond ; now that he has obtained both, his petition is changed to something else.

I am glad you incline to my way of thinking, in regard to my little girl *coming to the army this winter*. Why shouldn't she ? I have been pleading earnestly with her in my last letters to tell me when I can come for her. I can come whenever she bids me do so. Now don't you think she ought to tell me to come *soon ?* You know if I don't come this winter, it is not probable that I shall be granted a leave before next winter. Cannot you *threaten* her, or use your influence to induce her to do as she *ought*. If I was there, how I would talk to her ! She would be glad to say yes to get rid of me. . . . .

His petition was nearer to being granted than seemed possible a few months before. While the army lay quiet that winter, Custer's commission was confirmed in the senate, and he obtained leave of absence to go to Monroe, where he was formally married, February 9th, 1864, in the Presbyterian church, by the Reverend Mr. Boyd, pastor and schoolmaster, to Elizabeth, only daughter of Judge Daniel S. Bacon.

What a wedding that was. Mrs. Grundy talks of it to this day ; and all Monroe that could get inside the church crammed the pews and filled the aisles to suffocation. The Monroe papers were full of the wedding of " our distinguished townsman," and details of personal appearance of bride and bridegroom were plentiful.

Custer was attended by his staff, and wore, perhaps for the first time, his full uniform as a brigadier-general, sash and all. His hair had been cut, and he was no more the "boy general with the golden locks" of the reporters. How often he and his friends had laughed over that name, when they read it!

The bride, with veil and orange blossoms, a white figure of timid purity, won all hearts as she came into church on her father's arm; the Judge, tall, stalwart, with his grand old Webster head towering above the crowd, proud of his daughter, and now also of his son-in-law, yet had a hard struggle to choke down the desolate feeling which comes over a father giving up his only child forever.

It was a beautiful, a romantic wedding, such as seldom occurs in these humdrum days, and only one such could then occur, for there was only one Custer, only one knight of romance, brave and loving, famous and tender. No wonder Monroe was proud of him.

But what was the pride of Monroe to that of the brigade, a few days later, when Custer returned to camp, bringing with him his timid, child-like bride, with her innocent dark eyes, delighted and astonished at the novelty of everything. Ah, Custer was a wise man, and a patient one, to wait for his reward as he did, but it was worth all his trials at last, and proved the entrance, for him, to a life of perfect happiness thereafter. The gentle, timid girl, so scrupulously obedient to her father, proved to Custer a jewel above all price, when she became his wife. With a fidelity and devotion rarely paralleled, she followed him to the front and remained near there just so long as it was possible, in all his subsequent career. Only when the troops were in actual and fierce campaign, and her presence might have proved an embarrassment to her husband, did she consent to remain behind, and then she was always ready to hasten to the front as soon as there was the first sign of a long halt.

Her influence over the state of society at the headquarters of the Michigan Brigade, and subsequently in all the different commands to which Custer was assigned, was traceable in every instance, in a refinement of tone, an absence of the usual roistering drinking scenes too common in the army, in a standard of morality such as prevailed nowhere else. Before Mrs. Custer's arrival at the headquarters of Custer's brigade, the presence of respectable women was almost unknown in the army. While Hooker lay at Falmouth, after Chancellorsville, Miss Harris, sister of Senator Harris, of New York, with a few other noble disinterested women, had come out to take charge of the hospitals, within range of the enemy's shells, but these were the only exceptions, so far as I am aware.

When Mrs. Custer made her appearance, it was the prevalent belief that camp was no place for ladies, and many were the comments her visit created. It was only after observing the effect of her presence, that the sneerers were compelled to admit that it was altogether pure and elevating, and to wish that a similar blessed influence might extend over their own camps.

Like a good angel she came to the brigade at Stevensburg, like a good angel she remained with them till spring. All that Custer's already noble character needed of dignity and repose, of sweetness and patience, she gave him. Finding him good, she left him perfect, and her sweet and gracious influence can be traced on all his after life.

CHAPTER IV.

THE WILDERNESS AND THE VALLEY.

THE spring of 1864 witnessed a great change in the Army of the Potomac, and especially in the Cavalry Corps. Hitherto, there had been a marked difference in success between the conduct of the war in the eastern and western departments. In the latter, beginning with the capture of Fort Donelson, and the substantial repulse of the Confederates at Shiloh, the campaigns of the Union forces had resulted in carrying the war from the banks of the Ohio, where the Confederates once threatened Louisville, down to the borders of Georgia at Chattanooga, a substantial advance of over two hundred miles. The general success of the western generals had only been marred by the desperate and bloody battles of Shiloh, Murfreesboro' and Chickamauga. In all these three battles, the Confederate generals, starting with decided strategic successes, and beginning by driving the Union forces, had ended by retreating and losing the fruits of victory. In the case of Chickamauga alone, had Bragg held his own; and a few weeks later he was driven from his vantage ground in confusion by Grant.

Contrasted with this, the achievements of the Army of the Potomac were empty and barren of results. Beginning with the disastrous defeat of Bull Run, the eastern men gave their foes the advantage of *morale* at the start, and the flank movement of evasion made by McClellan, which terminated in the Peninsular campaign, had only provoked further disaster. Lee had entered Maryland, and three times threatened the capital of the nation, in as many years. Now, the experience of Meade's timidity, displayed in his October retreat and the equally unnecessary failure at Mine Run in November, showed plainly that he was not the man to whom an aggressive campaign could be committed. Excellent for defence, his aggressive ability was confessedly unequal to the task of driving Lee.

Under these circumstances, General Grant was called from the west, made Lieutenant General, placed in chief command of all the armies, and came himself to Virginia, to direct operations personally. He did not assume the direct command of the Army of the Potomac. The memory of Gettysburg saved Meade from the humiliation of removal, and his cheerful, uncomplaining obedience to orders on all occasions, so different from the independent ways and constant complaints of McClellan and Hooker, pointed him out as just the man to execute Grant's orders, whatever they were.

At the same time that Grant came to the field, General Pleasonton was removed from the command of the cavalry corps, which was given to a western man, of whom none in the Army of the Potomac had ever heard, an infantry division commander, named Philip Henry Sheridan. Grant, however, knew him as one of the very hardest fighters in the west, and his choice of men was never more abundantly justified. Other changes took place in the cavalry corps, no less radical. John Buford, the most capable of the division leaders, was dead, Kilpatrick was sent out west to join Sherman, and a young brigadier named Wilson was taken from staff duty and put in his place. Gregg was the only one left of the old set. Buford was replaced by Brigadier-General A. T. A. Torbert, who had for some time commanded the Jersey brigade of infantry, once trained by Phil Kearny.

To Custer the change was great. He was transferred with his " Michiganders," to the First division, and found himself under an infantry general, side by side with Devin, an old, steady-going man, not given to dash, in a place where his enthusiasm must necessarily be cooled to conform to the slower movements of his comrades. That spring, which witnessed a change in his surroundings, witnessed also a change in his personal appearance. He cut his long locks away, and began to grow side whiskers. The change was decidedly a disfigurement, and before the end of the summer he repented of it, for he allowed his hair to grow again, and became the old Custer once more, by October.

On the 3d May, 1864, the anniversary of the disaster of Chancellorsville, the Army of the Potomac was once more over the Rapidan, a part of it on the very same ground which had witnessed that defeat. The main body of the army, however, was higher up toward Orange Court House, and the fighting took place away from all houses in the midst of scrub woods, whence no view of the battle could be obtained. It was a haphazard sort of a fight, the heads of columns on the road feeling for each other; and it terminated only in a drawn battle; while Grant moved across Lee's front in the night, to get between him and Richmond. In the Wilderness fight the cavalry was on the left. Wilson, with the Third Division, had the lead, Gregg was next, Torbert third. Wilson ran into the enemy at Tod's Tavern and was driven back by Fitzhugh Lee, in some confusion. All the fighting was dismounted, the woods being so thick that any other method was impossible. The first serious fighting of Torbert's division was still further to the left, at Spottsylvania Court House. It took place after the main battle of the Wilderness was over, and was the first indication to Lee that his enemy was working round on that flank. It was sulky, stubborn bull dog fighting, entirely opposed to the brilliant methods by which Custer had gained his reputation, dismounted lines of skirmishers pressing grimly forward through tangled woods, firing at each other like lines of infantry, holding on to hasty breastworks of rails and fallen trees, and making but little progress.

One thing however was noticeable in all the battles. The Confederate cavalry were not fighting with the obstinacy and vigor which characterized them in 1863. They were in as strong force to all appearance, and would fight well in the morning, but the evening invariably showed a relaxation, very different from their old ways. This feature was clearly noticeable in the Wilderness, and after. The infantry fought as fiercely as ever but the cavalry was beginning to lose its backbone.

It is not our intention to dwell long on this period of Custer's career as a brigade commander. It was marked by less individuality than during the previous summer, and for a simple reason. Torbert was a slow and steady chief, who always kept his division close together, and never got it into scrapes; consequently Custer was generally alongside of some one else, and sharing the ordinary incidents of every fight, uninteresting save to professional readers. His only rival for dash was General Merritt, who had left West Point a year before Custer, and therefore ranked him. Merritt commanded the Regular Brigade of the same division, and was always trying to be side by side with Custer. Something, however, he lacked. It is hard to say what it was, except beauty of person and that chivalrous romantic spirit which pervaded Custer's every look and action. Certain it is, that Custer was idolized by his men, and could give by his personal presence weight to a charge of which Merritt could not boast, although, as a general, he was held in higher esteem by many, as not being thought so rash and reckless. There is little doubt that in this respect Custer had lost as much in reputation by his long association with Kilpatrick as he had gained in popular favor by being so frequently mentioned in the papers, however unjust the verdict of rashness.

The savage and determined fighting of the cavalry on the left of Grant's army lasted till the 7th of May, when the horsemen were relieved at Spottsylvania, and withdrawn to prepare for Sheridan's first raid. In his final report the general tells us his reasons for this step, and very good ones they were. Up to that time, save in the short Gettysburg campaign, the cavalry of the Army of the Potomac had been hampered by being always attached to the infantry, taking care of the latter, and engaged in indecisive actions, in which the infantry never supported it. Sheridan's idea was that it should operate as an independent body, raid around the enemy's rear, and fight his cavalry only, till that should be destroyed, living off the country meantime. Grant consented to allow him to try the experiment, and it succeeded so well that it was constantly repeated thereafter. The former raids of the cavalry, under Stoneman, had been made in detached bodies, liable to be crushed by superior force. Sheridan determined to act with his whole mass in unison, knowing it to be stronger than any cavalry force Stuart could bring against it.

On the 9th of May, 1864, accordingly, the whole cavalry corps, nearly twelve thousand strong, started out on its road to Richmond, and was soon well on its way, Custer's brigade in the extreme advance. Before the evening, Custer reached the North Anna River, at Beaver Dam Station, where the Richmond and Gordonsville railroad crosses the river. He at once charged right into the station, which was directly in the rear of Lee's centre, captured three long trains and two engines, and released four hundred Union prisoners, going to Richmond. The cars were full of rations for Lee's army, and were burned, and the railroad was destroyed for miles.

To reach this point, the cavalry column had made a march of over thirty miles, and had completely got the start of Stuart. During the afternoon the Confederate chief followed up the rear of the column, which was nearly ten miles long, and attacked it fiercely, but was easily beaten off. All that night Stuart marched on, to get ahead of the Union cavalry, with Fitzhugh Lee's and Wade Hampton's divisions of horse. The next day, Sheridan started again, and marched more leisurely to Ashland, about fifteen miles farther. He was quite safe from

Lee's infantry, for Grant had all that fully employed at Spott-sylvania, and he did not care much for the assaults of the cavalry. Ashland depot was burned, with more cars, and more track was torn up here.

On the 11th of May, the whole cavalry corps was within four miles of Richmond, on the Brooks pike, Custer once more in the advance. It was in this campaign that Sheridan or Torbert commenced the practice of giving Custer the advance whenever anything serious was to be done, and this day Custer fully justified it. Stuart had by this time got in front of Sheridan, and gallantly endeavored to stay his course.

Custer in his report says :—The Second and Reserve Brigades were first engaged, afterwards my brigade was thrown in on the left of the Reserve Brigade, connecting on my left with the right of the Third division. The enemy was strongly posted on a bluff in rear of a thin skirt of woods, his battery being concealed from our view by the woods. The edge of the woods nearest my front was held by the enemy's dismounted men, who poured a heavy fire into my line. The Fifth and Sixth Michigan were ordered to dismount and drive the enemy from the position, which they did in the most gallant manner. On reaching the woods I ordered Colonel Alger to establish the Fifth and Sixth upon a line near the skirt of the woods, and hold his position till further orders. From a personal examination of the grounds, I discovered that a successful charge might be made upon the battery of the enemy by keeping well to the right. With this intention I formed the First Michigan in column of squadrons under cover of the woods. At the same time I directed Colonel Alger and Major Kidd to move the Fifth and Sixth Michigan forward to occupy the attention of the enemy on the left, Heaton's battery to engage them in front, while the First charged the battery in the flank. As soon as the First Michigan moved from the cover of the woods, the enemy divined our intention and opened a brisk fire from his artillery. Before the battery could be reached there were five fences to be opened and a bridge to cross over which it was impossible to pass more than three at one time. Yet notwithstanding these obstacles the First Michigan advanced boldly to the charge, and when within two hundred yards of the battery charged it with a yell which spread terror before them. Two pieces of cannon, two limbers filled with ammunition, and a number of prisoners, were the fruits of this charge.

While this was going on in the First, Alger was at work with his Fifth Michigan, had driven the enemy through the woods into the open, and the order was given to cease firing, the enemy being worsted. Just at that instant a Confederate officer, who afterwards proved to be General J. E. B. Stuart, rode up with his staff to within four hundred yards of the line, when a man of the Fifth fired at him. John A Huff of Co A. remarked : " Tom, you shot too low and to the left," and turning to Colonel Alger, who was near, said,

" Colonel, I can fetch that man."

" Try him," said Alger.

Huff took a steady aim over a fence and fired—the officer fell. Huff turned to the colonel and coolly said : " There's a spread eagle for you."

Huff had previously been in Berdan's Sharpshooters, and was an excellent shot : he was killed a month later, at Cold Harbor.

After Stuart's fall the enemy rallied desperately for awhile, but finally gave way in a complete rout, before a general charge led by Custer, in which the First, Fifth, Sixth, and Seventh Michigan and the First Vermont all joined together.

Thus, once more, Custer had taken the brunt of the fighting for his whole division, and driven the enemy from the field.

That evening Sheridan was in a dilemma. He had beaten the enemy's cavalry, and was in front of Richmond, but he could do no more without infantry and heavy guns. He had one chance of success, however. Butler, with twenty thousand men, was known to be on the James River, south bank, near

15

Richmond, and it was possible that he might advance, capture
the city, and join the cavalry. The hope was vain, however.
Butler was too far away. Nothing was heard of him, and every
available Confederate infantry soldier was hurrying out of
Richmond to attack Sheridan in front, while Fitzhugh Lee and
Wade Hampton were pressing on his rear. Sheridan had two
courses left open. One was to march back, crushing the cavalry in the way, and join Grant ; the other to strike off to the
east, down the Peninsula, to Whitehouse Landing, and rest his
command till Grant's advance reached the head of the Peninsula. He chose the latter course for two reasons. First, he
did not care to march back, with a certain fight, while he was
out of forage, when a stubborn enemy could delay him sufficiently long to starve his command : second, having gone so far
it would hurt the *morale* of the whole campaign to recede. He
marched down the old and now deserted Peninsula to Whitehouse landing, where gunboats and supplies awaited him, and
rested in peace after his first raid.

After a few days' repose, the cavalry corps marched up the
Peninsula, and found the Union army drawn up near Hanover
Court House. On the 28th May, Sheridan, with a division of
the Sixth Corps and the cavalry, started off on the next flank
movement of Grant, which ended at Cold Harbor. By successive flanking movements, Grant's army had come in a slanting
direction, all the way from Orange Court House, crossing successively the Rapidan, North Anna, South Anna, and Pamunkey,
and now found itself just where McClellan was two years before,
at Cold Harbor not twelve miles from the centre of Richmond.
The position of the two armies was however different from the
days of McClellan. The latter's lines had been drawn east and
west, his rear being open to Jackson's attack, coming from the
valley. Grant's lines were drawn north and south, across the
head of the Peninsula, with his base indifferently at either
Whitehouse on the Pamunkey, or Harrison's Landing on the
James.

In this position the battle of Cold Harbor was fought. It began by the cavalry moving to the left, driving off Fitzhugh Lee and holding the enemy's infantry in breastworks. It ended, as at Spottsylvania, in the infantry coming up, relieving the cavalry, and making a savage attack on Lee's army heavily fortified, along the whole line. The assault was repulsed with heavy loss, as all the others had been, but the Army of the Potomac retained the advantage, for the first time in its history, of having always attacked and never retreated.

The disadvantage to the Southern infantry of the defensive attitude was great. As long as they had things all their own way, as during 1862, no soldiers fought better, and their attacks were heroic. The disaster at Gettysburg, on the other hand, when they were obliged to defend themselves, developed the great weakness of the Confederate armies, a tendency to scatter, each man for himself, and to surrender in small squads. The Union troops, under similar disasters, displayed an opposite tendency, to huddle together and look blindly to the Government for help. The disintegrating tendency of reverses, during 1864, did more to strip the Southern army of strength than the material blows of Grant's troops. Only the very best soldiers, under the personal lead of Lee and Johnston, held together. When any one else took them, as in the cases of Early and Hood, they broke all to pieces at the first serious defeat.

The close of the battle of Cold Harbor was marked by Sheridan's second raid. His first had been round Lee's right, and succeeded perfectly. Now he proposed to try the same experiment round his left. The army lay in front of Cold Harbor, sulkily watching Lee, and it is possible that the latter thought a second McClellan was about to begin a second siege. If so, on the 7th June he was undeceived, for on that day Sheridan, with the First and Second Divisions, started round his left flank, and very soon was roaming over the country lately occupied by Lee's army. He was compelled, after the first day, to march very slowly. The country was almost en-

tirely bare of forage for his horses, and when the grain that his
men carried with them was exhausted, they were obliged to
subsist by grazing their animals, to a large extent. Four days
after starting, Sheridan reached Trevillian Station, about five
miles from Gordonsville. He found Fitzhugh Lee there, drove
him away, burned the station, and tore up the track. It was
his intention while there to have effected a junction with General Hunter, who was ordered to come down through the
Shenandoah Valley to meet him. Hunter never got so far, for he
met Breckinridge, and was driven back. Sheridan, hearing that
Breckinridge was close to him, with a heavy force of infantry,
judged that he could not afford to fight a battle. His supply
of ammunition was not sufficient for more than one contest, his
horses were in poor condition, and in the event of a defeat he
would be in a bad plight. He therefore fell back in the night,
marched to the Peninsula, and finally rejoined Grant's army,
which had crossed the James at Petersburg on the 25th June.

In all these operations, Custer had no opportunity for the
display of any of his peculiar talents for brilliant success save at
Beaver Dam, and in front of Richmond at Yellow Tavern. The
rest was all grim hard work, weary march or straight ahead
assaults on breastworks, with nothing but hard knocks and a
few feet of ground to gain.

During the whole of July, the cavalry and Custer had little
to do. The position at Petersburg, where the siege was now going on, rendered them useless. At the end of June, they tried, in
conjunction with the Second Corps, to turn Lee's right flank,
by getting between Petersburg and Richmond at Deep Bottom,
but the attempt was frustrated by fortifications.

During July, however, Lee took the initiative into his own
hands once more. He did not dare attack Grant, but he did
dare attack Washington, by way of the Valley. His lines at
Petersburg were so strong that he could afford to send away
considerable force to the Valley, without compromising the
safety of Richmond; he did so. On the 3d of July, Early

marched up the Valley to Martinsburg, and soon after entered
Maryland and Pennsylvania. The raid, though made at first
by a small force, had the effect Lee intended it should have.
It caused Grant to detach the Sixth Corps from Petersburg,
and finally two divisions of his cavalry (Torbert's and Wilson's)
to the succor of Washington. Early fought one battle, at
Monocacy, against Lew Wallace, who had hastily gathered together a lot of militia and hundred days' men. He whipped
Wallace, and advanced to Washington, but the battle had detained him so long that it gave time for the Sixth Corps to
arrive and man the defences. Nearly at the same time, the
Nineteenth Corps also began to arrive, by sea, from Louisiana,
where it had been serving; and Early retreated down the valley with his plunder.

The Sixth Corps was again ordered back to Petersburg, and
had reached Washington, when the news came that Early was
again advancing, this time in heavier force. Lee had found his
first experiment so successful that he hoped to better it. Early,
with twelve thousand men, had called away Wright's corps : it
was probable that another twelve thousand might call out still
more, and weaken Grant sufficiently to enable Lee to even
attack him. Lee reckoned without his host. Instead of another corps, Grant sent Sheridan, on the 2d of August, 1864,
and, what is more, went himself.

NOTE. In the fight at Trevillian Station, mentioned shortly before, Custer's Brigade was at one time in great peril. It had been sent off to the left,
and had cut off a Confederate brigade from its led horses. On the right, Torbert and Wilson had driven back the force opposed to them, and as it happened, straight on to Custer's rear. The Michigan Brigade found itself
surrounded, its guns in peril, and finally the enemy were so close on Custer's colors that his color-bearer was shot, and the general only saved the
colors by tearing them from the staff and stuffing them into his breast.
We extract from Custer's and Sheridan's official reports of the operations of
his brigade, the main incidents of this fight. His column moved on Trevillian Station by a different road from that of the rest of the division, followed
at a respectful distance by Wickham's brigade of Confederate cavalry.
Coming to the station, Fitzhugh Lee was found in front, and a wagon train

was in sight. Custer ordered in that inevitable Fifth Michigan ; with the equally inevitable Alger, and as usual Alger went in on the charge. He captured a large number of wagons, ambulances, and caissons, and some eight hundred men with 1500 led horses. These were the horses of the enemy engaging Merritt and Devin on the other road. Had Alger obeyed his orders, to halt at the station, all was well ; but he was so transported with ardor, that he charged nearly a mile down the road. The enemy in front of Merritt and Devin came driving back on Custer's right, in great confusion. Wickham made a desperate assault on his rear, and a third force coming up to the support of Merritt's foes, made its appearance on the left and front, between Custer and Alger. Then the fight became lively for a while. Custer naively observes in his report, that his lines were " very contracted " and " resembled very nearly a circle." He was only intent on holding on to his captures till Merritt and Devin came in, for he could hear their firing steadily advancing. All his plans were frustrated by a single coward. The quartermaster in charge of the trains and captures, demoralized by his unaccustomed position under fire, moved out his train without orders, and ran right into the enemy. Everything was retaken with much of Custer's property, and the enemy broke into his lines. It is very satisfactory to record that this quartermaster was cashiered for cowardice. It was at this juncture when everything was in confusion on both sides, that Sergeant Mitchell Belvir, First Michigan Cavalry, Custer's color-bearer, was killed, right in the advance of a charge. His death grip on the color-staff was so tenacious, and the danger at the moment so imminent, that Custer was compelled to wrench the flag from the staff to save it. A little later, Merritt and Devin came in, and the enemy was driven in confusion. Alger cut his way back, but with heavy loss.

CHAPTER V.

WINCHESTER.

ON the 4th of August, 1863, Major Philip H. Sheridan reported in Washington to Halleck, Chief of Staff, for instructions. He was informed that he was assigned to the Army of the Shenandoah, and would receive further instructions from General Grant, personally, at Monocacy Junction in Maryland. He went there and received them, brief, and to the point. He was to find the enemy, drive him up the Shenandoah Valley as soon as he could, and to destroy all forage and provisions in that valley, so as to prevent the enemy from going that way again. Grant noticed that all Lee's raids went up this rich valley, not over the bare and desolated field of Bull Run, and he was resolved to strip the one as bare as the other.

The Army of the Shenandoah then consisted of the Sixth Corps, much reduced in numbers, one division of the Nineteenth Corps, two small divisions under Crook, a small division of cavalry one thousand strong, under Averill, and Torbert's cavalry division. Averill was off after McCausland's cavalry, which had just burned Chambersburg, Pa., and Torbert's men had not yet all reached Washington. The losses of horses and men in the raids had reduced them in number so much that the total effective force of Sheridan when he started down the valley, within a week of his arrival, was only eighteen thousand infantry, and three thousand five hundred horse.[*]

Opposed to these was Early, with a total force in the neigh-

* Sheridan's Report.

borhood of twenty-five thousand infantry, and five thousand horse scattered throughout the country. It is very difficult and almost impossible to verify Early's numbers, for the reason that his own final report, written after the war, avers that he had less men in his whole army, than were returned as prisoners by Sheridan's provost-marshal at the close of the campaign. Of this we shall speak further on.

Torbert was at once appointed chief of cavalry for the Army of the Shenandoah, and Merritt was given the First Division, in which he was now senior brigadier. Sheridan gathered his forces so quickly, that on the 10th of August, he was beyond Strasburg, driving Gordon's division before him, the First Union cavalry division in advance. All through the valley campaign, after this, whenever Sheridan wanted work done, he called on the remnants of his old cavalry corps, already "old" to him, though he had taken them for the first time in May, and it was now only August.

While at Strasburg, however, he heard that a column of the enemy was moving over the old campaigning ground, towards Front Royal, on his left rear; and on the 13th, he dispatched Devin's brigade to Front Royal, to find out what was the matter. The same day he received a special message from Washington, by an officer who rode all the way. The message was from Grant, who was already back at Petersburg, and informed him that Lee had certainly sent two divisions, and at least twenty guns, to join Early. To meet these, another division of the Nineteenth Corps, and Wilson's division of his own old cavalry corps, were coming to join Sheridan. He determined to fall back to the end of the valley while waiting for these, and hold the line of Halltown, in front of Harper's Ferry, which he did at once. The expected column of the enemy *did* come down on him at Front Royal, with Kershaw's infantry division, and Fitzhugh Lee's cavalry division, but Merritt, who was there by this time with his single cavalry division, beat the enemy back, Devin's brigade taking the honors, two flags, and some hundred prisoners. In this fight Devin won his star at last.

From the date of Front Royal to the middle of September, the movements of the two armies around Halltown were very confusing. Sheridan, by careful inquiry and reconnoissances, ascertained at last exactly what troops had joined Early. They were only Kershaw's and Fitzhugh Lee's divisions, the first foot, the second horse. This made his force superior to Sheridan's by a few thousands, but when the latter was joined by his own reinforcements, they were about equal.

The question now was, what to do. Sheridan was obliged to be very cautious. There was nothing behind him if he got beaten, and Early was a hard fighter. He was placed there to keep Early from going into Maryland, and he did his duty well, but with a caution in great contrast to his previous and subsequent career. He kept on his shifty tactics so long, marching and countermarching, reconnoitring and falling back, that Grant began to fear he had mistaken his man. It seemed as if "Sheridan the Bold" was paralyzed by the responsibility, and growing into a nervous engineer, afraid to move. So strong was this impression, that Grant actually left Petersburg, came to Washington, and travelled all the way to Harper's Ferry, to find what was the matter. He arrived on the 18th September, and found things so well settled, that, as he says, he never again interfered with Sheridan. The cavalry chief knew his business.

It turned out that Sheridan had learned beyond question from his scouts that Kershaw's division, of four brigades, at least five thousand men in all, was ordered back to Richmond, and he was patiently waiting, and had been for two weeks, for its departure. With all his usual impetuosity he was yet willing to wait, so as not to throw away a single chance. Another remark in Sheridan's report is very significant. "Although the main force remained without change of position from September third to nineteenth, still the cavalry was em ployed every day in harassing the enemy, its opponents being principally infantry. *In these skirmishes the cavalry was becoming educated to attack infantry lines.*"

This was worth more than all the rest, as was made evident on the 19th of September.

On the 15th, Sheridan heard that Kershaw's division was off, and he determined to strike. He allowed two days to pass over, so that Kershaw might be well out of reach; then, on the next night he gathered his men, and on the morning of the 19th of September marched on Winchester.

The battle of Winchester was perfectly simple in its nature, and was finally decided by the cavalry, the first instance in the civil war in which such was the case. Sheridan outnumbered Early, since the withdrawal of Kershaw, but Early had still four strong divisions of infantry, and five brigades of cavalry. With these he made a stand in front of Winchester, and his line was long enough to outflank Sheridan. The Union cavalry under Torbet, now consisted of Merritt's, Wilson's and Averill's divisions, numbering in all about seven thousand men. It began the action on Opequan Creek, nearly ten miles from Winchester, near Martinsburg, where it was met by Early's cavalry under Rosser, the "Savior of the Valley," as he was dubbed when he first came there.

It was considerably inferior to the veterans of Sheridan, both in numbers and composition; and was driven, together with Breckinridge's corps of infantry, found with it, steadily back along the pike to Winchester, and so on to Early's left flank.

During the day, till the arrival of the Union cavalry the fight between Early's and Sheridan's infantry was very even. The Sixth Corps was the only force that Sheridan could thoroughly depend on to stand, for the two divisions of the Nineteenth Corps, coming from Louisiana, where the enemy was very inferior, both in numbers and discipline, to Lee's army, was not yet used to the "stand up and take it" kind of fighting that had greeted the Army of the Potomac ever since its first campaign. Knowing its weakness, Sheridan held Crook's little force, only about three thousand men, in reserve; and it was well he did so. The Sixth Corps stood well up to its work, but the Nineteenth broke under the tremendous fire of musketry, and Sheridan's centre was all giving way. Then it was that he himself, seeing the danger, dashed in, and for the first time in his history in Virginia, treated the infantrymen to a taste of the tallest swearing they had ever heard. No one in the cavalry corps had ever heard him vituperate in such a manner, the general impression there being that he was a kind, indulgent chief. The only time he was heard to swear in such fearfully profane style was when troops were breaking, as in this instance, and the line in danger. Then he seemed to be beside himself. Ordering up a reserve brigade, which charged very gallantly, he threw himself among the fugitives and fairly cursed them back into the lines, raving in such a manner that they feared him more than the enemy. The line was restored, and once more advanced; and Sheridan, finding his right flank in danger of being turned, put in Crook, and by so doing extended his line so far as to turn his enemy's left. The influx of fresh troops on the flanks so dismayed and disheartened the stubborn infantry of Early that they broke and fell back in confusion. At the edge of the town they rallied desperately and seemed about to drive back their foes, when the clouds of dust and rattle of volleys, away to their left rear, announced the coming of Sheridan's cavalry, driving Rosser and Lomax before them. The crisis was come with the cavalry. How they came there let Custer tell, as also what followed.

My command, he says, was in readiness to move from its encampment near Summit Point, at 2 o'clock in the morning. It being the intention to reach Opequan, some five miles distant, before daylight, the march was begun soon after 2 A. M., and conducted by the most direct route across the country, independent of roads. My brigade moved in advance of the division, and reached the vicinity of the Opequan before day-light, unobserved by the enemy, whose pickets were posted along the opposite bank. Massing my command in rear of a belt of woods and opposite a ford, situated about three miles from the point at which the railroad crossed the stream, I awaited the arrival of the division commander and the re-mainder of the division. At daylight I received orders to move to a ford one mile and a half up the stream, and there attempt a crossing. This movement was also made beyond the view of the enemy, and my command was massed opposite the point designated in rear of a range of hills overlooking the Opequan. Owing to a reconnoissance made at this point by our forces a few days previous, the enemy were found on the alert, thereby destroying all hopes of securing possession of the ford by a surprise. Two regiments, the Twenty-fifth New York and Seventh Michigan, both under command of that reliable soldier, Lieutenant-Colonel Brewer, of the Seventh Michigan, were selected to charge the ford and obtain possession of the rifle-pits under the opposite bank. By request of the senior officer of the Twenty-fifth New York Cavalry, that regiment was placed in advance, and both regiments moved under cover of a hill, as near to the ford as possible without being exposed to the fire of the enemy. At the same time the Sixth Michigan Cavalry, Colonel Kidd commanding, advanced, dismounted, to the crest overlooking the ford, and engaged the enemy on the opposite bank. Everything promised success, and the order was given for the column of Colonel Brewer to charge.

Accordingly both regiments moved rapidly toward the ford. The advance of the Twenty-fifth New York reached the water, when the enemy, from a well-covered rifle-pit opposite the cross-ing, opened a heavy fire upon our advance, and succeeded in repulsing the head of the column, whose conduct induced this entire portion of the command to give way in considerable con-fusion. No responsibility for this repulse could be attached to

Lieutenant-Colonel Brewer, who had left nothing undone to insure success. Giving him orders to re-form his command under the cover of the ridge of hills before mentioned, and directing Colonel Kidd to engage the attention of the enemy as closely as possible, such a disposition of sharp-shooters was made as to quiet that portion of the enemy lodged in the rifle-pits covering the ford. The First Michigan cavalry, Colonel Stagg commanding, which had been held in reserve, was ordered to accomplish what two regiments had unsuccessfully attempted. No time was lost, but aided by the experience of the command which preceded it, the First cavalry secured a good position near the ford.

Colonel Stagg, detaching two squadrons as an advance guard, under Lieutenant-Colonel Maxwell, one of the most dashing and intrepid officers of the service, ordered the charge, and under cover of the heavy fire poured in by the Sixth Michigan, gained a footing on the opposite bank, capturing the rifle-pits and a considerable number of prisoners. The enemy retired about one mile from the ford in the direction of Winchester, and took a position behind a heavy line of earthworks protected in addition by a formidable chevaux de frise. My entire command was moved to the south of the stream, and placed in position along the ridge just vacated by the enemy. About this time, a battery of horse artillery, under command of Lieutenant Taylor, reported to me, and was immediately ordered into position within range of the enemy's works. Prisoners captured at the ford represented themselves as belonging to Breckinridge's Corps, and stated that their corps, with Breckinridge in command, was posted behind the works confronting us. Deeming this information reliable, as the results of the day proved it to be, I contented myself with annoying the enemy with artillery and skirmishers, until the other brigades of the division, having effected a crossing at a ford lower down, established connection with my left. Acting in conjunction with a portion of Colonel Lowell's brigade, an advance of the

First and Seventh Michigan and Twenty-fifth New York was ordered to test the number and strength of the enemy.

This movement called forth from the enemy a heavy fire from his batteries. It failed, however, to inflict serious damage. Lieutenant-Colonel Maxwell, who headed the charging column, as was his custom, succeeded in piercing the enemy's line of infantry and reaching to within a few feet of their artillery. Overwhelming numbers alone forced him to relinquish the intent of their capture, and he retired, after inflicting a severe loss upon the enemy. This advance, while clearly developing the position and strength of the enemy, was not without loss on our part. Among those whose gallantry on this occasion was conspicuous was Lieutenant Jackson, of the First Michigan cavalry, who, while among the foremost in the charge, received a wound which carried away his arm and afterwards proved mortal. He was a young officer of great promise, and one whose loss was severely felt. At this time the engagement along the centre and left of our line was being contested with the utmost energy upon both sides, as could be determined by the heavy firing, both of artillery and small arms. While it was known to be impossible to carry the position in my front with the force at my disposal, it was deemed important to detain as large a force of the enemy in our own front as possible, and thus prevent reinforcements of other parts of their line. With this object in view, as great a display of our forces was kept up as circumstances would allow. At the same time, skirmishing was continued, with little or no loss to either side. From the configuration of the ground the enemy was enabled to move or mass troops in rear of his position, unseen by my command. Either divining our intentions of delaying him, or receiving orders to this effect, he abandoned the position in our front and withdrew towards our left. In the absence of instructions I ordered a general advance, intending, if not opposed, to move beyond the enemy's left flank and strike him in reverse. I directed my advance toward Stevenson's Depot, and met with no enemy until within two miles of that point, when I encountered Lomax's division of cavalry, which at that time was engaged with Averill's division, advancing on my right on the Martinsburg pike. Our appearance was unexpected, and produced such confusion upon the part of the enemy that, though charged repeatedly by inferior numbers, they at no time waited for us to approach within pistol range, but broke and fled. Soon after a junction was formed with General Averill, on my right, which, with the connection on my left, made our line unbroken. At this time five brigades of cavalry were moving on parallel lines. Most, if not all, of the brigades moved by brigade front, regiments being in parallel columns of squadrons. One continuous and heavy line of skirmishers covered the advance, using only the carbine, while the line of brigades, as they advanced across the open country, the bands playing the national airs, presented in the sunlight one moving mass of glistening sabres. This, combined with the various and bright-colored banners and battle-flags, intermingled here and there with the plain blue uniforms of the troops, furnished one of the most inspiring as well as imposing scenes of martial grandeur I ever witnessed upon a battle-field.

No encouragement was required to inspire either men or horses. On the contrary it was necessary to check the ardor of both until the time for action should arrive. The enemy had effected a junction of his entire cavalry force, composed of the divisions of Lomax and Fitzhugh Lee. They were formed across the Martinsburg and Winchester pike, about three miles from the latter place. Concealed by an open pine forest, they awaited our approach. No obstacles to the successful manœuvering of large bodies of cavalry were encountered. Even the forests were so open as to offer little or no hindrance to a charging column. Upon our left, and in plain view, could be seen the struggle now raging between the infantry lines of each army, while at various points the small columns of light-colored smoke showed that the artillery of neither side was idle. At that moment it seemed as if no perceptible advantage could be claimed by either, but the fortunes of the day might be decided by one of those incidents or accidents of the battle-field which, though insignificant in themselves, often go far towards deciding the fate of nations. Such must have been the impression of the officers and men composing the five brigades now advancing to the attack. The enemy wisely chose not to receive our attack at a halt, but advanced from the woods and charged our line of skirmishers. The cavalry were here so closely connected that a separate account of the operations of a single brigade or regiment is almost impossible. Our skirmishers were forced back, and a portion of my brigade was pushed forward to their support.

The enemy relied wholly upon the carbine and pistol ; my men preferred the sabre. A short but closely contested struggle ensued, which resulted in the repulse of the enemy. Many prisoners were taken, and quite a number of both sides were left on the field. Driving the enemy through the woods in his rear, the pursuit was taken up with vigor. The enemy dividing his column from necessity, our forces did likewise. The division of General Averill moved on the right of the pike, and gave its attention to a small force of the enemy which was directing its retreat towards the commanding heights west of the town. My command, by agreement with General Averill, took charge of all forces of the enemy on the pike, and those in the immediate vicinity of the ground to its left. Other portions of the first division made a detour still farther to my left, so that that which had lately been one unbroken line was now formed into several columns of pursuit, each with a special and select object in view. Within three-fourths of a mile from the point where the enemy had made his last stand, he rallied a portion of his force. His line was formed beyond a small ditch, which he no doubt supposed would break, if not wholly oppose, an attacking column. Under most circumstances such might have been the case, but with men inspired with a foretaste of victory, greater obstacles must be interposed. Without designating any particular regiments, the charge was sounded, and portions of all the regiments composing my brigade, joined in the attack. The volleys delivered by the enemy were not enough to check the attacking column, and again was the enemy driven before us, this time seeking safety in rear of his line of infantry. Here he re-formed for his last attempt to check our advance. The batteries of the enemy were now enabled to reach us, an advantage they were not slow to improve. At this time a battery of the enemy, with apparently little support, was being withdrawn. My command, owing to the repeated charges, had become badly broken, rendering it impossible for me to avail myself of the services of a single organized regiment. With detachments of each regiment, a charge was ordered upon the battery, which, but for the extreme smallness of our numbers, would have proved successful. Lieutenant Lounsbery, Fifth Michigan cavalry, with great daring, advanced with a handful of men to within a few paces of the battery, and was only prevented from capturing it by an infantry support, hitherto concealed, and outnumbering him. Sergeant Barber, Fifth Michigan cavalry, clerk at headquarters, distinguished himself in this charge as my color-bearer. He carried the colors in advance of the charging column, and was conspicuous throughout the engagement until severely wounded in the latter part of the day. It being necessary to re-form my regiment before attempting a further advance, advantage was taken of a slight ridge of ground within one thousand yards of the enemy's line of battle. Behind this ridge, and protected from the enemy's fire, I formed as many of my men as could be hastily collected. Two guns, which had been annoying us on our right, were now charged and taken by the First and Second regular cavalry. This gave us possession of a portion of the main line of the enemy's fortifications. At the same time our infantry on the centre and left had, after our successes on the right, been enabled to drive the enemy, and were now forcing him

16

towards the town. Still determined to contest our further advances, the enemy now contracted his lines. This gave me an opportunity to move my brigade to a small crest, within five hundred yards of the enemy's position.

" This movement was entirely unobserved by him, his attention being drawn toward the heavy lines of our infantry, now advancing in open view far to our left. At this moment I received an order from the division commander to charge the enemy with my entire brigade. Having personally examined the situation, and knowing that a heavy force of the enemy was lying down behind these works, facts of which I knew the division commander was ignorant, I respectfully requested that I might be allowed to select my own time for making the charge. My reasons for this course were, that I was convinced that the advance of our infantry on the centre and left would compel the force in my front to shift its position to the rear, and the most favorable moment to strike it would be after this movement had commenced, not while they were awaiting us in rear of their works. My opinions were verified. Watching the enemy until his force had arisen from behind their works and commenced their retrograde movement, I gave the command to charge. The order was obeyed with zeal and alacrity by all. The First, Fifth, Sixth and Seventh Michigan, with a portion of the Twenty-fifth New York, advanced in one line, using the sabre alone. Officers and men seemed to vie with each other as to who should lead . . . The enemy, upon our approach, turned and delivered a well directed volley of musketry, but before a second discharge could be given, my command was in their midst, sabreing right and left, and capturing prisoners more rapidly than they could be disposed of. Further resistance on the part of those opposed to us was suspended. A few batteries posted on the heights near the town continued to fire into our midst, fortunately killing more of their own men than ours. Their fire was silenced, however, as we advanced toward them. Nothing more remained but to collect the prisoners and other trophies of the victory. No further resistance was offered : the charge just made had decided the day, and the entire body of the enemy, not killed or captured, was in full retreat up the valley. Many of the prisoners cut off by my command fell into the hands of the infantry, whose advance soon reached the ground. My command, however, which entered the last charge about five hundred strong, including but thirty-six officers, captured over seven hundred prisoners, also fifty-two officers, seven battle flags, two caissons, and a large number of small arms. Night put an end to the pursuit, and the brigade bivouacked on the left of the valley pike, three miles from the battle-field. Our loss was by no means trifling."

So closed the battle of Winchester, the first decisive field victory won in the civil war, made decisive only by the proper use of cavalry. It must not be imagined that Custer's brigade was all alone in its glory, but it had a large share of it. How it appeared in the last charge to a neighboring brigade is told so well by a participant, who was taken prisoner, that we can not forbear the transcription.*

" While awaiting in suspense our next movement, the enemy's infantry was distinctly seen attempting to change front to meet our anticipated charge. Instantly, and while in the confusion incident to their manœuvre, the Second Brigade burst upon them, the enemy's infantry breaking into complete rout, and falling back a confused and broken mass." General Merritt in his official report, writes : " The brigade emerged from the fray with three stands of colors and over three hundred prisoners. This blow, struck by General Devin, was at the angle of the line caused by the enemy refusing his left to meet our attack. Soon Colonel Lowell (Reserve brigade, which formed to the left of the old position from which Devin charged) entered the lists. His heroic brigade—now reduced to about six hundred men—rode out fearlessly within five hundred yards of the ene-

* From " Everglade and Cañon," a history of the Second U. S. Dragoons by General Rodenbough, used by permission of the author.

my's line of battle, on the left of which, resting on an old earth-work, was a two-gun battery. The order was given to charge the line and get the guns.

It was well toward four o'clock, and, though the sun was warm, the air was cool and bracing. The ground to our front was open and level, in some places as smooth as a well-cut lawn. Not an obstacle intervened between us and the enemy's line, which was distinctly seen nervously awaiting our attack. The brigade was in column of squadrons, the Second United States Cavalry in front.

At the sound of the bugle we took the trot, the gallop, and then the charge. As we neared their line we were welcomed by a fearful musketry fire, which temporarily confused the lead-ing squadron, and caused the entire brigade to oblique slightly to the right. Instantly officers cried out, " Forward ! forward ! " The men raised their sabres, and responded to the command with deafening cheers. Within a hundred yards of the enemy's line we struck a blind ditch, but crossed it without breaking our front. In a moment we were face to face with the enemy. They stood as if awed by the heroism of the brigade, and in an instant broke in complete rout, our men sabring them as they vainly sought safety in flight. In this charge the battery and many prisoners were captured. Our own loss was severe, and of the officers of the Second, Captain Rodenbough lost an arm and Lieutenant Harrison was taken prisoner.

It was the writer's misfortune to be captured, but not until six hundred yards beyond where the enemy were first struck, and when dismounted in front of their second line by his horse falling. Nor did he suffer the humiliation of a surrender of his sabre ; for as he fell to the ground with stunning force, its point entered the sod several inches, well-nigh doubling the blade, which, in its recoil, tore the knot from his wrist, flying many feet through the air.

Instantly a crowd of cavalry and infantry officers and men surrounded him, vindictive and threatening in their actions, but unable to repress such expressions as these : "Great God! what a fearful charge! How grandly you sailed in! What brigade? What regiment?" As the reply proudly came, "Reserve Brigade, Second United States Cavalry," they fairly tore his clothing off, taking his gold watch and chain, pocketbook, cap, and even spurs, and then turned him over to four infantrymen. What a translation—yea, transformation! The confusion, disorder, and actual rout produced by the successive charges of Merritt's First Cavalry division would appear incredible, did not the writer actually witness them. To the right a battery, with guns disabled and caissons shattered, was trying to make to the rear, the men and horses impeded by broken regiments of cavalry and infantry. To the left, the dead and wounded, in confused masses, around their field-hospitals— many of the wounded, in great excitement, seeking shelter in Winchester. Directly in front, an ambulance, the driver nervously clutching the reins, while six men, in great alarm, were carrying to it the body of General Rhodes. Not being able to account for the bullets which kept whizzing past, the writer turned and faced our own lines to discover the cause and, if possible, catch a last sight of the Stars and Stripes.

The sun was well down in the west, mellowing everything with that peculiar golden hue which is the charm of our autumn days. To the left, our cavalry were hurriedly forming for another and final charge. To the right front, our infantry, in unbroken line, in the face of the enemy's deadly musketry, with banners unfurled, now enveloped in smoke, now bathed in the golden glory of the setting sun, were seen slowly but steadily pressing forward. Suddenly, above the almost deafening din and tumult of the conflict, an exultant shout broke forth, and simultaneously our cavalry and infantry line charged. As he stood on tiptoe to see the lines crash together, himself and guards were suddenly caught in the confused tide of a thoroughly-beaten army—cavalry, artillery and infantry—broken, demoralized, and routed, hurrying through Winchester."

The battle of Winchester possessed some remarkable features, considered in a scientific point of view, especially when contrasted with those which had previously been fought during the American Civil War. It was the first which resembled in any degree one of those actions which, under NAPOLEON and FREDERICK, have become models for the military student; the first which displayed on the Federal side the possession of a real *general*, capable of planning and executing every movement of an engagement, and of personally handling all his troops. Up to that time, the history of every American battle on both sides, with the exception of the valley campaign of Stonewall Jackson, had been the history of a number of nearly independent corps commanders. It has been said that VON MOLTKE once remarked about the American war, that "the struggles of two armed mobs were of no service to a military student." Although the general has "officially" denied that he used such scornful language; there is a strong probability that he did, in *private conversation*, say something very like it. There was much truth in the remark, whoever made it, even if it was severely expressed. A "mob" is a crowd without absolute chiefs. It follows different leaders from time to time with a certain degree of docility, but always requires persuasion, resists command, and is subject to sudden changes. Instead of one impulse, it has fifty or more. While this latterly ceased to be true of the lower ranks of the American army, it remained to the very last among the general officers, especially the corps commanders. Each had his own notion of what ought to be done, and each would do things in his own way. Meade could not control his corps generals, and their lack of quick obedience marred more than one battle in 1864, and nearly at one time spoiled the success of 1865. In the valley, Sheridan changed all this. He made his generals obey his orders, without following opinions of their own, and his army consequently pulled together. Winchester was won, and what was more, *improved*, because Sheridan was a man who *would be obeyed*.

FIFTH BOOK.—THE THIRD CAVALRY DIVISION.

CHAPTER I.

WOODSTOCK RACES.

ON the 26th September, 1864, Brigadier-General Custer was relieved from the command of the famous Michigan Brigade, in the First Cavalry Division Army of the Potomac, and transferred to the head of the Second Division, West Virginia Cavalry, hitherto operating under General Averill. At the time of the transfer, the whole valley was in confusion. Early's army, scattered and demoralized after the crushing disasters of Winchester and Fisher's Hill, was slowly gathering itself together at the very head of the Valley, from Port Republic to Staunton, and the Union Cavalry, spread out fanlike, was operating by independent brigades, on the old Donnybrook Fair principle of hitting every head they could see.

Custer, accordingly, found himself separated from his new command, which had gone on up the pike towards Staunton and turned to the left in the direction of Piedmont. The country was full of guerillas and scattered parties of Confederate cavalry, and it was not so easy to open communication between the different divisions, without proceeding bodily and in force, one toward the other. All through the valley campaigns, from the days of Banks downwards, the same trouble was met by the Federals, as soon as they neared Staunton. Their line of supply was so long and easily cut, that it was impossible to go further

in safety with a regularly organized army. The only solution
of the problem was that afterwards adopted, of cutting loose
from the infantry and trains, and moving as an independent
raiding column, living off the country. Even this was not
practicable for long, for the country was so much impoverished
by the near neighborhood of Richmond, that two or three days'
subsistence for a cavalry corps was its utmost capacity.

Under these circumstances, Custer was doomed to several
days of inaction before he could reach his command, and having left his beloved Michigan Brigade, was obliged to remain
with General Torbert, at cavalry headquarters, till the Second
Division was near enough to be reached. On the 26th, he
entered Staunton with that General, accompanied by Wilson's
Division, (the third) and the Reserve Brigade, (the regulars).
At Staunton fifty-seven prisoners were made, and a quantity
of stores destroyed.

On the 27th, Custer, impatient to reach his command,
started with a single regiment to reach it at Piedmont, but
was compelled to return the next day, with the news that Early
had again massed his forces, and was trying to cut off the
cavalry from the rest of the army. It turned out that Early
had been reinforced from Richmond by Kershaw's division, and
was coming through the gaps to which he had retreated,
resolved on revenge. The main Union army was concentrated
some miles back, behind Harrisonburg, and each brigade of
cavalry, as it successively struck the enemy, found him in such
force that they could make no impression. It was exceedingly
tantalizing, for the troopers had become so used to victory that
when they saw the enemy's trains in plain sight, as they often
did, blocked in the mountain roads, they would charge recklessly
in, only to find a heavy force of infantry in the woods, pouring
in such volleys as showed that Early was yet far from being
whipped.

On the 28th the Confederates came down to Staunton and
Port Republic, and did their best to drive out the First and

Third Cavalry Divisions, passing by the Second, which was out near Brown's Gap. The cavalry fought them till dark, holding on to their positions, but during the night Torbert fell back toward Harrisonburg with Wilson's division, leaving Merritt and Powell, with the First and Second, out on the left still. On the 29th the enemy fell back from Port Republic to the gaps of the Blue Mountains, and on the 30th Sheridan's army was again concentrated, the infantry at and beyond Harrisonburg, at the head of the valley pike, the cavalry spread out fanwise around the head of the column.

On this day occurred the second important change of Custer's life. General Wilson was relieved from the command of the Third Division, and sent to join Sherman in the west. Custer was at the same time transferred from the Second Division, which he had not yet been able to join, and placed at the head of the same division in which he had first won his star. It was the same old Third, which under Kilpatrick had done such service in the Gettysburg campaign, always ready for hard knocks, dashing pellmell into the enemy, no matter what the odds, and trusting to the wonderful luck which never deserted it to get out of its scrapes.

Under Kilpatrick, this division had done more fighting, killed more horses, marched further, and charged oftener, than perhaps any other in the army. The reckless valor and want of discretion of its first leader had both their bad and good sides. Had infantry been handled in the same way, the division would long before have been annihilated, but the traditions of the cavalry service are essentially different. Kilpatrick had acted from the first as if he thoroughly believed the maxim of Seidlitz, that under no conceivable circumstances can a mounted cavalry officer be justified in a surrender. Charging in and cutting out were the every-day experiences of the division under his orders, and their losses had been proportionately heavy.

When Wilson took command of the division, in the spring of 1864, he found it depleted by the loss of its crack brigade,

Custer's "Michiganders," and the real secret of its previous
high fighting reputation was shown in the summer campaigns.
Custer, the lance-head of Kilpatrick, had become the lance-head
of Torbert, and it was the First Division that was to do most of
the fighting and charging, while he was with it. As good as
ever, the Third had still lost much of its old fiery fame, under
the more cautious lead of Wilson. It was Custer and Merritt
who were now in people's mouths when the cavalry was mentioned, as the previous year it had been Buford, Kilpatrick and
Custer. There is something so fleeting and hard to grasp, in
this phenomenon of public favor and fame, that it is difficult to
assign a reason for the fact, but it was none the less patent during
the Shenandoah campaign and before. Torbert, the division
commander of Custer and Merritt, was lost to public view in a
large measure, through the lustre of his subordinates, who engaged in a fierce rivalry with each other which resulted in
splendid successes.

Now Custer and Merritt were again to engage in the same
rivalry, but as division commanders, the latter having the additional advantage of retaining the brigade which Custer had made
so famous. Custer was to take up the division which had so
far, under Wilson's lead, only held its own with respectability,
and was to transform it into the most brilliant single division
in the whole Army of the Potomac, with more trophies to show
than any, and so much impressed with the stamp of his individuality, that every officer in the command was soon to be
aping his eccentricities of dress, ready to adore his every motion
and word.

The accession of Custer to the command of the Third Division took place at a time when a change in Sheridan's policy
was impending. He had come to the Valley to clear out Early;
he had done his work, and the question remained—what next?
Concentrated at Harrisonburg, he was at the end of his tether.
The whole valley is traversed by a single long turnpike, which
forms a splendid avenue of communication, perfectly dry and

hard in the muddiest winter. At Harrisonburg it ceases and beyond it are "dirt roads" only. The enemy was waiting in the Blue Ridge gaps, prepared to dispute any further advance to Richmond. The course of action necessary is indicated by Sheridan himself in his subsequent report.

He says: "The question that now presented itself was whether or not I should follow the enemy to Brown's Gap, drive him out, and advance to Charlottesville and Gordonsville. This movement I was opposed to for many reasons, first that it would have necessitated the opening of the Orange and Alexandria Railroad, and to protect this road against the numerous guerilla bands would have required a corps of infantry . . . Then there was the additional reason of the uncertainty whether the army in front of Petersburg would be able to hold the entire force of General Lee there, and, if not, a sufficient number might be detached and move rapidly by rail to overwhelm me, quickly returning. I was also confident that my transportation could not supply me further than Harrisonburg, and therefore advised that the valley campaign should terminate at Harrisonburg, and that I return, carrying out my original instructions for the destruction of forage, grain, etc., give up the majority of the army I commanded, and order it to the Petersburg line, a line which I thought the Lieutenant General believed if a successful movement could be made on, would involve the capture of the Army of Northern Virginia. I therefore, on the morning of the 6th of October, commenced moving back, stretching the cavalry across the valley from the Blue Ridge to the eastern slope of the Alleghanies."

On the way, the horsemen were directed to burn all the forage, but to spare the houses. These orders were obeyed to the letter, as the infantry moved back towards Winchester. Merritt marched on the pike, while Custer took the side road, next the Blue Ridge. Of course this was nearest the enemy, whose cavalry had not yet suffered very much. It consisted of Rosser's division (three brigades) and the extra brigades of Lomax and Bradley Johnson. Rosser had about thirty-five hundred, Johnson and Lomax about fifteen hundred together, a total of five thousand men.

It must be conceded to the Confederate forces in the last valley campaign, that they fought and were fought with the most obstinate heroism and skill by all concerned, and that they showed in these days of disaster, more conduct and skill against heavy odds than they had ever shown before. When Sheridan first arrrived in the valley, Early considerably outnumbered him, but every day strengthened the former and weakened the latter. When finally Kershaw's division was withdrawn, a few days before the battle of Winchester, the scale was turned, and as soon as Sheridan had certain intelligence of its departure, he gave battle with heavy odds in his favor, though by no means so great as Early insists. During the whole valley campaign, thirteen thousand prisoners were taken from Early, which, added to the eleven thousand men he claims, gives about twenty four thousand. Added to these the sick, wounded, extra duty men, stragglers, etc., and it is probable that in real truth Early had at Winchester at least twenty-six thousand men, infantry, artillery and train, which, with Rosser's cavalry, gives a total of about thirty thousand men, outside of Kershaw's division, which was not engaged till Cedar Creek. When this came, it was probably about enough to fill up the gaps of Winchester and Fisher's Hill. This is hardly the place to enter into a complete analysis of the figures on both sides, but reason and statistics seem to point, after making all allowances, to an effective total for Early about this time of at least twenty thousand infantry and five thousand horse.

Opposed to these, from the nearest figures attainable at present, it seems that Sheridan must have had about seven thousand cavalry in his three divisions, and twenty-five thousand infantry. These figures are derived from a comparison of his force in August, when, with the First and Second

Cavalry Divisions, Sixth Corps, Nineteenth, and Crook's force, he reported 18,000 infantry and 3,500 cavalry. He was afterwards joined by a division of the Nineteenth Corps, and by the Third Cavalry Division, with such recruits as could be sent from Remount camp. In one of these detachments the present writer arrived at Harper's Ferry, the evening of Winchester fight, and after scraping up every available man and horse, the result was less than three hundred men.

The odds in Sheridan's favor were heavy enough for practical purposes, though by no means enough to account for the succession of complete and crushing blows delivered on the devoted Early, without admitting conduct and capacity of the highest kind to Sheridan and his officers, especially those heading the cavalry.

Rosser, overmatched in numbers as he was, on this occasion did his duty heroically. The feelings of himself and his men were excited to the highest pitch of fury at sight of the remorseless destruction meted out to the valley by the retreating foe. True, that foe was part of the terrible army that had punished them so fearfully ever since the 19th September, but the arrival of Kershaw's division had put new heart into them, and they followed the cavalry down the valley, constantly attacking them. Lomax and Johnson followed Merritt at a respectful distance, but Rosser hung on Custer's skirts with vindictive tenacity. The first night of the retreat he fell on Custer's, camp at Turkeytown, near Brooks' Gap, but was repulsed. Next morning, as Custer moved on, Rosser was again after him, Custer proceeding leisurely towards Columbia Furnace. His rear-guard was fighting Rosser all day long, in the peculiar style developed by Virginian warfare. The main body, in column of fours, was in the road, detaching parties to right and left to burn every barn and haystack to be seen. Ordinarily, the rear-guard followed at a slow walk, the greater part deployed as skirmishers. When the enemy pressed too close, the men would halt and face about, a brisk fusillade lasting some minutes when the advancing grey-coats would be repulsed. Then trotting on, the rear-guard would halt at the edge of the next hill or belt of woods, to repeat the operation.

Not far from the Union rear-guard could be seen a brilliant group of cavaliers, headed by the same bright debonair figure we remember at Aldie and Brandy Station. As usual, there are the bright brazen instruments of the band near him, the men not much of players perhaps, but what is better, capable of sticking to their posts under fire, and playing "Yankee Doodle" to the shrill accompaniment of whistling lead. Whenever any trouble is anticipated, when Rosser becomes too bold, the flaming scarlet neckties of Custer and his staff are seen coming, and the bright-haired warrior comes trotting leisurely along the skirmish line, whistling a tune, and tapping his boots with his riding whip, his blue eyes glancing keenly about, his short curls, just growing again, flung from side to side, as he jerks his head in his peculiar nervous manner. There is no more trouble about standing the assault.

But this mode of fighting was peculiarly irksome to one of Custer's impatient temperament, and when he knew, as he soon did, that it was his old classmate Rosser, who was following him so persistently, he was doubly disgusted. All that long day of the 7th October, he was compelled by his orders to retreat from the face of a foe he was only too anxious to fight, and even till dark his pickets were annoyed.

All this time, Merritt's column pursued its way without fighting, only observed by Lomax and Johnson. The reason was very simple. The two Union divisions each numbered about two thousand five hundred effective men, and Powell's Second Division about two thousand more. Powell was off to the right of Merritt following the Luray valley, separated from the rest by hills and gaps. Consequently, the forces in the main valley of the Shenandoah were equal, and thus divided, roughly speaking. Custer's two thousand five hundred against Rosser's three thousand five hundred were falling back: Merritt's two thousand five hundred against Lomax's one thousand five hundred, were also falling back, but quite unmolested.

The next day, 8th October, General Torbert, in command of the cavalry, thinking Custer had had about enough, halted Merritt in the afternoon, sent back one of his brigades about a mile on the pike, to develop Lomax, and the other two to relieve Custer, who all that day had been suffering even fiercer assaults than before. The experience of the three days had given the enemy confidence, and Custer had been retreating in the face of a superior force who fancied they were driving him. The arrival of Merritt's brigade checked Rosser, and the fighting ceased at dark, when Merritt withdrew his men to his own camp.

The position on the night of the 8th was as follows: Merritt was in camp at Brook Creek, on the pike, at the foot of Round Top Hill. The pike runs up the middle of the valley. Custer camped at Tumbling Run, on the back road, some six miles off, to the left and retired. Powell was further off still, to the left and rear, having crossed behind the others to Front Royal. Rosser lay opposite Custer, Lomax and Johnson opposite Merritt. The back road so often mentioned is a dirt road, nearly parallel to the pike, between it and the Blue Ridge, and about three miles from the pike.

That night "Little Phil" came up to the front to see how things were going on, and soon learned the exact posture of affairs. The enemy, grown bold through impunity, was becoming too troublesome. He must get a lesson. The story of the orders to Torbert for next day is thus told by both parties.

Sheridan says, "On the night of the eighth, I ordered General Torbert to engage the enemy's cavalry at daybreak, and notified him that I would halt the army till he defeated it."

Torbert says, "I had received orders from Major-General Sheridan to start out at daylight, and whip the rebel cavalry, or get whipped myself."

The difference in the literalness of the stories is in favor of

Torbert, but there is no question as to the way in which the order was obeyed. When it was given, the cavalry was in front of Strasburg, where the infantry was concentrated. Merritt was ordered to move one brigade on the pike and two more to the left, to open communication with Custer.

At daybreak the movement commenced, soon to become famous under the name of "Woodstock Races." The forces were not far from equal, the difference in favor of the Federal cavalry being but slight. In guns they were about the same. Each division had a battery, and Rosser and Lomax were similarly equipped, six guns on the pike, six on the back road.

Now Custer was to avenge himself for his long suffering. His experience, it must be confessed, since he had taken command of the Third Division, was peculiarly mortifying. For the first time since Meade's retreat, he had been obliged to retrograde in face of the enemy, and to suffer severe punishment while doing it. As in the former however, nothing but orders had compelled him to do so, and now had come the far more congenial orders to advance.

Out swept, as at Winchester, side by side, Custer and Merritt to attack Rosser and Lomax ; and to Custer's share fell the greater part of the force of his old classmate Rosser.

On the pike moved the steady old Reserve Brigade, the Regulars, under Lowell. Next to them was Devin's Brigade, the Second, with "Old Tommy," or the "Old War-Horse," as he was nicknamed, at its head. Then the Michiganders, Custer's old brigade, connected Merritt's line with that of their former division, under their own commander of a few days back, and the union of the line was perfect. Old and new were only impatient to pay off the enemy. In front of each brigade stretched a regiment, deployed as skirmishers, then a second line of two regiments, deployed in double rank, behind each wing, finally a fourth regiment in close column, to the rear of the centre, with the brigade commander and staff in its front. Merritt rode in rear of the centre of his division, with his battery near him, Custer was up even with his skirmish line, his own guns following.

In this order the two gallant looking divisions swept over the beautiful level surface of the valley. It was a magnificent place for a cavalry fight, and very different from the scrub woods of Central Virginia, where all the fighting had to be dismounted. There was room to deploy, smooth ground to ride on, all the rail-fences had long ago vanished for soldiers' fires, and the field was clear.

Rosser and Lomax were met on the other side of Tom's Run, a rivulet too small to intercept the movement of either force, and both sides were drawn up and ready for the fray. That it was to be a severe and decisive fight, both knew. The Southerners had recovered from the demoralization of their first reverses; and their apparent successes of the last few days had further elated them. They were part of the same cavalry that once, under Stuart, had raided round the Army of the Potomac, and captured Pope's headquarters; and they were burning to avenge the destruction of their homes, which they had lately witnessed.

Both sides deployed within plain view of each other, and the skirmishers opened with their carbines, in the dashing and picturesque style that makes a cavalry fight so pretty a sight at its outset. Very little harm is done, but the long lines of horsemen go trotting on, waving to and fro as the individuals halt to take aim, fire their pieces, and trot on, loading as they go. At the first gentle knoll that presents itself on either side, the batteries gallop up, and unlimber on the crest, opening fire and mingling their crashing reports with the sharp crack of the rifles. Not much smoke, the order is too open, and the breeze strong, the bright sunlight and clear air of the autumn day aiding to inspire every one to do his best. It is exciting, romantic, intoxicating. The little white puffs of smoke on the skirmish line, the dark bodies following in rear, all fringed with the steel of their drawn sabres, the little groups of general

17

officers and their staffs at regular intervals in the three mile line, the white clouds round the four opposing batteries as points of peculiar interest.

Rosser's position for his main body was well chosen, and as his pickets fell back and revealed it, this became evident. He occupied a low but abrupt range of hills on the south bank of Tom's Run, and had posted his dismounted men behind stone fences at the base of the ridge. A second line of barricades· crowned the ridge, also defended by dismounted men. On the summit he had six guns in position strongly supported, and he had the great advantage of being able to see all of Custer's movements.

And now occurred one of those little incidents that stamp the innate romance of Custer's character on his biography, like the echo of his famous last speech at the Academy, " Let's have a fair fight, boys." Here it was, fair and square and no favor, perhaps the first in the war. No infantry to bother the horse, numbers about equal, his first fight as a division commander, and Rosser in sight. Out rode Custer from his staff, far in advance of the line, his glittering figure in plain view of both armies. Sweeping off his broad sombrero, he threw it down to his knee in a profound salute to his honorable foe. It was like the action of a knight in the lists. A fair fight and no malice.

On the ridge before him he had seen Rosser, his classmate at the academy, with whom he had held many a wordy contest in days of old, and who had been his great rival at " the Point." Rosser had but just come to the valley and was already hailed as its savior. He saw Custer and turned to his staff, pointing him out, " You see that officer down there," said he. " That's General Custer, the Yanks are so proud of, and I intend to give him the best whipping to-day that he ever got. See if I don't."

And he smiled triumphantly as he looked round at his gallant Southern cavaliers.

CUSTER AT "WOODSTOCK RACES."

Then Custer lifted the hat and clapped it on his head, turned to his line of men, and the next moment the Third Division was sweeping on at a trot, the flaming scarlet necktie and bright curls of Custer before all, followed by his staff, all with swords out. Now the pace quickens. Rosser's and Lomax's guns open furiously at shorter range, and the rattling of volleys rolls along the Confederate line. The bullets go pattering around, whistling overhead, knocking up the dirt, killing or wounding a few horses and men, but doing surprisingly little damage, all things considered. The trot has become a gallop, and as the pattering of bullets becomes heavier, a wild savage yell breaks from every throat in that long wave of cavalry, and away they go, the lines lost in confused clumps of horsemen, with waving sabres, the horses crazy with excitement, leaping half out of their skins as they race for the Confederate batteries and lines of cavalry.

Custer's attack, arranged in full sight of Rosser, yet proved triumphantly successful. One brigade in front, another to the right, the third to the left, they swept on at a charge, not heeding the fire, curled round Rosser's flanks in a moment, and before he could tell what had happened, had him enclosed in a semi-circle of charging horse. Vain all his efforts when his flanks were threatened. Had the attack been made on foot he might have had time to think, but the sudden and impetuous rush of a whole mounted division completely demoralized the Confederates. Despite Rosser's efforts, away they went in the wildest confusion, driven back at a gallop for nearly two miles, when one brigade, shamed by the frantic appeals of their leader, made a desperate stand, and the lately fugitive battery opened a furious fire, which staggered Custer's advance and threw it into momentary confusion. Rosser was not whipped yet. Seizing his moment, he charged with his remaining brigades and forced Custer's advance back half a mile, when Custer's battery of four guns made its appearance, and checked Rosser again.

Now was Rosser's time to fight, and now was the time he

missed it. Disappointed in his charge, he again trusted to a defensive battle, while Custer reformed his three brigades for a second grand charge, and once more advanced at the trot in a long sweeping line of steel.

Ill fared it with Rosser and his men then that they received the charge at a halt, and trusted to fire for their defence. Through the dust, turmoil, and confusion of the Northern charge, could be seen, far in advance, another cloud of dust, out of which the glittering horseshoes are shining, as the squadrons flee from the charge. The Confederates were thrown into immediate confusion, and behind them was nothing but an open field, as far as Mount Jackson, twenty-six miles away. Every gun opposite Custer is taken, and only one of Lomax's escapes, by being limbered up in desperate haste, and taken off over the hill at full speed. It was no longer a fight. " Woodstock races" had begun. All the way to Woodstock, now at a gallop, anon at a trot, occasionally at a walk, to breathe the reeking horses, the Union lines swept on with scarcely a pause, the Confederates fleeing before them like sheep.

Sheridan sums up the victory in a portion of a sentence, stating that " the enemy was defeated with the loss of all his artillery but one piece, and everything else which was carried on wheels. The rout was complete, and was followed up to Mount Jackson, a distance of some twenty-six miles."

Torbert says, " The First division (Brigadier-General Merritt) captured five pieces of artillery (all they had on the road except one), their ordnance, ambulance, and wagon trains, and sixty prisoners. The Third division (Brigadier-General Custer) captured six pieces of artillery (all they had on the back road) all of their headquarter wagons, ordnance, ambulance, and wagon trains. There could hardly have been a more complete victory and rout. The cavalry totally covered themselves with glory, and added to their long list of victories the most brilliant one of them all, and the most decisive the country has ever witnessed. Brigadier-Generals Merritt and Custer, and Colonels

Lowell and Pennington commanding brigades, particularly distinguished themselves . . . . . My losses in this engagement will not exceed sixty killed and wounded, which is astonishing when compared with the results. The First division returned to Woodstock and camped for the night, the Third returned about six miles and camped for the night."

Thus ended "Woodstock Races," the first pitched battle in which the Third division took part under Custer's command. As always, before and after, he and Merritt were in close rivalry as to distance and results, but Custer was just a little ahead. The completeness of the victory was owing to two things, the open ground, and the vicious cavalry school in which Rosser and his command had been reared. All through the Virginia campaign, the Confederate cavalry displayed the same taste for fire-arms, and the same distaste and contempt for the sabre as a weapon. In the West the case was even worse, for the cavalry in that vicinity abandoned their sabres entirely, and trusted to nothing but fire-arms. Out in the woods, this method of warfare is possible, but on a plain suicidal. The only place in Virginia besides the Valley, where open fields exist, adapted for mounted cavalry fighting, is around Brandy Station, where the sabre had always proved triumphant. Rosser, in common with most of the Confederate officers, distrusted the sabre, which was rarely used by the Confederate cavalry after Stuart's death, and not enough during his life.

Custer, on the other hand, was never more in his element than in a sabre charge, and the same thing was true of the whole of the First and Third divisions, especially the former. Custer's influence soon gave the same taste to the latter, and they became excessively fond of rapid mounted work, wherein pistol, carbine and sabre were used, one with the other, with the happiest effect. The moral impetus of that day of charges never left the Third division. Henceforth they became imbued with a certain contempt for the Confederate cavalry. They had found the certain way to drive it in confusion. It never afterwards gave them serious trouble. The time was coming, and not far distant either, when the cavalry of the Shenandoah Army was to measure itself with a more stubborn foe, the infantry, and be the means of achieving the last and most glorious victory of all at Cedar Creek, only ten days later. Meanwhile, let us leave it to its hard earned repose, after "Woodstock Races."

CHAPTER II.

CEDAR CREEK.

FOR about ten days after "Woodstock Races," the cavalry and army in general enjoyed comparative quiet. Sheridan and Grant were in correspondence as to further movements, and it was almost determined by the latter that Sheridan should continue his advance and operate on Charlottesville and Gordonsville, through Manassas Gap. Sheridan, on the other hand, wished to send back the Sixth Corps to Grant; and on the 10th of October, it actually started and marched toward Front Royal, on its way to Washington. On the 12th, it was at Ashby's Gap; but the same day news came that Early had once more advanced to Fisher's Hill. The Federal army was encamped at Cedar Creek, near Strasburg, and the Sixth Corps was recalled. On the 13th, Rosser, not yet discouraged, came down on the extreme right of the army, and drove in Custer's pickets. He had three brigades of cavalry and one of infantry, but retired when Custer moved out of camp. From thence to the 18th, all was quiet. Merritt and Custer sent frequent reconnoissances up the pike and the back road, but found no enemy nearer than Fisher's Hill. The Confederate cavalry was in the Luray Valley, and occasionally annoyed the extreme right of the army. Everything seemed to point in Wright's opinion to a quiet sulky enemy, with a possible attack on their right rear. On the 16th, Sheridan was summoned to Washington to see Secretary Stanton. As he was at Manassas Gap, and about taking the train, he received a note from General Wright of the Sixth Corps, who was left in command of the army. It enclosed a dispatch which the signal officers had just read off the Confederate signal flags on Three Top Mountain, near Fisher's Hill. It ran thus:

" *To Lieutenant General Early :*
Be ready to move as soon as my forces join you, and we will crush Sheridan.

LONGSTREET,

Lieutenant General."

The Union cavalry was at this time moving toward Front Royal, preparatory to going through Manassas Gap, on a raid towards Gordonsville. Wright asked that it might be recalled, as he expected an attack on his right. Sheridan was inclined to believe the dispatch a ruse, as it turned out afterward to be. He sent back the cavalry, however, told Wright to be careful, and proceeded to Washington, from whence he returned to Winchester on the night of the 18th October.

During the same night, Early, plucky and enterprising to the last, a general who fully deserved, if he did not attain, good fortune, left Fisher's Hill, crossed the Shenandoah, and came down on Wright just where he was least expected, on the almost unguarded left of the Federal army. Powell, with the Second Cavalry division, small as it was, should have been there. In Sheridan's last dispatch, dated the 16th, he had distinctly told Wright to "close in Colonel Powell," who was then at Front Royal. Powell was *not* closed in. One brigade of his skeleton force, commanded by Colonel Moore was moved near the infantry, the only cavalry on that side of the army.

Early attacked at dawn, nothing between him and Wright's camps but a line of infantry pickets, only a few hundred yards out. He swept them away like chaff, fell on Crook's demoralized camps, drove his half-dressed men in utter rout, then falling on the Nineteenth Corps in front, drove that, and finally crushed the left of the Sixth Corps, next in line. In less than an hour, Wright's army was all driven in confusion, twenty-four guns taken, the camps in possession of the enemy, and the Confederate line, in an enveloping crescent of flame, was pressing on, driving the scattered remains in confusion toward Winchester.

The only force left untouched was the cavalry, on the extreme right of the army, and the only infantry division not broken to pieces was Getty's, of the Sixth Corps. Wright had been thus far completely deceived. Expecting an attack on one flank, he had received it on the other, and by 10 o'clock the battle was virtually over. Between 9 and 10, Wright, seeing his first mistake, tried to remedy it by ordering the cavalry to the left of the army, against Torbert's opinion. The latter, however, obeyed the order, but, on his own responsibility detached three regiments on the flank he was leaving, to protect it. The enemy had been trying Custer's pickets on the extreme right, since daylight, but without success, being evidently in small force there. When the Union cavalry left, he began to press harder, and the three regiments were put to their utmost efforts to keep Rosser from breaking in, and capturing the streams of fugitives going to the rear from the infantry.

Meantime, Moore's little brigade, which we noticed as being the only cavalry on the left of the Union army, had been cut off from the rest in the first attack, and was confronted by Lomax's brigade, stronger than himself. In no wise daunted, the plucky Moore sent back his trains to Winchester, and boldly attacked the Confederate infantry in rear, till Lomax attacked him in turn. Then he formed across the pike, and stubbornly contested every foot of ground all the way to Middletown, thus saving the trains and fugitives from being broken in upon by Lomax, just as the three regiments on the other flank were doing with Rosser.

Merritt and Custer, recalled from the right and put in on the left, flung themselves on the advancing infantry, and stayed the course of Early's victory. Colonel Powell, with the rest of his division, had joined Moore by this time, and the strange spectacle was beheld of six or seven thousand cavalry, with a few batteries, holding in check and repulsing charge after charge from an army of nearly twenty thousand infantry flushed with victory, and acting as a shelter, behind which, at several miles distance, Wright's broken infantry was hastily re-forming. The only infantry on the line with Custer and Merritt was Getty's division of the Sixth Corps. On this line the enemy was held till 12 o'clock, by which time Wright had restored a semblance of order in the rear, and it seemed as if the battle was turning. From that time till 2 o'clock, Early ceased to advance, and at 2, General Sheridan arrived on the ground, re-formed his whole line, and finally ordered the advance which culminated in that crushing defeat of Early, so famous in history.

In the meantime, let us see what Early had been doing. His first conception and execution of the battle had been masterly. He had completely surprised Wright, and practically annihilated all the Union infantry but a single division. This and the cavalry, ten thousand men at most, were all that was left to oppose Early's infantry, strengthened by Kershaw's arrival to at least eighteen thousand men, while the Confederate cavalry, still four or five thousand strong, was untouched. Yet Early ceased to advance, and his men began to plunder the Union camps, giving his enemy time to recuperate and reörganize. For this conduct the general offers the excuse that his men were uncontrollable, and that to their plundering solely the after disaster was attributable. A calm review of the battle points to another cause, Early's improper use of his horse. Had he concentrated it at first on his right, he could have swept away the feeble resistance of Moore's brigade, and cut in on all the stragglers and trains that continued their flight quite unmolested. Had he done that, the two hours delay of his infantry would not have mattered. Infantry are not supposed to pursue a defeated foe.

As it was, the same stragglers that under a vigorous pursuit of cavalry would have surrendered by whole brigades, were gathered up and re-formed by Wright, and subsequently by Sheridan. When the latter arrived, the rout was over, and Wright was entitled to claim that he had retrieved his first misfortune, and was ready to advance once more.

Sheridan's arrival, and his immense enthusiasm, effected a wonderful change in the beaten army. Much of the work of reörganization was already effected, but there was little hope that an advance would be made. A stand, and a stubborn defence of what was left, was the utmost that could apparently be hoped for. It required the magic of Sheridan's name and genius to transform defeat into such a complete victory. The enemy was skirmishing without much vigor, but preparing for a new advance. Early had gathered up most of his plunderers. Sheridan's first step was to send his cavalry to its true post, on the flanks. It had been holding the infantry long enough. Accordingly, Custer's division was called out and sent off to the extreme right, while the rest of the Sixth Corps moved up to fill the gap. Merritt was sent off to the extreme left, and the Nineteenth corps moved up to take his place. There was but little left of Crook's two divisions, but what there was went in with the rest, and the stragglers began to pour in from the rear once more. From two till four they kept coming in, and Getty's line was prolonged further and further, and hasty breastworks being thrown up.

About three, Early's troops, flushed with victory, resumed their advance. They assaulted the centre of the line, and were repulsed. Their line was longer than Sheridan's, especially on the right, showing that fresh troops must have come in there. No sooner was the assault repulsed, and the battle again languishing, than Sheridan ordered a general advance, at 4 P. M., October 19th, 1864. That order may be said to have sounded the death knell of the Southern Confederacy, for it was the signal for the almost instant and total destruction of its last aggressive army in Virginia. The only parallel to the utter ruin of Early, is found in that of Hood's army, two months later, by Thomas at Nashville.

It was moreover, as sudden as the rout of the cavalry of Rosser and Lomax at " Woodstock Races," but with this difference : Rosser and Lomax saved most of their men alive, only losing their guns and wagons. Good horses and spurs saved the rest. At Cedar Creek, Early's infantry was not so lucky. It was scooped in by hundreds. Just what Early had failed to do at 9 o'clock in the morning, Sheridan did at 4 in the evening. He used his cavalry as it should be used, and *completed his victory.*

The history of the last advance is thus told by Sheridan : " The attack was brilliantly made, and, as the enemy was protected by rail breastworks and stone fences, his resistance was very determined. His line of battle overlapped the right of mine, and by turning with this portion of it on the flank of the Nineteenth Corps, caused a slight momentary confusion. This movement was checked, however, by a charge of McMillan's brigade on the reëntering angle, and the enemy's flanking party cut off. It was at this stage of the battle that Custer was ordered to charge, with his whole division, but though the order was promptly obeyed, it was not in time to capture the whole of the force thus cut off, and many escaped across Cedar Creek. Simultaneously with this charge, a combined movement of the whole line drove the enemy in confusion to the creek, where, owing to the difficulties of crossing, his army became routed."

Torbert's account explains more fully the part taken by the cavalry. "In the general advance, Brigadier-General Custer, commanding Third Division, left three regiments to attend to the cavalry in his front, and started with the balance of his division to take part in the advance on the enemy's infantry. Thus the cavalry advanced on both flanks, side by side with the infantry, charging the enemy's lines with an impetuosity they could not stand. The rebel army was soon routed and driven across Cedar Creek in confusion. The cavalry, sweeping on both flanks, crossed Cedar Creek about the same time, charged and broke the last line the enemy attempted to form (it was now after dark) and put out at full speed for their artillery and trains."

The captures were forty-five guns (twenty-four being Union guns, lost in the morning and now recaptured) besides weapons, horses, prisoners, and battle-flags. Only night saved the whole of Early's army from capture. From thenceforth it may be said to have ceased to exist as an organized body of any importance, Lee ceased to make any more efforts to save it, and all that there was of any value in the troops composing it was recalled to the Army of Northern Virginia, especially Kershaw's division.

The battle of Cedar Creek completed the noteworthy commencement of Custer's fame as a cavalry division leader. Woodstock Races and Cedar Creek showed his abilities to give weight to a charge, obstinacy to a defence. In all his valley experience, he and Merritt were in constant rivalry as to results, and a comparison of their losses and captures will show just how they stood. It comes from Torbert's report.

The First division lost, during the whole campaign, 186 killed, 778 wounded, 594 missing, total 1558. The Third division lost 67 killed, 385 wounded, 321 missing, total 773.*

The captures were as follows:—First division, 29 guns, 12 caissons, 36 wagons, 40 ambulances, etc., 306 horses and mules, and 14 battle-flags.

Third division 29 guns, 30 caissons, 44 wagons, 23 ambulances, etc., 602 horses and mules and 6 battle-flags.

* The smaller proportion of loss was probably due to the more rapid style of fighting adopted in the Third division, but largely also to the fact that in the early part of the campaign it generally operated as an unit, while the First was pretty often cut up in detachments, on one occasion losing nearly the whole of a single regiment, that was cut off and surrounded while guarding an ambulance train. The assailants were Mosby's guerillas and two regiments of Ransom's cavalry, and the regiment lost nearly 200 men, the rest cutting their way out.

During this winter, Custer received, for his brilliant services in the campaign, the brevet of Major-General. Merritt was similarly decorated, and Colonels Gibbs of the Regular brigade, and Devin, of the Second brigade, First division, were made brigadiers. Both were comparatively elderly men, and deserved their promotion. Colonel Devin had been the senior colonel of the cavalry corps, and in command of his brigade, as early as January, 1863. General Gibbs was an old regular cavalry officer of many years experience. At the close of the war, Devin was brevetted major-general in the regular army, and made lieutenant-colonel of the Eighth cavalry, at the same time that Custer and Merritt received the same rank in the Seventh and Tenth cavalry respectively. Merritt is now Colonel of the Fifth Cavalry. He graduated from West Point the year before Custer. Devin's regiment was the Sixth New York cavalry, to which he was promoted in November, 1861, having before been captain in the First New York Militia cavalry.

NOTE. At the close of this campaign, the flags captured by the cavalry were sent to Washington in Custer's charge, carried by the different men who had taken them. Custer, on his arrival in Washington, where Mrs. Custer had been during the campaign, hurried away to find her. By a curious instance of cross purposes, Mrs. Custer went to the War Department on purpose to see him, hearing of his coming with the flags. She was kindly received by Mr. Stanton, but was dreadfully frightened when she found herself among strangers and that her husband was not there. To add to her confusion, in came the sergeants with the captured flags, and a great deal of speechifying followed, ending by Mr. Stanton publicly introducing her to the brave fellows as the wife of their beloved general. While much embarrassed, the dear little lady acquitted herself splendidly, and said something appropriate to each. During the winter she was able to remain with the general at his headquarters near Winchester.

CUSTER IN 1865.

CHAPTER III.

THE LAST RAID.

DURING the fall and winter of 1864-5, after the battle of Cedar Creek, nothing of importance occurred, the army of Sheridan being concentrated around Winchester. The Sixth Corps was sent away to join Grant, and Merritt's division was sent through Chester Gap to raid on the interior. He met the enemy near Gordonsville, took a couple of guns, destroyed the railroad, and returned. Custer raided out to Harrisonburg and returned about the same time, the middle of December. Both columns suffered very much from the cold, and no more movements were made during January, the cavalry receiving recruits, doing its best to feed up its horses, and get ready for spring work.

On the 5th February, Lieutenant-Colonel Whittaker of the First Connecticut cavalry, Custer's division, went out with Colonel Young, Sheridan's chief of scouts, and they succeeded in capturing the renowned Harry Gilmor, the most active and enterprising partisan chief of whom the Confederates could boast, after Mosby. The latter had by this time ceased to be capable of serious mischief; and Gilmor's capture cleared Sheridan's rear.

He began to think it was time to advance, and called in all his cavalry from cantonments around Winchester, starting out, on the 27th February, on the last raid to be made by Sheridan's cavalry. The chief took with him Merritt, now Brevet Major-general, as chief of cavalry. Brigadier-General Devin, commanded the First division, 4,787 men, and Brevet Major-

General George A. Custer commanded the Third, 4,600 men. Each division had one section of artillery, and the train consisted of three baggage wagons, eight ambulances, twenty ammunition wagons, and about three miles of pack mules. The horses were in good flesh, and each carried thirty pounds of grain, with five days' rations for the men and coffee and sugar for ten days. One extra wagon, laden with coffee and sugar, accompanied the force, and that was all the train, except eight pontoons.

As it turned out, all the lightness and strength of the column was needed. Its destination was no less a place than Lynchburg, and thereafter it was to march into North Carolina, to join Sherman, who was then moving north. This part of the programme was afterwards altered, through the impossibility of crossing the James River, the bridges being destroyed. Failing Lynchburg, the orders were to destroy all that was left of the Virginia Central Railroad and the James River Canal, then to return to Winchester. These orders Sheridan took the liberty to exceed, by joining Grant, just as the latter needed him worst.

On the 27th February, 1865, the great raiding column, with a total strength, including teamsters and artillerymen, of nine thousand four hundred and eighty four men, started up the valley. Before it was the valley pike, a splendid hard road, on which, in one or two spots, there was actually dust: on each side were broad fields, softened by the early spring thaw into quagmires, in which the horses sunk over their fetlocks. This pike lasted to Harrisonburg, and beyond, some seventy miles, followed "dirt roads," in red Virginia clay. The first day's march was to Woodstock, thirty miles, and nothing of interest occurred. All day long the steady clatter of hoofs was almost uninterrupted, a bright sky overhead, the men talking and singing, everybody in high spirits. Occasionally, on the side roads, on either flank, a glimpse could be caught of small parties of horsemen in grey, keeping pace with the column and evidently

watching its movements. Once, a few men left the column to
chase the nearest of these gentry, who kept almost within carbine range, but the state of the fields prevented active pursuit,
and the enemy were left unmolested. They were a few of
Mosby's guerillas, latterly joined by some of Rosser's cavalry,
but no damage was done by or to them. Sheridan's policy to
the guerillas in general was to leave them alone. They served,
as he naively tells us in his reports, as "a very good provost
guard for his army," and prevented straggling. Next morning,
at daybreak, the column moved on, twenty-nine miles further,
to within nine miles of Harrisonburg. At daybreak of the
1st of March, the advance pressed on through Harrisonburg and
Mount Crawford, to Kline's Mills. The advance that day was
given to Custer's division, and the march was long and weari-
some, the mud beginning to be troublesome. Devin's rear did
not get into camp till four in the morning. Next day, by
right, he should have had the advance, but work was growing
nearer now, and Sheridan told Custer to press on. Rosser's
men had come out during the day, and tried to burn a bridge
over one of the forks of the Shenandoah. Rosser had about
three hundred men. Colonel Capehart's brigade, of Custer's
division, came up in time, swam the river above the bridge,
charged Rosser, sent him flying, saved the bridge, and cleared
the way for their comrades. Kline's Mills are seven miles
from Staunton, where Early had his headquarters; and he, poor
fellow, seeing his rest so rudely disturbed, left Staunton and
went to Waynesboro', ten miles further on, leaving word at
Staunton that he was "coming back to fight." Now it was
that a man of rapid decision and fiery energy like Custer was
worth his weight in gold. A slower and more methodical man
would have utterly failed in the task set him next day. It
was to reach Waynesboro' seventeen miles off, in the midst of
a driving rainstorm, on a dirt road, mud up to the horses'
knees everywhere, and up to their bellies in the mud holes, to

18

cross a river of unknown depth, and to attack and whip Early who had an unknown force.

He did it with the triumphant success that always marked his independent efforts. He had three brigades, each about 1,500 strong, commanded by Colonels Wells, Pennington, and Capehart; and Devin was to follow with Gibbs', Fitzhugh's and Stagg's brigades, of Merritt's old division. Sheridan's record is brief and to the point. "General Custer found General Early as he had promised, at Waynesboro', in a well chosen position, with two brigades of infantry, and some cavalry under General Rosser, the infantry occupying breastworks. Custer, without waiting for the enemy to get up courage over the delay of a careful reconnoissance, made his dispositions for attack at once, sending three regiments around the left flank of the enemy, which was somewhat exposed by being advanced from, instead of resting upon, the bank of the river in his immediate rear; he, with the other two brigades, partly mounted and partly dismounted, at a given signal boldly attacked and impetuously carried the enemy's works, while the Eighth New York and First Connecticut cavalry, who were formed in columns of fours, charged over the breastworks, and continued the charge through the streets of Waynesboro', sabring a few men as they went along, and did not stop until they had crossed the South Fork of the Shenandoah, which was immediately in General Early's rear, where they formed as foragers, and with drawn sabres held the east bank of the stream. The enemy threw down their arms and surrendered, with cheers at the suddenness with which they were captured. The general officers present at this engagement were Generals Early, Rosser, Long, Wharton, and Lilley; and it has always been a wonder to me how they escaped, unless they hid in obscure places in the houses of the town." Custer pushed on after Early's trains, and did not halt until he got to the Blue Ridge.

The results of this capture, made by Custer, single-handed,

were eleven guns, complete with caissons, teams, etc., two hundred wagons, sixteen hundred prisoners, and seventeen battle-flags. He had fully balanced his account of rivalry with the First division, and passed it fairly. His loss was insignificant, owing entirely to the dash and rapidity of his fighting. That night he crossed the Blue Ridge and encamped on the other side, in full view of that mysterious land which had been a sealed book for the Federal army, the country where lay Charlottesville, Gordonsville, Columbia, the upper James, never visited since the short and hasty raid of Stoneman at the time of Chancellorsville, and then only hastily skimmed, in fear and trembling. Thanks to Custer, it was now open to our forces in every direction, with not an enemy nearer than Petersburg, and the end was coming fast.

Devin's division camped at Waynesboro' that night, and the cavalry corps was divided. The horses had been suffering fearfully from grease-heel and scratches, ever since they had left the pike and entered the mud roads. The great fatigue, the poor food, and finally the change from oats to corn, when they used up their first forage and lived off the country, was running them lame by fifties and hundreds. Only the toughest were able to march well enough to be trusted on a further raid through the mud of the low countries, and the next day's work to Charlottesville promised to be worse than the road to Waynesboro'. It was necessary to send back the Confederate prisoners and train to Winchester, and with that object a column of 1,500 men, under Colonel Thompson, First New Hampshire cavalry, was detached at Waynesboro', and ordered back to Winchester. Colonel Thompson went off, followed by Rosser, who made a fierce attack on him at Mount Jackson, thirty miles from Winchester, trying to rescue the prisoners. Rosser failed to do this; and lost instead some of his own men, whom Thompson took safely in with him.

The valley being tranquil, Sheridan resumed his march, Custer ahead as usual. The young general did not seem to like to give up the advance, rule or no rule, and Sheridan indulged him. Custer marched to Charlottesville, and was met outside the town by a polite deputation, headed by the Mayor, who brought him the keys of the public buildings. Here the whole command rested two days, till the train could be brought up, the roads being in horrible condition. The two divisions, now reduced to about eight thousand men, all told, enjoyed themselves hugely at Charlottesville, forage and food being plentiful. Parties were sent out to destroy the railroads, and did so in the most effectual manner, but the necessary delay caused Sheridan to abandon all idea of reaching Lynchburg.

On the 4th of March, the real business of the raid began. Merritt took the First division, went up the James River Canal to Scottsville, and returned to Columbia. Sheridan took Custer's division to Amherst Court House. Each column on its way destroyed every piece of public property likely to be of use to the enemy, blew up the locks of the canal, ruined it utterly, burned the flour mills and factories, and made a dash for the bridges at Dugaldsville and Hardwicksville. It was Sheridan's intention, had he saved the bridges, to have crossed the river, struck for Appomattox Court House, and so forced Lee to come out, and probably surrender, a month earlier than he afterwards did. But the bridges were burned before he could get there, and he was left complete master of all the country north of the James. He could no longer get at the enemy, nor could the latter get at him either. When the columns united at New-market, on the James River, Sheridan finally determined on his grand stroke of joining Grant. His plan involved marching down the north bank of the James, destroying the canal as he went.

Only one danger remained. The railroad from Richmond to Gordonsville remained open for some distance, and it was probable that Lee might send out a heavy force of infantry, to crush Sheridan. Custer and Devin were ordered to spread out in different directions, and cut this road as near Richmond as they could get. They accomplished the feat successfully, and Sheridan's scouts soon brought him news that showed him what he had escaped by not crossing the James. It turned out that Pickett's division of infantry and Fitzhugh Lee's cavalry were waiting for him on the Southside Railroad, but that no movement had been made from Richmond to the north.

When Custer struck the Gordonsville Railroad at Frederickshall, he came on some very agreeable intelligence in the telegraph office. It informed him that the irrepressible Early was not either dead or sleeping. The telegram was from Early to Lee, stating that he was following Sheridan with two hundred cavalry, and intended to strike him in rear about daylight. The news tickled Custer immensely. He at once dispatched a regiment after the unfortunate Early, caught and destroyed his party, and nearly took Early himself, the latter swimming the South Anna to escape, accompanied by a single orderly, after a campaign in which he lost all his army, every piece of artillery, and all his trains.

Through the country to the north of Richmond, Custer and Merritt now roamed at will for more than a week. On the 14th March, Custer's scouting parties burned a railway, within eleven miles of Richmond itself, while Merritt burned the bridges over the North and South Anna Rivers. By this time Sheridan's scouts had reached Grant, and returned with the welcome news that supplies awaited the cavalry at Whitehouse Landing on the Peninsula. The way there was open. Lee was at Petersburg, on the other side of the James, and could not send much force through to the north of Richmond, but what he had he sent. Another telegram was captured, dated at Hanover Junction. It was from Longstreet, addressed to a Colonel Haskell, presumably a cavalry officer hovering round Sheridan. It directed Haskell to " follow the enemy if he goes east," and to observe whether he struck for the Rapidan or the Peninsula. Next day Custer and Devin struck Ashland, to the northwest of Richmond, on the Gordonsville road. Prisoners taken reported Pickett's and Johnson's divisions of infantry, at least 12,000 men, with Fitzhugh Lee's cavalry division of 4,000 men, only four miles off, waiting to bag Sheridan, Longstreet in command. This was all Sheridan wanted to know. By his feints he had drawn the slow moving infantry far away from Whitehouse Landing, which is on the Pamunkey River, on the north side of the Peninsula. He pretended an attack with Pennington's brigade of Custer's division, and moved off towards the Whitehouse. Longstreet soon saw it was no use for him to follow with infantry, and Fitzhugh Lee did not dare, single handed, his force being so far inferior to Sheridan's. The latter took his time, reaching Whitehouse on the 19th March, to be welcomed by gunboats and supplies.

Longstreet returned to Lee. He knew how much he was wanted. The end was coming faster and faster. Sheridan rested at Whitehouse five days, feeding his horses on all the oats they could eat. Supplies were prodigal, and with reason. The government had saved nearly a month's subsistence for ten thousand men, and the Confederates had during the whole raid fed Sheridan's men on the fat of the land. On the 24th March, the refreshed column started, crossed the Peninsula, and reached the James, filed over the long pontoon bridge, and finally on the 26th, went into camp at the rear of Grant's army, which lay in front of Petersburg. The last raid was over, and Custer was coming to that brief and brilliant campaign which was to complete his glory, and leave him a full major-general at twenty-six years of age.

CHAPTER IV.

FIVE FORKS.

ON the 27th of March the cavalry corps went into camp behind the extreme left of Grant's Army of the Potomac, at Hancock Station. This station was the terminus of the military railroad, which ran from flank to flank of the besiegers, occupying, as they did, a line of nearly fifteen miles in length. There they had lain in front of Lee's lines at Petersburg for some nine weary months, in the monotony of siege operations, wherein incessant picket firing and equally incessant artillery duels by day, were alternated with pauses of sulky repose, after a more than common expenditure of ammunition. The only reliefs to the monotony had been found in the occasional attempts of the Federals to extend their left wing and turn Lee's right. These attempts had taken place at various intervals, the most desperate and successful having been made by the Second Corps, under the lead of Hancock. This cause led to the naming of the last station of the military railroad after that dashing corps commander.

So far Lee had succeeded in maintaining his main position intact, in spite of the inferior numbers with which he confronted Grant. His skillful use of fortifications made his lines impregnable, and he was able to hold them one against ten, with little difficulty or danger. Thus he could always spare for the threatened flank sufficient force to repel any assault and prevent the turning of his position. The country on that flank was for some distance much like the Wilderness he had found so favorable for defence—a desolate land of scrub woods, abandoned tobacco fields and dirt roads, where the defence and attack were alike depressing to the spirits, and where knowledge of the country was the one point of importance.

When Sheridan, with Custer's and Devin's divisions, went into camp at Hancock Station, he received an accession of force. The old Second Cavalry division, once Gregg's, was restored to its old comrades, this time under the command of General Crook. Poor Crook was, at the moment of joining, under a cloud. He had done very well in the Valley, under Sheridan's command, till late in the winter. Then, owing to inexcusable negligence, he was one night snapped up in his headquarters by a party of guerillas, carried off, and made a prisoner. At the close of the winter he was exchanged, and found himself at Petersburg, where he was given the command of this little division.

The curious and very unphilosophical grades of rank in the Federal army at that time, as contrasted with those of the Confederates, was illustrated by the number of major-generals in the cavalry corps. Sheridan, Crook, Merritt, and Custer, were all major-generals, the last two being brevets assigned. Devin and Gibbs were brigadiers. The assignment to command of each was curious. Sheridan seemed to have a sort of roving commission to go where he pleased, and Merritt was in the same interesting condition. Devin, Custer and Crook each had a division, though each held a different rank, the first a brigadier, the second a brevet major-general, the third a full major-general. Gibbs, although of the same rank as Devin, had only a brigade, and all the other brigade commanders under Custer and Devin were colonels. Crook's division was the only one that was properly and philosophically officered, having three brigadiers for the brigades, and a major-general for the division.

Apart from all these confusions of rank, the anomalous position of Merritt in the campaign, as well as that of Sheridan, was marked. Nominally Merritt had been commander of Custer and Devin, but inasmuch as both seemed to be able to take care of themselves, he really became very much like the fifth wheel on a caisson, only useful in case of accidents. Actually, he was most of the time occupied as a sort of dry nurse for Devin, who was a slow and cautious officer, new to the control of a division, and, in the mixed movements of the following campaign, very apt to get confused and miss opportunities. Devin was one of those safe, steady men who always like to keep their enemy straight in front, and who lose their heads if they find themselves surrounded. For a stubborn defence or straight ahead movement no one was better, but he always did best where he could see his whole battle-field. In the midst of such haphazard combinations as distinguished the campaign before Gettysburg, so long as Devin was united to the division to which his brigade was attached, he did splendidly; and under the fostering care of John Buford, who knew well how to develop his officers, the steady old colonel of volunteers, all guiltless of West Point as he was, became a first-rate brigade commander, who could be trusted out alone on his own responsibility.

For such a series of movements as distinguished the Five Forks campaign to Appomattox, Devin was too slow, and when compared to the brilliant keen-witted Custer, appeared to singular disadvantage, save at the battle of Five Forks, where his division had nothing to do but straight bull-dog fighting. He utterly lacked that keen instinct, which seemed inborn in Custer, that told him where an enemy might be safely pushed, and when the most reckless audacity would *pay*. While Devin was reconnoitring and getting ready to fight, Custer was already half through his battle; and before Devin was fairly engaged, on several occasions he found Custer had snatched away the prize from under his very nose, gaining glory, guns, and flags, with little comparative danger, while Devin was wondering what it was all about, and when the enemy were going to charge. The trouble was that Devin was old, and Custer

young. The quick wit of the latter made him invincible ; and
Merritt, who was paralyzed by the divided nature of his command, appeared to the same disadvantage as Devin. The result
of the whole campaign was that Custer was invariably triumphant. Everything he did succeeded, failure seemed unknown
to him, and the surrender at Appomattox left him with the
highest individual fame as a cavalry commander of any man except Sheridan. His name and figure, when only a division commander, were better known all through the Union, and attracted
more compliments from Confederates, than those of any corps
commander then in the Army of the Potomac, and we question
much whether at that time there was not far more curiosity to
see Custer than either Meade, Hancock, Burnside, or Hooker,
or indeed any one short of Grant, Sherman, and Sheridan.
Custer came right behind them in the popular favor, and enthusiasm ; and it was mainly owing to his series of brilliant
successes in this, his last campaign against a civilized foe.

Of course this fact (popular favor) attracted much envy to
Custer, and much detraction from him. Hardly a cavalry officer
outside of his own commands but was intensely jealous of him,
and detraction was ready to belittle all of his exploits. A great
deal of this was due to the boasting and sarcastic remarks of
his injudicious friends, who could not be satisfied with praising
their own chief without depreciating others. This caused a
good deal of bitter feeling at the time ; and, added to the fact
that part of Custer's success in the last campaign was due to
his perception of the demoralization of the enemy, gave rise to
many sneers at Custer's captures, which were ascribed by his
detractors to mere luck, without serious fighting. A cool and
candid examination of the evidence however, shows that " Custer's luck " was peculiar to Custer himself, and, coming to other
men, would have been lost. It consisted mainly in the quickness
with which he seized every opportunity as soon as it occurred, and
this quickness was entirely owing to the difference of his method
of directing a battle from that adopted by most general officers.

The prevalent custom among commanders, whether of companies, regiments, brigades, divisions, corps or armies, when their commands are in a battle, is to take post in rear of the centre of the line, whence they can see all or most of the line of battle of their own men, and be able to order in reserves to any threatened part of the line. For a defensive position this is well, and if an eminence can be secured for the commander, from which he can survey the field, so much the better. If the country is open and the enemy in plain sight from the commander's post, nothing better could be desired. The ideally perfect position for such a general would be up in a balloon, from whence he could see both armies spread out as on a chess board, and direct the operations of his own by telegraph. Unfortunately, no means has yet been found by which a balloon can be anchored at a great elevation, in any weather except a dead calm, and consequently the balloon plan has been abandoned, lofty hills being preferred. Some commanders, like McClellan at Antietam, take the highest ground in the neighborhood, no matter how far back it is, and trust to their glasses to tell them of the movements. This again, is only possible in an open country. In a heavily wooded place, such as the Wilderness or the vicinity of Five Forks, no chief, in rear of the centre of his line, can learn anything of what is going on, save by listening to the firing and requiring constant reports to be sent in from the skirmish line.

There is, however, another position, which may be taken by a leader in any country and which offers special advantages in a closely wooded one. This position was the one habitually taken by Custer. It was *up with the skirmish line itself, keeping in constant motion from end to end of the line*. This position has many advantages over the rear centre post. The general sees more, and knows by experience over what ground his men are going. He sees as much as any one can, for he is nearest to the enemy. If the latter falters or presses, he is on the spot, and gives suitable orders, *viva voce*, not through an aide-de-camp.

The only orders he needs to *send*, are those which go to the reserves in rear. Moreover, his constant presence is a great encouragement to the soldiers, who value kind words exactly in proportion to the rank of the person from whom they come. The general who shares their dangers they are ready to adore, after one or two battles, as Custer always found.

The objections to this position for a general are two. First, it is fatiguing, and uses up horses very fast. Second, the general may get shot. These risks Custer always took, along with Sheridan, Phil. Kearny, and one or two others in the army who followed the same plan. To be *always in the advance, and always in rapid motion*, was their secret. It showed them the opportunities, the moment they occurred. This was the secret, the real secret, of Custer's wonderful success in Sheridan's last campaign, and the difference between him and Devin. While the latter was watching his own line, Custer was watching that of the enemy. Who shall deny that his laurels were fairly won?

It was a fine sight to see Custer and his staff on the field, during that last campaign. The appearance of the leader had slightly changed, since he was brevetted major-general. The old blue shirt, with its star in the corner, remained, but the velvet jacket was replaced by a blue sack with major-general's shoulder straps, and his trousers were now of the regulation sky-blue. The cavalier hat, long curls, and flaunting red necktie, were as conspicuous as ever, and every man in the division had apparently mounted the same insignia, with an attempt to imitate the careless grace of their leader. There were more shocks of long, shaggy, unkempt hair in the Third Division than anywhere else in the army. As for neckties, Custer's division could be recognized a mile off, by its fluttering, scarlet handkerchiefs, and they were to be met with all over the country.

With his forces under this leadership, Sheridan left camp on the 29th of March, starting out to the extreme left of the army. It was Grant's first intention that the cavalry should only make a raid in Lee's rear, cut the Southside Railway, and, after ravaging the country, join Sherman's force. It was expected that this raid would be a long and weary one, and Sheridan weeded his force of all weak and broken down horses and dismounted men, who were left at Petersburg. It will give some idea of how tremendously severe the last raid through the mud had been on Sheridan's horses, to note the numbers he now took with him. The First and Third divisions had started from Winchester, a month before, 9484 strong. They had been weeded of 1500 men at Waynesboro, leaving about 8000 men; and now all they could muster was 5700 men, all told, fit for a march. To this 5700 was added Crook's 3300 men, and at a later date McKenzie's skeleton cavalry division from the Army of the James, 1000 strong. This made Sheridan's total cavalry force 10,000 men, and to his command was subsequently added the Fifth Corps. Sheridan was no longer attached to the Army of the Potomac. He took his orders direct from Grant, without the interposition of Meade, and the fact of his having been made a major-general in the regular army made him senior to every one but Meade. Grant gave him a sort of general command over the left wing of the Army of the Potomac during the subsequent operations.

On the 29th March, the cavalry moved out of the lines, striking off to the southwest. The first night they crossed Hatcher's Run, and moved on in the direction of Dinwiddie Court House, which was reached by Devin, who had the advance, about 5 o'clock. Devin and Crook went into camp there. Custer was left behind at Hatcher's Run (called Rowanty Creek there, having been joined by Gravelly Run). It had begun to rain, the roads were horrible, the creek was only bridged by pontoons, and it was supposed that Fitzhugh Lee's cavalry was off to the south, ready to pounce on Sheridan's trains if he saw an opportunity. It turned out that this was an error. The Confederate cavalry was really to the north, inside of Lee's lines, on the very right of his army. Sheridan, by his rapid

march, had left a gap of about ten miles between himself and
the head of the Union column of infantry. This was composed
of the Fifth Corps, near Custer, and the Second Corps next
behind it.

For a clear understanding of what follows, a rough formu-
lated diagram of the country, showing the general direction of
points of subsequent importance, will be found of use. It is
taken from General Warren's sketch, annexed to his subsequent
vindication of himself. [See map, end of chapter.]

In this sketch the curves are roughly indicated, but it will
show the directions in straight lines, with sufficient accuracy.

On the morning of the 30th of March,* Sheridan sent
Devin, together with Davies' brigade of Crook's force, from
Dinwiddie, due north, to gain Five Forks, on the White Oak
road. Sheridan himself remained behind, to help out Custer
and the trains, a job which was not over at dark of the 30th.
Devin came to Five Forks, and found the enemy in such force
that he could not dislodge him. It rained all day, and Devin's
pickets were fighting all the time, but made no impression.

The position on the morning of the 31st was this. [See map.]
Sheridan was at Dinwiddie, about seven miles from the head
of the infantry, over roads so muddy that the distance must be
doubled to give an idea of the time necessary for help to reach
him. Grant's column was curling round Lee's left, but the latter
saw an opportunity for a brilliant stroke. It was to send down
a heavy force by the White Oak road to Five Forks, smash
Devin, roll him back on Sheridan, and crush the latter, separating him from Grant by entering the gap between them. To
do this, Lee detached Pickett's division, part of Johnson's, and
all the Confederate Cavalry. The whole force was about

---

* During the night of the 29th March, Grant changed his mind as to
Sheridan's ultimate disposition, and sent him word to that effect. He had
passed the flank of Lee's army. Instead of sending him off to ravage the
country and join Sherman, Grant now ordered him to turn on Lee's right
flank. This order was the one that sent Devin to Five Forks, and determined
the issue of the campaign.

11,000 men. The only trouble was, Lee did it too late. Had he struck Devin and Sheridan on the 30th, the Fifth Corps was still out of supporting distance. On the evening of the 31st, it was within five miles of Sheridan.

He tried it on the 31st, in the style in which Lee always delivered his attacks. It was carefully and secretly prepared, and executed about two in the afternoon. Striking Devin, whose total force did not exceed four thousand men, of which one-fourth were horse-holders, the fighting being dismounted, the Confederates drove him out of the woods into the road to Dinwiddie, with crushing force. They formed a perfect horseshoe of fire around the little division, and resistance was useless. It was made, however, with that savage obstinacy peculiar to dismounted cavalry, covering the retreat of their horses. The men held on till the beasts were out of danger, rallied and charged again and again, and finally emerged in the fields, repulsed but not conquered, having saved every horse and gun, and without the loss of a prisoner.

This was the last brilliant move Lee's army, or any portion of it, ever made. This dashing corps of eleven thousand men, starting from the White Oak road, first drove back the head of the Fifth Corps, then swung over and beat Devin, followed him down the road and charged Crook, and was only brought to a final halt in front of Dinwiddie Court House, by the rest of the cavalry corps, deployed in the open fields, dismounted. Devin's division was separated from the rest. Custer brought up two brigades from the belated train, and with three others managed to hold the victorious foe till night, when Pickett rested on his arms in front of Dinwiddie Court House.

Such was the position at nightfall of the 31st. Sheridan was isolated, and Pickett was in front of him, but a glance at the diagram will show that Pickett was also isolated from Lee, and that Warren, with the Fifth Corps, was right behind Pickett. All Warren had to do was to move down the Boydton plank road, to strike the enemy directly in the rear.

Sheridan saw this plainly enough, and sent another officer to Warren, telling him to " attack Pickett at daylight." It appears, from General Warren's "Narrative," that Sheridan misconceived Warren's position, imagining that he was about two miles nearer to Five Forks than he really was. Actually, the bulk of the Fifth corps was nearly six miles off, but Warren's headquarters were only four miles from Sheridan's, on the Boydton plank road. We have been careful to take, in regard to the subsequent battle, the exact statements of fact of General Warren as true, and it seems quite clear that the difficulty which ensued between the two generals was one of temperament wholly. Warren was a cool, cautious, methodical man, whose training as an engineer had assisted to make him, like McClellan, careful and painstaking. He did his very best, but his temperament rendered it an absolute impossibility for Warren to do anything in a hurry. Sheridan, on the other hand, was rapid and impetuous, and his contact with such a totally dissimilar character as Warren was sure to bring difficulty, unless indeed the latter, like Devin, was willing to obey orders blindly, no matter what the consequences to himself. This, however, was just what Warren's character again rendered him incapable of doing. Being a polished and perfectly educated soldier, who had graduated high at West Point, he set a value on his own notion of how a thing should be done, and this is very evident in his "Narrative." When Sheridan asked him to hurry, he replied in effect that he was doing the best he could ; he differed in opinion from Sheridan as to the proper place of a general on the battle-field ; and whenever the opinions of the two came in conflict, as they did on almost every point of real importance, Warren stuck to his own opinion, and tacitly implied that he was going to do as he pleased. This fact develops itself in his subsequent " Narrative," in one very important point, on which we have already touched in speaking of the difference between Custer and Devin.

Sheridan's idea of the proper place of a general was *at the front, in rapid motion,* where he could see for himself. Warren's idea was that of *rear of the centre, and out of fire.* He justifies it in the following sentence in his narrative. " While giving orders thus, I did not think it proper to leave my place in the open field, because it was one where my staff officers, sent to different parts of the command, could immediately find me on their return, and thus I could get information from all points at once, and utilize the many eyes of my staff and those of my subordinate commanders, instead of going to some special point myself, and neglecting all others."

This sentence shows the radical difference between the two men. It was a clash of wills, and Warren would not yield. Sheridan sent word to him, that night, where the cavalry was, and where the enemy was; also that he, Warren, was behind the enemy. He concluded, " I will hold on here. Possibly they may attack Custer at daylight: if so, attack instantly, and in full force. Attack at daylight anyhow."

He pointed out that by so doing Sheridan and Warren could bag the whole of Pickett's isolated force. The message reached Warren at 4.50 A. M. April 1st; too late for obedience. The Fifth Corps could not get to Sheridan by daylight, as the nearest brigade was four miles off, and the sun rose at six. It seems too, that although Sheridan knew Warren was under his orders, Warren did *not.* It was not till an hour and a half after receipt of Sheridan's order that Warren received one from Meade, the immediate commander of the Army of the Potomac, directing him " to report to Sheridan."

As it happened, no harm was done. Pickett was just as astute as Sheridan. He saw his danger, and quietly left in the morning, falling back to Five Forks, where he held a line of breastworks to the north of the White Oak road; and there the cavalry followed him. The position was some three miles to the north of Dinwiddie, and about three miles and a half to the west of Warren. The latter did not join Sheridan, under his orders, *till eleven o'clock.* One can fancy how this must

19

have irritated the impatient cavalry leader. His men had been out since six o'clock, pushing Pickett back to Five Forks, and here was Pickett before him, separated by a gap of about five miles from Lee's army, while Warren, with 15,000 men, ready to occupy that gap, was letting the precious moments slip. It seemed almost impossible that Pickett could be fool enough to stay where he was, to be trapped; and it was much more reasonable to suppose, from his obstinate attitude, that Lee was bringing up more forces behind, to serve Sheridan as he had served Devin. In such a case, an ugly and disheartening check to the Army of the Potomac, such as had happened so often before, was pretty certain.

When at last Warren was up, Sheridan did not hurry him unduly. McKenzie's little division reported to the general at the same time, coming down the White Oak road, and brought the news that the country in that direction was clear, so that it was settled that the gap between Lee and Pickett really existed. Sheridan sent back McKenzie to Dinwiddie as a reserve, and to guard the trains, while Custer and Devin, under Merritt's orders, proceeded to assault the works at Five Forks, threatening especially to turn the right flank of the enemy. Not till one o'clock did Sheridan deem the attack sufficiently serious to hold the enemy; then he sent word to Warren to bring up his infantry, which was lying about half a mile from the works. It was ordered to advance in the following order:

Ayres and Crawford's divisions in the first line, and Griffin's behind Crawford, were to strike the left of Pickett's line, and sweep down behind the breastworks, while Custer and Devin were to charge home in front. Crook was not engaged. It must be remembered that Custer and Devin, with only 5,700 men, had been fighting and driving the enemy all the morning, and that the Fifth Corps had not yet struck a blow that day. Imagine then, the impatience with which Sheridan saw Warren bringing up his corps of 15,000 men, the order given at *one* o'clock, and he not ready till *four*. Three whole hours consumed in putting a single corps, already massed, into line of battle, were more than enough, and we can see the sarcasm of the remark which Sheridan made to him, as Warren reports in the "Narrative." "General Sheridan expressed to me his apprehension that our cavalry, which continued to fire on the enemy, *would use up all their ammunition before my troops would be ready.* I informed him that they would not all be in position before four P. M."

Here the difference of the two men was again manifest. Sheridan was all hurry, with no such word as "impossible"; Warren, with a constitutional inability to hurry, was finding so many things impossible.

At last, however, Warren was ready, and advanced. After that he had no more trouble. With a simultaneous charge, Pickett's men and Wise's brigade were swept out of existence as an organized body, and Five Forks was won. As soon as Warren entered the fight, Sheridan at once possessed twenty thousand men to Pickett's ten, and the surrender of the Confederate infantry was a foregone conclusion. When the Fifth Corps charged, Custer and Devin followed suit, swept over the breastworks, and captured all the guns and battleflags in the works. Pickett was no longer a division commander.

No sooner was the fight fairly over, than Sheridan sent a curt note to Warren.

"*Major-General Warren, commanding the Fifth Army Corps, is relieved from duty, and will report at once for orders to Lieutenant General Grant, commanding armies United States.*"

It came like a thunderbolt to Warren. He had evidently not expected it. He, even in his "Narrative," seems to be seriously impressed with the idea that the victory at Five Forks was owing to *his* exertions, and that he had done his whole duty, for which he should have been praised. He complains, in this "Narrative," of the peculiar hardship and injustice of relieving him, at the very moment when he had done his work and was triumphantly successful. After a careful examination and comparison of his account with that of Sheridan, the conduct of the latter is easy to explain. Sheridan was above all things a practical soldier, with little solicitude for any one's feelings, in a matter where success was involved. When he found, as he early did, that he and Warren could not pull together, there is little doubt that he determined to relieve him, as he had the power to do. But to have relieved Warren from command at the *commencement* of a movement like this—an assault in force—would have been very perilous. Had he been suddenly removed, it would have involved a change of leaders, all through the corps, unfamiliar officers, and a prospect of failure, with a perfect certainty of delay, even greater than Warren caused. Through Sheridan's own activity in reaching Dinwiddie Court House in a single day, he had gained time on the enemy, and Lee's hesitation to abandon Petersburg had given him more. It was clear that the cavalry could hold Pickett stationary till night, and a single hour was time enough to consummate the victory of Five Forks, once the combined attack was made. Sheridan weighed his chances and calculated that he would have just about enough time, even if he gave Warren his own way, which he did. Success attained, he had no further need to keep Warren, and every reason to get rid of him. In the further prosecution of the campaign, activity and hearty coöperation were absolutely necessary, and neither of these was to be looked for from Warren. Sheridan wanted a man who would obey orders, not dispute them, and Warren's weakness lay in the latter direction. By the sudden exercise of arbitrary power, there is no doubt that Sheridan made a bitter enemy of Warren, and excited much ill-feeling in the whole Fifth Corps, but the practical success of the future movements in pursuit justified him to the country. Rightly considered, the relief of Warren was no discredit to that officer, as a soldier employed in scientific warfare. He was as good a commander as he had ever been, but in the pursuit of Lee, scientific warfare was not needed so much as unremitting activity. The enemy had little or no force left to fight in open country; the only difficulty was *to catch him.* Warren was an engineer, Sheridan a huntsman, and the latter needed more huntsmen, not engineers. The best proof that Warren's relief was not regarded by Grant as an indication of incapacity, was afforded by Warren's almost immediate assignment to the command of the Department of the Mississippi. He was as good as ever for any purpose, except the one for which Sheridan needed him, that was all.

We have been somewhat lengthy in our account of the difficulty between Warren and Sheridan at Five Forks, because it is essential to the complete understanding of the campaign in which Custer bore so important a part. Another thing must be taken into account in estimating the subsequent operations, to explain the difference between the cavalry and infantry.

When Sheridan arrived at Petersburg, he came from a campaign in the open field, wherein intrenchments had played no part. He was used to activity, as were his cavalry. He found the Army of the Potomac enfeebled by a long siege, of which the effects are well known. They disincline men to long marches and active exertions. What was a mere bagatelle to Sheridan's riders, was a terribly long march to the infantry, fresh from winter quarters, out of condition and heavily loaded as they were. Infantry generals are so much used to being hampered by the exhaustion of their men, that they are apt to sink down and pronounce a long march "impossible," especially at the beginning of a campaign. It needed all the fiery energy of Sheridan and the example of the cavalry to nerve the infantry up to their work. They would fight as well as ever, but had got out of the habit of marching; and it was marching that was now needed. Moreover, so used was the whole army to encountering a foe rendered formidable by fortifications, and always ready to fight, that it was not dreamed of by any, till some days after, that Lee was on his way to surrender. Besides

Grant, Sheridan seems to have been the only man who had the idea, and it was he who suggested it to Grant, in his laconic dispatch, "I think, if things are pushed, Lee will surrender." The still more laconic reply of Grant is equally well known— "Push things." Sheridan *did* push them, and his right arm was Custer.

The present chapter, while part of the life of Custer, has unavoidably wandered away from him to the principal actors in the battle of Five Forks. Custer's division had not had the advance on the march to Dinwiddie, and the difficulties with road and train had kept it back to Rowanty Creek, all of the thirtieth of March, and till evening of the thirty-first. Even then, only two of Custer's brigades were able to get up to help Crook's two brigades and one of Devin's, and it was these five brigades that held Pickett's entire force that evening. In the morning of the first of April, Custer and Devin did all the fighting in advance, Crook being held in reserve. Custer's division held the extreme left of the line, threatening Pickett's right. The fighting was dismounted, and quite severe, the cavalry driving back the enemy from two lines of defence to the last breastwork at Five Forks. Here they stopped, a lull taking place in the fight at noon, till one o'clock, when the assault was resumed and seriously pressed.

The dismounted lines of skirmishers never dreamed but what it was their duty to carry the works unassisted, and with that notion, savage over the reverses of the day previous, they made two desperate charges over the tangled brushwood, piled in front of the works, right in the teeth of the rebel infantry. The heaviest fire fell on Devin, who occupied the centre, but Custer's men, by their audacity in trying to turn Pickett's flank, suffered nearly as heavily. It was their bitter and determined assaults that caused Sheridan's sarcastic remark to Warren about the ammunition. When at last the rolling volleys of the Fifth Corps, to the right of the enemy, showed they were really at work, the excitement of the cavalry rose once more.

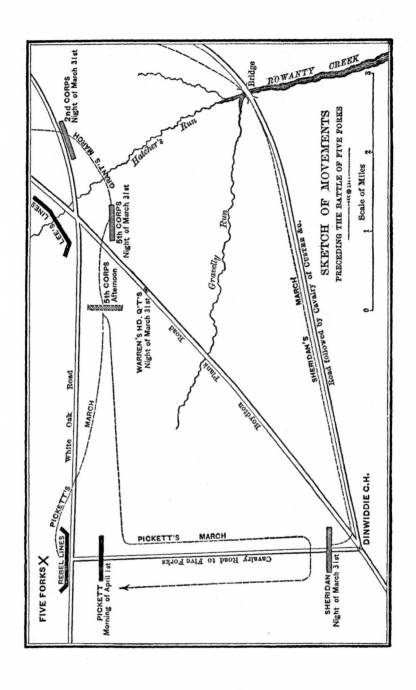

Twice they had been repulsed before the fearful fire from the works, but now they rose again. Their eagerness was changed to a perfect frenzy, a moment later, when Sheridan himself, with his battle flag behind him, and all his staff, came galloping down the line, through a storm of bullets, waving his sword and pointing onwards. In a moment, every brigade commander caught the impulse and dashed forward, while Custer, his red necktie and golden curls shining like a star, galloped out in front of his line, and rode right at the breastwork. Such a yell was never heard as then burst from the whole line of men, as they swept forward. The volleys of the enemy were answered by a perfect hell fire from the carbines, and the works were taken with a rush.

What a spectacle presented itself then! A crowd of fleeing men in grey, running wildly and confusedly together from side to side, while a long line of fire and smoke was coming through the woods from the right, sweeping away the hapless Confederates.

Only for a moment that sight was seen, and the next the grey-coated crowds were throwing down their arms and waving their handkerchiefs, or any thing white, in token of surrender.

The battle was over, the Confederate infantry annihilated. What was left of the cavalry made its escape to the left of Custer, and struck off to the west, followed by McKenzie's and Custer's men, for about six miles, after dark.

The last fight had been fought. The pursuit was now to begin, and Custer had the advance.

CHAPTER V.

APPOMATTOX.

THE night of the 1st of April was passed in serious work, and events were still in a doubtful condition. Lee's main army, of unknown strength, was still intact, and Pickett's defeat was after all only the capture of a detachment. Sheridan was on Lee's flank, with 25,000 men, including cavalry and Fifth Corps, but they were facing *west*, while Lee's main force was at Petersburg, to the *northeast*, and probably not more than five miles off. Obviously, it was still possible for Lee to crush Sheridan in the morning, if he turned on him with all his force. Sheridan perceived this so clearly that he at once sent back two divisions of the Fifth Corps to open connection with the Second, and to face toward Petersburg. They found the advance of the Second Corps before they had gone two miles on the White Oak road. That night, the sound of heavy guns was incessant from Petersburg, all night long, and at 4 A. M. increased to a tempest. At daybreak, came the news that Wright, with the Sixth Corps, had assaulted Lee's lines in front, found them to be weakly guarded, that Petersburg was taken, and that Lee had evacuated all his positions, and was moving away to the open country, in the hope of joining Johnston for an offensive campaign.

On the morning of the 2d of April, the pursuit began. The cavalry pushed on to the westward, and reached Ford Station, on the railroad from Petersburg to Lynchburg. In order to understand the further movements of the pursuit, a clear idea of the country is necessary.

Previous to the battle of Five Forks, Lee's lines were nearly north and south, running between Petersburg and Richmond, a distance of nearly twenty miles. His army was now concentrated and moving west. There were two railroads crossing the country he was in. One ran from Richmond, southwest to Danville, North Carolina, known as the "Danville road." The other ran from Petersburg, nearly due west, to Lynchburg. These roads crossed each other at Burke's Station, some forty miles west of Petersburg. Lee's first plan was to move on the Danville road, so as to get to North Carolina and join Johnston. The way to block his game was for the cavalry and Fifth Corps to push for Burkesville, throw themselves in his way, entrench, and fight, to give time for the rest of the army to come up and take Lee in rear. On the 2d of April, Custer, in advance, reached Ford Station, about half-way to Burke's Station, on the Lynchburg road. On the 3d, the Union cavalry pursued its march. Nothing was met but Fitzhugh Lee's cavalry, which gave way wherever struck. Lee's main army was pressing on in a parallel line, some six or seven miles north, toward Amelia Court House, on the Danville road. This place is about ten miles northeast of Burke's; Custer and Devin pursued the road to Burke's, but Crook and McKenzie were sent out towards Amelia Court House, along with the Fifth Corps, and soon found the enemy's infantry and trains. Lee was come to the turn of his fortune. He was encumbered by an enormous train, full of all that accumulation of rubbish that marks the exit of troops from winter quarters. He had been compelled to leave in such a hurry that this train was perfectly unmanageable, and entirely unfit to go on campaign. Grant was able to move out with only the pick of his troops and trains, leaving the rest in safety at his lines before Petersburg. Lee had to take everything, good and bad, or leave it to be captured.

The result was quickly visible to the cavalry and Fifth Corps. The enemy was completely demoralized. Prisoners

dropped in by dozens, fifties and hundreds, giving themselves
up without resistance, wagons were found abandoned, and—
surest sign of all—guns, limbers, and caissons *full of ammunition*, were found all along the road. Custer pushed on, and by
the evening of the fourth, cavalry and Fifth Corps had struck
the Danville Road, and interposed, at a village called Jetersville, between Lee and Burke's Junction. Sheridan arrived at
Jetersville at dusk, and learned without doubt that Lee was at
Amelia Court House, hardly five miles off. The Second Corps
was moving right in Lee's rear, and the Sixth Corps was coming up between the Fifth and Second.

That night was Lee's last chance. It was a desperate one
at best; but the Lee of Chancellorsville, who had Stonewall
Jackson to back him, would have seized it. The chance was to
march down on Sheridan with all his force, and crush him out
of the way, then go ahead to Danville. This Lee feared to do.
He was still encumbered with his long train, and the worst
part of his position was, that the train *carried no rations.* His
army was already short of food. Sheridan that very night in-
tercepted a despatch from the sorely tried Confederate general
to the commissaries at Danville and Lynchburg, ordering
200,000 rations to be sent to Burkesville. They never reached
there. Next morning Lee, finding his road to Burkesville
barred, stretched out for Lynchburg, directly across country,
hoping to strike the railroad at Appomottax Court House, forty
miles from Amelia.

Sheridan had first curled around Lee's right at Five Forks,
compelling him to fall back. Now he had again curled round,
blocked his *southern* road, and left his only way open to the
west. Very soon he was to bar even *that* way.

During the fifth of April, the cavalry and Fifth Corps lay
quiet at Jetersville. Crook was sent out on the left, to the
northwest, to find what the enemy was doing. Davies' brigade
of his division struck a wagon train, going west towards Appomattox, by way of Deatonsville. It was guarded by cavalry.

Davies took the train and five guns. In the afternoon, Lee came down and attacked Jetersville, but without vigor. His old pluck was gone. He simply desired to gain time by the demonstrations, to get his trains off. The road to the west was still free. Had Sheridan staid at Jetersville, Lee might have got off yet.

That evening, the rest of the army came up from Petersburg and the Fifth Corps was taken from Sheridan, to be replaced by the old Sixth, with which he had fought in the valley. This was done at Meade's request, as we are informed in Sheridan's report.

On the morning of the 6th of April, the Second, Fifth and Sixth Corps struck north towards Amelia Court House, only to find that Lee had gone, and was already past Deatonsville, and near Farmville, on the road to Appomattox.

Away went the cavalry after him, Crook leading, Custer and Devin following. It was only five miles to Deatonsville; and there, in the bright spring morning, the whole Confederate army was to be seen, its trains stretching for miles and miles, trying to escape. Close to Deatonsville ran the little stream known as Sailor's Creek, which gave its name to the fight that followed. Now was the time to catch Lee's trains, and capture at least his rear guard. If the whole Confederate army stopped to fight, so much the better. The Union infantry was moving off towards Amelia Court House, but a dispatch reaching it, the direction of the columns was speedily changed, and it only remained for Sheridan's cavalry to hold Lee long enough for the infantry to catch up.

Sheridan's method of action was very simple, as he records it in his report. " Crook was at once ordered to attack the trains, and if the enemy was too strong, one of the divisions would pass him, while he held fast and pressed the enemy, and attack at a point farther on, and this division was ordered to do the same, and so on, alternating, and this system of attack would enable us finally to strike some weak point. This result was obtained just south of Sailor's Creek, and on the high ground over that stream. Custer took the road, and Crook and Devin coming up to his support, sixteen pieces of artillery were captured, and about four hundred wagons were destroyed, while three divisions of the enemy's infantry were cut off from their line of retreat."

The description that follows of the part taken by Custer's division in this fight is taken from the account of one of Custer's staff officers. It is so picturesque and life-like as to be worth full quotation:

Early on the morning above mentioned our command was watering and massing, when a staff officer from General Wesley Merritt, then commanding the cavalry corps, came with orders directing General Custer to move forward at once with his command and attack the enemy's wagon train at a certain point which he, the staff officer, would designate. General Custer, turning to his staff, selected me to convey the order to cease watering the command and direct the different brigade commanders to forward their commands at a trot. When I reached the road again, after having delivered the order, I found General Custer at the head of his column, returning. I learned from him afterward that he had gone forward, as directed, but did not like the position designated as the attacking point, and seeing in the distance a position, in his opinion, more desirable, he rode forward just in time to meet the Confederates placing a battery of nine guns in position. He immediately charged the battery, capturing the nine guns before they could be placed in position, and with the guns he took 800 prisoners. Still charging, a mile beyond, he cut the enemy's wagon train, capturing and destroying nearly 1,000 wagons. Returning he took up his position in a sort of a ravine. Here he re-formed his command for the very active work that was to follow. Just over the brow of the hill the enemy had thrown up earthworks behind which was stationed the Confederate General Kershaw, one of the best generals commanding the finest division of the Confederate army. All day, until dark, General Custer was charging these works, always retreating to and re-forming his command in the ravine first selected. He knew they must give way sooner or later, as the Sixth Corps were doing excellent execution just beyond and would soon have their flank turned. About five o'clock in the afternoon

I rode out toward our battery, which had been in position all day shelling the enemy. My attention was attracted to a large batch of prisoners off to the left of our position, and, my curiosity being somewhat excited, I rode out to the guard for the purpose of inquiring whether there were any distinguished officers among the captives. But a short distance from me, mounted on a thorough-bred mare, I saw what I at once knew to be a rebel officer of distinguished rank. In a moment his eye caught mine, and he beckoned me to come within the enclosure, as he desired to talk with me. I did so, and the following conversation ensued :—

"Are you not one of General Custer's staff?"

"I am, sir; a surgeon, however."

"Sir, I desire to surrender my sword to General Custer. A non-commissioned officer is continually demanding it, but I consider that I have the right to request the privilege of surrendering it to a commissioned officer."

"Whom have I the honor of addressing?" I asked.

"My name," said he, "is Kershaw—General Kershaw, sir."

"General," I said, "I am glad to meet you. I assure you, sir, we always had great respect for you and your command when you confronted us in the valley."

"I look upon General Custer as one of the best cavalry officers that this or any other country ever produced. I shall, indeed, consider it an honor to surrender my sword to him." He continued, "Ever since the battle of Cedar Creek, when he and General Sheridan embraced each other after the battle, I have had a most perfect admiration for the man. I read a full account of it in the New York Herald some days after the engagement. All through to-day's battle I directed my men to concentrate their fire upon his headquarters flag, knowing he was there always at the front. While I should have deprecated the idea of killing a man so brave, good and efficient, yet I knew it was my only hope."

"General," I said, "you merely succeeded in killing his best horse. Now, if you will accompany me outside the guard, I will take you over to Woodruff's Battery, and leave you in charge of its commanding officer, while I communicate your desires to General Custer."

In company with two or three other rebel generals of minor importance, he followed me. As General Custer was then making another charge, I awaited the result. It was the last and proved to be the grandest success of the day, as the balance of the enemy's command surrendered.

The capture of the day was upward of 7,000 prisoners, thirty-seven battleflags, and a large number of guns. The Third Cavalry division at no time during the day had more than 600 engaged against the enemy. As General Custer was returning from the charge with his prisoners, battleflags, etc., I rode forward and met him. After congratulating him, I communicated the desires of General Kershaw. The general seemed very much pleased, and rather accelerated his movement in direction of the battery. In presenting his sword General Kershaw was exceedingly complimentary in his remarks. After the surrender General Kershaw and friends, by invitation, spent the night with Custer and his staff, and in the morning they were sent to the rear with the rest of the prisoners.

This account gives a very fair idea of Sailor's Creek. Custer was its grandest figure. Crook struck the enemy first, and then Devin, but neither could make an impression, and did not demonstrate seriously. Custer passed Devin, and took up the first real attack, charging again and again, mounted.* All the while, the infantry was coming up. When Custer was hotly engaged, Devin was withdrawn, and sent on still further, but only one of his brigades charged mounted. This was Stagg's Michiganders, Custer's old brigade. As Devin left, the Sixth Corps came up. Succor had been delayed a long time by Meade's withdrawal of the Fifth Corps. In the morning, the Second, Fifth and Sixth Corps had started to the north, the Second nearest Sheridan, the Fifth next, the Sixth furthest of all. Instead of ordering in the Second to help Sheridan, Meade trans-

* It was in one of these desperate charges that Tom Custer, the general's brother, took with his own hand, his second flag within ten days. Tom had been a private soldier in an Ohio infantry regiment, in which he enlisted at the age of sixteen. The general procured him a commission in the Michigan cavalry in the winter of 1864, and put Tom on his staff, where he was serving at Sailor's Creek. In the charge Tom leaped the breastworks, seized the flag, and at the same moment was shot by the color-bearer, the bullet entering his cheek and going right through out of the back of his neck. Nothing daunted, Tom shot the color-bearer, took the flag and got back safely, when the doctor ordered him to the rear. His previous flag was taken at Namozin Church.

ferred the Sixth all the way over from right to left, thus losing valuable time, according to his own report. When it came into action however, as with the Fifth at Five Forks, it finished the battle in a very short time. Humphreys, with the Second Corps, also joined in, at a further point to the north, on his own responsibility. All through the campaign indeed, he seems to have acted with more energy, without orders, than any of the corps commanders.

When Humphreys came up, Lee's rear guard was surrounded. One of Stagg's Michigan men, in the last charge, went right over the Confederate breastworks, and dashed through their whole line, reaching Sheridan, who was on the other side, hurrying up the infantry.*

General Ewell and all his corps were taken bodily, and so ended the battle of Sailor's Creek. Sheridan says, " I have never ascertained exactly how many prisoners were taken in this battle. Most of them fell into the hands of the cavalry, but they are no more entitled to claim them than the Sixth Corps, to which command equal credit is due for the good results of this engagement."

That night, nearly the whole of the old Army of the Valley encamped together by Sailor's Creek. Sheridan, Merritt, Custer, Devin, Crook, and Wright, were all there, and their old success had attended them.

Next morning, away went the cavalry again, after Lee, Crook in advance. By this time, another corps had come up, Ord, with the little Army of the James, once Butler's command. Sheridan, still thinking Lee was as bold as ever, and knowing well that the Confederate leader's objective point must be Danville, if he hoped to join Johnston, imagined that he would cross the Lynchburg railroad, and move south through the open country.

In the morning of the 7th April, therefore, he sent Custer

Sheridan's Report. This incident would seem almost incredible did not Sheridan personally vouch for it.

and Devin off, under Merritt's command, to the southwest, away from the railroad, to Prince Edward Court House. Crook was pushed directly after Lee, in the direction of Farmville, which lies due north of Prince Edward Court House, and some seven miles therefrom.

It turned out that Sheridan had overrated Lee's boldness, and still more his supplies. The Confederate leader was only intent on his western road to Appomattox, where, at last, provisions awaited him. Crook struck him at Farmville, and attacked him with his division, but it proved too weak to capture the whole rebel army, and was driven back, badly punished, General Gregg, one of the brigade commanders, being taken prisoner. As it happened, he was only held for a couple of days.

Devin and Custer arrived at Prince Edward Court House, to find the country deserted.

The part taken by Custer shall be told by Custer's surgeon, already quoted.

Nothing of importance in the way of an engagement occurred until the afternoon of the 8th. Among the prisoners captured was one who seemed to be well posted and desired to give information. From him the general learned that the enemy were loading four trains of cars at Appomattox station with artillery, ammunition, etc. Just as we had learned these facts a staff officer came from General Merritt directing General Custer to halt, mass his command and rest. By the same staff officer General Custer sent his compliments and requested him to state to General Merritt what he had heard from this prisoner, and say to General Merritt that " unless I get further orders from him I shall continue my march and capture those trains of cars." Immediately after the departure of General Merritt's staff officer General Custer despatched two of his own staff officers to reconnoitre. They quickly returned, reporting everything as the prisoner had stated. We were now only two miles away from the station. General Custer directed two regiments of the division to move forward at a trot as advance guard. The balance of the command followed at the same gait. The advance had orders to charge the station the moment they

20

came in sight of it and capture the trains. As we were nearing the station, and surely not a mile away, an exciting incident occurred which I must stop a moment to relate, as it helps to illustrate the noble character of the man of whom I am writing. Two young ladies came running, screaming, down the walk leading to the road, from a large and elegant mansion.

"They are robbing us!" "They are robbing and trying to murder us!" they screamed with all their might. General Custer without saying a word, stopped short, and, quickly dismounting, ran up the walk just in time to catch a man in United States uniform running from the front door. With his fist he almost annihilated the miserable scalawag. Then, running through the house, he caught another making his exit from the rear door. Catching up an axe, he threw it, hitting the brute in the back of his head, thus quickly disposing of the two wretches. In a moment he was in his saddle again, and after hurriedly directing Captain Lee, the provost marshal, to place a guard on the premises, he charged down the road at terrific speed, capturing the four trains in less than five minutes after this event. Now commenced a brisk cannonading from some rebel guns near the station. General Custer, through colored prisoners, learned of their position, and, although he was advised by one of his brigade commanders and other officers not to attempt their capture that night, he at once dismounted his command, as he was obliged to go through the woods and heavy undergrowth, and caught up his headquarters flag, saying, "I go; who will follow," and the result was that, after hard fighting, some thirty guns were brought in by hand that night. The next morning General Lee surrendered. The flag of truce— a towel on a pole—was brought to the command of General George A. Custer, and to him the desire of General Lee to surrender was first communicated. The towel is still in possession of the family, along with many other relics of that noted event.*

This account is confirmed by Sheridan's report, and the action closes Custer's career during the war. The incidents of

---

* This famous towel, the flag of truce which so suddenly terminated a bloody four years' war, is still in Mrs. Custer's possession, together with the little table on which the agreement was signed. Both are accompanied by letters of authentication, and were given to Custer by Sheridan, as the most proper person to possess them, he having been first in the pursuit all the time, and having received the first flag.

CUSTER RECEIVING THE FIRST FLAG OF TRUCE ON THE SURRENDER OF LEE.

the surrender are too well known to need enlarging on. Once more, by his wide sweep, Sheridan had headed Lee, and the slower infantry, following directly, had come up in time to bag the game the cavalry had brought to bay. In all the pursuit, Custer had been the foremost and he was fairly entitled to wear his laurels, for by his audacity he had taken more trophies than any man in the army. We can hardly close this part of his life better than by a literal copy of his farewell order to the Third Division, written the same day. It rings like one of Napoleon's:

HEADQUARTERS THIRD CAVALRY DIVISION.

APPOMATTOX COURT HOUSE, VA., *April 9*, 1865.

Soldiers of the Third Cavalry Division :

With profound gratitude toward the God of battles, by whose blessings our enemies have been humbled and our arms rendered triumphant, your Commanding General avails himself of this his first opportunity to express to you his admiration of the heroic manner in which you have passed through the series of battles which to-day resulted in the surrender of the enemy's entire army.

The record established by your indomitable courage is unparalleled in the annals of war. Your prowess has won for you even the respect and admiration of your enemies. During the past six months, although in most instances confronted by superior numbers, you have captured from the enemy, in open battle, one hundred and eleven pieces of field artillery, sixty-five battle-flags, and upwards of ten thousand prisoners of war, including seven general officers. Within the past ten days, and included in the above, you have captured forty-six field-pieces of artillery and thirty-seven battle-flags. You have never lost a gun, never lost a color, and have never been defeated ; and notwithstanding the numerous engagements in which you have borne a prominent part, including those memorable battles of the Shenandoah, you have captured every piece of artillery which the enemy has dared to open upon you. The near approach of peace renders it improbable that you will again be called upon to undergo the fatigues of the toilsome march, or the exposure of the battle-field ; but should the assistance of keen blades, wielded by your sturdy arms, be required to hasten the coming of that glorious peace for

which we have been so long contending, the General commanding is firmly confident that, in the future as in the past, every
demand will meet with a hearty and willing response.

Let us hope that our work is done, and that, blessed with the
comforts of peace, we may be permitted to enjoy the pleasures of
home and friends. For our comrades who have fallen, let us
ever cherish a grateful remembrance. To the wounded, and
to those who languish in Southern prisons, let our heartfelt
sympathy be tendered.

And now, speaking for myself alone, when the war is ended
and the task of the historian begins—when those deeds of daring
which have rendered the name and fame of the Third Cavalry
Division imperishable, are inscribed upon the bright pages of our
country's history, I only ask that my name may be written as
that of the Commander of the Third Cavalry Division.

G. A. CUSTER,

Brevet Major General Commanding.

OFFICIAL :

    L. W. BARNHART,

       Captain and A. A. A. G.

Custer had his wish. It is as commander of the Third Cavalry Division that his name will be cherished as long as there
are survivors of the war. When that memorable flag of truce
came into his lines it was an honor well deserved that he should
be the first to receive it, and none more fitting than he to keep
it, for as Sheridan said in his letter accompanying it, "I know
no one whose efforts have contributed more to this happy result
than those of Custer."

CHAPTER VI.

THE GREAT PARADE.

THE negotiations for surrender and the tedious operation of paroling Lee's army occupied several days, and then the cavalry started on their return to Petersburg, living on the country as they proceeded. So great had been the hurry of the last nine days, that supplies were short, and the trains had not arrived with forage. They were met, however, at Nottaway Court House, where also something else was met, in the shape of a dispatch which thrilled the whole country and army with horror and indignation. It conveyed the news of the assassination of President Lincoln, at a theatre in Washington, by John Wilkes Booth. At the same time came news that Sherman had been outwitted by Johnston in the latter's surrender, and that the capitulation was annulled. Then came fresh orders. The work of the cavalry was not quite over yet, and away they went again to the Roanoke, marching rapidly towards Johnston's army. The advance had actually reached the Roanoke, and looked into North Carolina, when the order was recalled. Johnston had surrendered on the same terms as Lee, and the war was over.

Once more the cavalry corps took up its march for Petersburg, which was reached without special incident. There it remained a few days, resting, and then parted forever from its beloved chief. Sheridan was called to Washington, and ordered away to Texas. The work of the volunteer army was done, but that of the regulars was only just commencing. The last glimpse the volunteers caught of Sheridan was when he rode through their camps, as they lay above Petersburg, just before his departure. Little did the men dream they would never see him again, or they would have been crazy with excitement. As it was, the sight of "Little Phil" brought them out from their tents to look at him, but it was remarkable that little cheering greeted his progress. The men looked happy to see him, and he conversed freely as he passed along, but all the cheering business seemed to have died out of the cavalry corps except in action. None the less their love and confidence in their leader was greater than any other chief had known, since McClellan's removal, and Sheridan never encouraged cheers, rarely bowed in response, generally laughed at the men who cheered him, or made some good humored "chaffing" response.

After some days' rest at Petersburg,* the cavalry corps under the command of General Crook, started on its homeward way by easy stages, passing through the long sought city of Richmond in parade style. How proud they all felt, few can realize but those who marched with them. Their toils were over and they were going home to be disbanded; that was in every one's heart. Some regret at the loss of a life of excitement and adventure troubled a few, but as a rule every one was thinking of home and civil life. The column passed through Richmond, gazed at by curious crowds, and thence over the back country, where the men had raided and fought so often. They passed Trevillian Station, and found the ruined railroad just as they

---

* No one needed this rest more than Custer, whose work during the past campaign had been tremendous. It was one of his peculiarities that when under strong excitement he could do with very little sleep or food, but the last campaign had nearly worn even his iron frame out. His portrait, taken just after the surrender, shows the effect of the hard work in his gaunt, haggard appearance. Petersburg restored him, however. He was met by Mrs. Custer before he got there, the brave little woman being the first Northern woman who went out on the Southside Railroad, after the surrender of Richmond. Together with Mrs. Pennington, wife of one of Custer's brigade commanders, Mrs. Custer made the whole of the march to Washington with the cavalry corps, the ladies riding on horseback at the head of the column, where the author first saw Mrs. Custer.

had left it a year before, crossed Rappahannock Bridge, the old battle grounds at Brandy Station, and camped on the Bull Run battle field. Every where the landscape was full of memories, sad and joyful, glorious or disastrous, but every where they were now sources of pleasure. They visited all the old friends they had made at the different places where they had sojourned during four years of strife, these wandering raiders, and congratulated each other that the " war was over." Then at last they reached Alexandria, and were dispersed all over the landscape, some in the very camps they had occupied in 1861 or 1862, when they were first mounted and sent to the front.

For several days the different regiments rested in their camps, and then they were ordered over the river, to take ground near Washington. Clothing awaited them by the car load, provisions were plentiful, they drew everything needful to make a good appearance. For the first time in years they began to experience the pleasant part of a soldier's life, the pomp and circumstance of war, with all its glitter and glory. Then at last came the order for the grand parade at Washington. The whole Army of the Potomac, with Sheridan's cavalry at the head of the column, was to pass in review before the President, through the streets of Washington, and Sherman's army was to follow next day, in the same ceremonies.

And what a review that was! The first, and it may be well hoped the last, of its kind in America, the passage of two armies of veterans, who had fought for four years, in such a series of battles as had not been seen in Europe for half a century. There was no sham about that parade. Every man was a veteran soldier. It might have been swelled to much larger proportions if need be, for every regiment had been joined, since it reached its safe camp, by crowds of recruits, malingerers, quartermaster's men, and all those who had been left back at Remount Camp. But in the review, as a rule, only those who had shared in the last campaign took part, and the camps were left behind full of men. There you might see regiments reduced to a single squadron, tattered banners muffled in crape for the President's death, but every man a veteran. The uniforms were neat and quiet. Every man wore the undress uniform, blouse and fatigue cap, in which the army was arrayed for work. The only difference was that all were neat and clean, boots inside trowsers, sergeants' stripes fresh and new, bright brass letters and numbers on every cap, buttons brightly brushed up.

In the parade, as in the pursuit, Custer had the advance, and, not to be behind his men, he had, for the first time, doffed his careless attire, and wore a full-dress major-general's coat, over the collar of which his bright curls played merrily. The broad hat was the only remnant of his old careless yet dandified costume. He submitted to regulations otherwise.

The route of the column was from the east of Washington to the Capitol, where it turned to the right and swept straight up Pennsylvania Avenue. At this turning point, the regiments of cavalry successively drew their sabres as they passed, and here the crowd began.

Such a crowd as that was, will never be seen again. They seemed to be crazy with joy, and they shouted and hurrahed at every fresh regiment. There was a perfect jam on the sidewalks, and halfway into the road, and every window was crammed. Girls in white, in large bands, were singing sweet songs of welcome and throwing flowers and garlands to the soldiers.

The girls thought how gallant the soldiers looked : they little dreamed how nearly divine they appeared to the soldiers, who had not seen a pretty girl for so long. Still it was these very floral angels that caused Custer's mishap at this place, a mishap which attracted more attention, admiration, and cheering to him than anything else could have done. It is thus described by one of the bystanders, who calls it " One glimpse of Custer," and the incident is correctly told in the main.*

* Detroit Evening News.

One bright May morning in 1865, when the very sky seemed brighter and the air lighter and purer for the exultant sense of the fact that the war was over and that thousands had gathered under the shadow of the capitol's dome to welcome the nation's children— the dust-stained, battle-scarred veterans of the Union army—the writer caught a glimpse of the brave, yellow-haired chief, whose fate has so recently thrilled the hearts of all who admire true heroism and sublime courage. Never can the picture made by the gallant Custer that day be forgotten. Soon after the formal head of the line, Provost-Marshal Gen. Patrick, had ridden down the broad avenue, bearing his reins in his teeth and his sabre in his only hand, and had passed by a few rods, a cry was raised, "See him ride!" "That's Custer and his raiders," and like a flash came a gallant Arab* horse up the avenue, bearing in its headlong gallop a young officer, on whose shoulders shone the stars of a major-general, and as Custer dashed past the President's stand and the stand for the wounded soldiers, the latter caught up the shout, and such a scene as followed! The gallant cripples staggered to their feet or crutches and hailed him with cheer after cheer, and then looked about for his gallant followers—but they were not there. The secret soon became plain. Soon after the column had set in toward Pennsylvania Avenue a bevy of white-clad maidens, stationed near the side of the street (there were 300 of them), had, as the brave fellow drew nigh, risen simultaneously, and bursting into the song, "Hail to the Chief," each threw a bouquet or wreath at him. It was the first surprise he ever had, but instead of dodging the floral missiles he began trying to catch them. The sudden rush, the pelting of bouquets and the peal of the 300 voices frightened his steed, and before he could gather up the reins the excited animal had made the rush we saw from the other end of the Avenue. As the gallant general flew past the

---

* Quite a history belongs to this horse. He was a thoroughbred "four mile racer," who had run thirty-three races, of which he had won twenty-six. Just before Appomattox surrender, Custer's scouts captured this horse, who was named "Don Juan," from the stable on the stud farm, and brought him to Custer. The horse was regularly appraised as captured property, contraband of war, and sold to Custer by the Quartermaster, Custer holding the receipt. The horse was a magnificent dark bay stallion, of a most furious temper. Custer sent him home to Monroe, and had him exhibited at the State fair, where "Don Juan" killed a groom. The horse finally dropped dead in his stall of heart-disease a year later.

President's stand he bethought him to salute Johnson and Gen. Grant, but in doing so, in the rush his sabre caught in his wide hat, and sabre and head-gear fell to the ground. Then, with his long, yellow, curly hair floating out behind, he settled himself in the saddle as if he grew there, and by one of the most magnificent exhibitions of horsemanship he in a moment reined in the flying charger, and returned to meet his troops. An orderly had picked up his hat and sword, and pulling the hat down over his eyes Custer dashed back past the assembled thousands, and soon reappeared at the head of his division. Will those of us who saw that last grand review ever forget those two pictures—Custer conquering his runaway horse, and Custer at the head of the well "dressed" lines of the most gallant cavalry division of the age, as with the hot flush of victory yet visible on their bronzed faces, he led it through the capital at a gallop march? It was but a momentary vision, but one that has fixed itself upon at least one memory in indelible lines.

That very evening, Custer was going to fresh labors in the Southwest, while his old comrades were to disperse to their homes: the close of the review was also the close of his connection with the Third Cavalry division. As soon as the column left the front of the Grand Stand it filed off toward its old encampment, and was drawn up on the familiar parade ground; then the officers of that proud little division were summoned to the front to take their last leave of their beloved general. The solemnity and mutual affection of that parting has been beautifully described by one of the participants: it was such a leave-taking as comes to few in a lifetime, like the parting by death of near relatives, sad and solemn. When it was over, Custer rode slowly down the line and off the ground, while many of the rough men in the ranks could not cheer for the choking in their throats. He passed from their view as a beloved chief, and all felt, as we feel to-day, that never shall we look on his like again.

SIXTH BOOK.—AFTER THE WAR.

CHAPTER I.

THE VOLUNTEERS IN TEXAS.

THE close of the war found the forces of the United States in a very curious and anomalous position. The sudden collapse of the rebellion, while it took every one by surprise, still had its disadvantageous side. The armed occupation of the Southern States that followed the surrender of Lee, assumed the attitude not so much of a fair conquest as of a mere military progress. There was no more fighting to do. The same men who had been so stubborn up to the 9th of April, suddenly abandoned all hope, and voluntarily dispersed to their homes, in apparent peace and quietness.

Then it was found that the real strain on the wheels of government was to begin. The United States was not a kingdom, but a republic; and a large party of the people held that just as soon as the population of the revolted States chose to cease armed opposition to the government, they were entitled to resume their old relations with the general body of the nation, with all rights unimpaired. To these views another party objected that self-preservation was the first law of nations, as well as of nature, and higher than any written constitution; and that it was manifest folly to invite men who had fought the general government till all hope was lost, to become legislators for their conquerors. Thus the few months next after the surrender of Lee witnessed the two new parties taking shape. One was the "constitution party," headed by the President, the

other was the "expediency party," which held the majority of
Congress in both houses.

The uncertainty and excitement of the contest that ensued
had its effect on the army, and especially on that portion
of the volunteers that remained in the service. As long as
the war lasted, these men had been to all intents and purposes
regular troops. Their term of service, their pay, rations, dress
and privileges were the same, and it was difficult to distinguish
one from the other, in the case of old regiments. So long
as the duration of the war was uncertain, the feelings and
esprit de corps of the volunteer service were identical with
those of the regulars. They were simply soldiers, and entirely
different from militia, who are always looking forward to the
termination of their brief terms of service, as a release from
irksome slavery.

The close of the war changed all this, as if by magic. At
once it became the universal desire of the volunteers " to go
home." They were enlisted " for three years or during the war,"
and the war was over : they ought to be disbanded forthwith
and sent home. This was the universal logic of their reasoning,
and it must be admitted that it was sound on the premises.
The only trouble was, who should decide that the war was
over. The President at one time undertook the job, and
was formally rebuked by Congress, after which followed the
long contest between the Executive and Legislative branches of
the government, culminating in the President's impeachment,
and terminating in the election of General Grant. But in the
meantime, the close of the year 1865 and the early part of
1866 were distinguished by uncertainty and disorder, which to
a great extent affected the troops in the field.

After the surrenders of Lee and Johnston, there still remained a third army to the Confederacy, and towards this
Jefferson Davis was making his way when he was captured.
This army was commanded by Kirby Smith, the very man
who had brought up the Confederate brigade which decided the

battle of Bull Run. His numbers were larger than those of either Lee or Johnston, his force well equipped, and—most favorable circumstance of all—the State of Texas in which he was stationed was entirely untouched by the war, and offered excellent strategic positions for a defensive fight. There is little doubt that had Davis, with his indomitable pride and energy, succeeded in reaching Kirby Smith, the two might have continued the war for some time to come, with a fair prospect of making an independent slave State out of Texas. The capture of Davis, however, put an end to any such schemes, and Kirby Smith, in his turn, peaceably surrendered his army to General Sheridan.

On the events of the surrender and subsequent occupation of Texas we do not intend to dwell, save so far as they concern Custer and the volunteers, and especially the latter. In the state of uncertainty which still prevailed as to the ultimate state of affairs in the South, it was found necessary to retain a considerable force under arms, to meet expected insurrections. It was fully anticipated that the ex-Confederates would resolve themselves into bands of guerillas, and harass the country. In order to guard against this possibility, considerable forces retained their army organization in brigades and divisions, and were stationed at railroad junctions and other strategic points, instead of being scattered at small company posts through the country. These forces were largely composed of volunteers. Any other arrangement would have been an impossibility. The regular army, which had entered the war less than 16,000 strong, hardly mustered that number now, after all its recruiting, and was totally unequal to the task of holding such an immense territory as now demanded military occupation.

But the volunteers, almost without exception, were clamorous to be discharged and sent home. The officers, who were receiving good pay and doing easy duty, were comparatively reconciled to their lot, but the men were sullen and discontented. The weakness of the volunteer organization, which had not re-

vealed itself during the war, became plain now. It was only
a temporary make-shift, after all, and the close of the war
showed it. The same men who in campaign had been docile
soldiers, in perfect discipline, became once more the same self-
opinionated mob which had been beaten at Bull Run. The
men resumed their functions as citizens, began to think and to
grumble, disputing orders, disobeying them, and fast sinking
into a state of demoralization that would appear incredible when
compared with the experience of a few months back, were it not
recorded. During the war, it seemed as if America had
become a military nation. Peace revealed the fact that it had
not done any such thing. Some million of citizens, under the
pressure of national pride and self-preservation, had consented
to play the part of soldiers while necessity existed. Now they
had done their work, were heartily sick of the unnatural life, and
wanted to return to a natural one.

The disgust and anger of the volunteers who were retained
in the service was further increased by the disbandment of so
many of their comrades. Most of the eastern regiments were
mustered out, and the Army of the Potomac entirely broken
up, while the regiments retained in service were generally from
the West. This was in consequence of their being nearer to
the dangerous places in the southwest, and in no sense a dis-
crimination against them, but they would not listen to explana-
tions. They heard of their friends who had gone home, who
were now in business and prosperous, while they felt only too
keenly that they were wasting their own time, that opportunities were slipping away and could never be replaced, and that
by the time they got home all the avenues to employment
might be filled, and they turned out to starve. All this grumbling and discontent increased daily among the volunteers, while
among the regulars it was unknown.

A calm retrospect of the facts, at this late day, ten years
after the event, shows the cause to be very simple. The real
trouble was that the volunteer organization, coming as it did

from the individual States, was merely a temporary loan to the United States. New York, or New Jersey, or Michigan, or Illinois, as the case might be, had lent the government a regiment bodily, officers and all, for a certain purpose, and the men keenly realized that the purpose was accomplished. They enlisted to end the war, not to help in reconstruction. A new force was needed for this. In a regular regiment, with different traditions, the case was different. The men enlisted to serve their time out individually. The organization was fixed and perennial. No matter if every man in the regiment was killed: something invisible,—the —— United States regiment —remained: all it needed was to be recruited. With the volunteers it was different: they could not be recruited: the war was over, and there was no authority for them to recruit under. As the men deserted, the regiments dwindled. Then consolidation was tried, but with even worse effect. The members of the old regiments had a bond of union, *esprit de corps*. It kept many a man from desertion, for fear of disgracing his old command, that carried the name of so many battles on its flag. For the new regiment, the "provisional" organization, they cherished no feeling but dislike. Even the officers hated it. They secretly sympathized with the men, and connived at disorder, or only checked it feebly. The new regiments dwindled away even more rapidly than the old. The only thing that kept most of the men in the service was the fact that the government owed them many months' pay, and that they did not care to forfeit that by desertion. At last the government was obliged to give up the attempt to make professional soldiers of the volunteers, and to do what it should have done at first, increase the regular army. The last of the volunteers were not discharged, however, till the spring of 1866. During this time, Custer found his hands pretty full, as far as discipline was concerned. He was first sent from Washington, after the great parade, to follow Sheridan to Texas. Mrs. Custer was able to travel with him, and his old staff accompanied him. At the

time Custer left for the Southwest, he was very much pulled
down by the tremendous labor which he had imposed on himself during the last campaign, and the relaxation of the present
journey was very pleasant to him. Before he had arrived at
New Orleans, the news of Kirby Smith's surrender announced
that all was safe, so that he was no longer obliged to hurry;
and the trip was consequently delightful. For the first time in
his life Custer was tasting the sweets of a major-general's life,
which he had not hitherto enjoyed. With a large staff, free
transportation, plenty of horses, ample pay, his family with
him, travelling luxurious, he began to enjoy life thoroughly.

The party went from Washington by railroad to Parkers-
burg, on the upper Ohio, where they took one of the great luxurious western river boats, and thence travelled down the Ohio and
Mississippi all the way to New Orleans. Of all methods of
travel, this is perhaps the pleasantest, on account of the ample
and commodious quarters, the beauty of the scenery passed
through, and the length of time occupied in the passage, just
sufficient to form pleasant acquaintances. There is always
ample room on the three or four different decks for all the
exercise one needs, the dinner table is plentifully and well supplied, the evenings are enlivened by a band of music in the
main saloon, while the passengers almost invariably get up a
dance. It resembles life on an ocean steamer, without the
formidable drawback of sea-sickness, and is altogether delightful. Custer and his little wife found it entirely so.

Hitherto their life had been strange and peculiar. To Custer, with his earnest, impatient temperament, his different steps
of promotion had brought little of luxury and enjoyment, but a
great deal of hard work, which had at last completely worn him
out. He owns as much in a letter written home to his sister
from Petersburg, just after Appomattox surrender. He says
that he feels completely exhausted, and needs rest badly. During the easy marches back to Washington, together with his
little wife, he obtained some rest, and this long pleasant boat

journey was another resting time. He enjoyed it with a perfect dreamy delight, such as he had never felt, and all the more because he could not help feeling that he had earned it.

Arrived at New Orleans, he stepped ashore a new man, fit for any amount of work, and already tired of rest. He was sent up the river to Alexandria, Louisiana, there to take charge of a division of cavalry, gathered from the Western States. Here his troubles commenced. Very few of these troops had been in action to any great extent. They were green regiments, and therefore all the harder to discipline. For all that, Custer set to work at them, as he had with his Michigan Brigade in old days, and established the most rigorous discipline from the first. The sort of success he had was not very gratifying, however: no one could have hoped that in those days. The trouble lay in the penny-wise, pound-foolish policy of Congress, which preferred the temporary employment of half a million of discontented volunteers, to the authorization at once of a permanent standing army of a hundred thousand regulars, such as could then have been organized in three weeks. To Custer, with his memories of the perfect adoration extended to him by his former commands, the present experience was very trying. The men under his orders all hated him furiously. He needed a battle to make them love him, and there were no more battles to be fought. His charging days were over.

What he could do he did, to get his troops into decent order, and accomplished a great deal, but nothing satisfactory to himself, when the division was finally ordered to Austin, Texas. The transfer was made by easy marches, and once on the road there was not so much trouble with the troops. They had something to do, and were not so full of discontent. The great difficulty then, as always after the war, was to keep the men from marauding. They were so used to living off the country in war time, that it required a powerful provost-guard to patrol the flanks of the column to keep the stragglers from going off to plunder.

21

Apart from these troubles, the march was delightful. Mrs. Custer marched at the head of the column, riding on horseback nearly all the way. A large roomy spring wagon, with a team of four matched greys, belonging to the general, accompanied headquarters, and was so fitted up that it could be used as a tiring room or a sleeping apartment while on the march, should the delicate little woman get tired out. She used it but little, however, making the journey as well as any of the men. At last they arrived at Austin, where their command, still called the "Third Division," found itself with Merritt's, still known as the "First." The state of affairs there was worse than at Alexandria, Merritt's division aggravating the troubles of Custer's.

A little extract will give an idea of the state of things. It is quoted from the correspondence of the New York Times, March, 1866. The correspondent gives an explanation of the unpopularity of General Custer with the enlisted men :

Every one who glances at the heading of this paragraph will say, " Well, there's no discount on him." But there is, though, in the estimation of some. The soldiers are down on him like a thousand of brick, and so are their friends. And why ? I'll tell you. As a general thing, the Volunteers wanted to go home as soon as the war was over, and that portion of them who were sent out have acted badly, and were encouraged in such performance by their friends in the North, who wrote them letters, in which they told them to come home—that the war was over, and that it would not be desertion. General Custer, knowing that the trial for desertion was a farce, tried every humane way to save his army from going to pieces, but failed. He then tried a new way; and flogged several men and shaved their heads. This had the desired effect, but brought down the friends of these soldiers upon him, who charge him with being disloyal, inhuman, and everything that is bad. Now, I leave it to every one if Custer didn't do right. The Volunteers are not acting in a good spirit here, while nearly half of them have deserted. This state of things operates badly in the two regular cavalry regiments which are stationed in this section, nearly one-third of whom have deserted. These deserters turn murderers and robbers and horse-thieves, and are a terror to the traveling community. Scarcely a night passes but that some poor fellow is waylaid and killed. The great necessity of the increase of the Regular Army, and the discharge of all the Volunteers—white and colored—must be apparent to all.

He also gives an account of the mutiny of the Third Michigan Cavalry, for the truth of which he vouches:

It is pretty well known that this regiment has had the reputation of being one of the best bodies of cavalry in the service. For fighting, marching or drilling it is unequaled by any cavalry regiment in the United States. Like all of the Volunteers, the men composing this regiment wanted to go home. A few weeks ago, while upon parade, General Thompson complimented the regiment in eloquent terms, and stated to them that it was an honor to be kept in the service. Says the general: " To say nothing about your past services, no inspector in the army would permit such a well-organized, well-dressed and well-disciplined regiment to quit the service as long as any necessity exists for retaining the services of Volunteers." It happened that the next day they were to be inspected by one of General Sheridan's staff officers, and they prepared themselves accordingly. Such a crowd never before appeared upon inspection, except the Ancients and Horribles. Some had on caps, some had on hats with the corners jammed out or stuck in, some had on boots, and some had on shoes covered with oil and ashes; some had on coats, some had on jackets, and some were in their shirt sleeves ; some had their breeches stuck into their boots, some had their belts and cartridge boxes on bottom side upward; and, on the whole, presented a most wry appearance. All those men who were not dressed in this manner were ordered to arrest their " Horrible " companions, when they refused, and the whole regiment mutinied. Subsequently the thing was fixed up, and ninety of them are in confinement and are to be tried for mutiny.

As may be imagined, the trial for mutiny amounted to very little, and the regiment was at last disbanded, to its own relief, and that of every one else.

In this matter, just as before and since the war, Custer and the regular army officers suffered in common with their comrades, from the incompetency and stupidity of their management by Congress. During the war, this sapient body was confined to its true functions, as regards the army. These were to legislate on general subjects, and to provide money: the executive arranged all the details. Instead of many masters, the army had but one, Stanton, a harsh and severe ruler, sometimes, but generally just and sensible. Good or bad, every man knew what to expect, and as a whole, the army was managed by men who knew their business. Now all this was changed. The law, whether good or bad, had to be obeyed, and expediency was no longer consulted. Troops were governed not according to necessity, but according to what Congress chose to order; and Congress, like all deliberative bodies, halted and hesitated and did nothing, while discontent increased. This state of things is peculiar to a republic, and especially to a federative government like the American. It is part of the price paid for personal liberty.

To a king or emperor, the situation would have offered no difficulties, either at the beginning or close of the war. He would have levied his troops, used them, and disbanded them, as seemed fit to him: the increase or diminution of his army would not have affected its stability. President Lincoln could not raise a company: he was obliged to ask the States for regiments. President Johnson could only return the regiments lent him, and the fact of his needing many of them made no difference. He could only retain them by a legal fiction, for the rebellion had ceased. Had Congress, on Kirby Smith's surrender, at once increased the regular force, and authorized the change of volunteer regiments into regular regiments, leaving their formation to volunteering from the "natural soldiers" of the old regiments, and retaining the traditions of the war, the trouble would never have arisen. A change from temporary to permanent organization was needed, and it came too late to save the volunteers from unmerited reproach. Custer, among the rest, paid the penalty of doing his duty, in unpopularity among the men who had adored him. At last, Congress thought better of it, and passed the bill of 1866, " to increase and fix the military establishment of the United States."

CHAPTER II.

THE REGULAR ARMY.

IT is one of the consequences of republican institutions as affecting modern civilization, that the standing army of a republic is pretty sure to be constantly abused. The fact is that republics and standing armies are incompatible, and always will be so. The one theory of government is predicated on the liberty of every man to go where he pleases, and do what he pleases, so long as he does not hurt his neighbors. The other is founded on the duty of every man to obey his superior officer without question, and to stir no step without permission. The only footing on which standing armies have ever been tolerated in free republics has been as a police force, to control the criminal classes. As such the regular army of the United States before the war acted. It was kept up solely to control the dangerous Indians, and to keep burglars out of the nearly deserted forts. The people at large saw but little of it, soldiers being rare spectacles in the *ante-bellum* days.

During the war, this little police force practically vanished from the struggle. A brigade of cavalry and a division of infantry in a single army, both mere skeletons, constituted all the regulars, except in the batteries of artillery and the headquarter escorts of a few generals. These, from the feebleness of their numbers, attracted little attention. It might have been and probably was expected, that this small force, by its innate superiority, should fill to the volunteers the office of Napoleon's Old Guard to the rest of the French army, to be the last reserve, steady and invincible, capable of deciding every battle.

This expectation, if entertained, was disappointed. The regulars, after Bull Run, ceased to be distinguished for any special valor or constancy, and merely fought alongside of the rest of the army, neither better nor worse.

The cause for this state of things was simple. At Bull Run, the small force of regulars present was made up of veterans, and shone by contrast with the rest of the army. As time went on, the veterans grew less and less in number, and were replaced by green recruits. Worse still, the regular officers, instead of remaining with their old commands, sought, and easily obtained, volunteer commands, far higher than any the regulars could offer. Lieutenants and captains were jumped to colonels, and field officers became generals of brigade and division, to the benefit of the volunteers and the detriment of the regulars. The vacancies thus created, were either unsupplied, or filled by new appointments, and more than half of these latter were from civil life. The "civil appointments," as a rule, were perfectly green young gentlemen, precisely the same as those who entered the volunteers as officers and privates, but they happened to possess political influence, to know a senator or representative, and so they were commissioned. Thus it very soon resulted that, as a rule, only the poorest of the old officers remained with the regulars. The energetic and ambitious had left for the volunteers; what remained may be divided into three classes. First were the lazy ones and plodders, who preferred the old groove; second were the few who looked down on the volunteers, and fancied themselves of a superior class; third were the new officers, who needed training. To these must be added, however, a fourth class, of modest and capable officers, who had not sufficient influence to secure high volunteer commands, and who remained with their old regiments from necessity.

It was the influence of this last class that kept up the reputation of the little skeleton force of regulars, and enabled them to hold their own with the volunteers. It is indeed surprising how strong was their influence over the new material from civil life. The same men who came in, raw unlicked cubs, proud of their political friends, and chiefly anxious for every one to understand that they were " regulars," at a time when their ignorance would have disgraced a squad of country militia, found their level in a very short time. Within a year from their first entrance, it was hard to recognize, in the quiet and self-possessed officer, in command of his picket post or scouting party, the rude gawky bumpkin who had joined in 1861. The old hands had licked him into shape, while the veterans in the ranks had done the same kind office for the recruits below. In the old regiments, which dated from before the war, this change was very marked, in the few new regiments that had been authorized since the commencement of hostilities, much less so. Even there, however, there was some difference, and it was noticeable at the very close of the war. It consisted chiefly in a different standard of discipline, a difference of condition between officers and men, which was most prominent in camp. At the close of hostilities it made itself visible in the different behavior of regulars and volunteers.

On the march and in the battle there was nothing to choose between the regulars and the old first class regiments of volunteers, especially where the latter had been commanded by a West Point graduate. On the drill ground, if any thing, the volunteers were smarter, and they almost always attacked in battle with an energy slightly superior to that of the regulars. Their camps were often much handsomer than those of the regulars, and at permanent camps they always displayed far more taste in adorning their habitations, while in cleanliness there was little to choose between the two.

But between the officers and men of volunteers, there was always, even to the last, a kindly and cordial feeling, which was the perfection of ideal relations. It was very different from the loose style prevalent at the beginning of the war, when the men elected their officers, or the latter were appointed to exercise duties of which they were totally ignorant. That class had vanished. What remained of officers were men of experience, who had either risen from the ranks, or from being subalterns had become field officers. The men knew that in case of vacancies in the lower ranks these would be filled from among themselves. The career was open to all, and while the war lasted was excellent. This bred between the two classes a certain mutual respect which was noticeable. The men were punctilious in saluting, neat in their dress, and obeyed orders promptly. The officers were kind in their manner, and only maintained the due distance essential to discipline in public. When an officer and a sergeant, formerly comrades and tent mates, were alone together, with no one to see them, they talked like the old friends they were, while the presence of a third party, especially an enlisted man, would instantly freeze up the sergeant into haughtily profound respect. The secret of subordination was that *every man respected the rank he hoped to attain himself.* During winter quarters there was little or no trouble in maintaining perfect discipline among the old volunteer regiments, on this account.

In the regular regiments a very different state of things prevailed. Officers and men were practically distinct classes, with lines of demarcation irrevocably fixed. The distance between them was impassable. The youngest subaltern newly joined was entitled to the same respect shown to a general, and the marks of respect enforced were and still are decidedly slavish. A little instance will show the contrast.

A company of regulars is in barracks. Their captain is detailed on staff duty, the first-lieutenant is on a court martial, the second lieutenant is in his quarters, smoking a pipe, when some citizen friends arrive to pay him a visit. After a cigar, and a visit to the bar-room, " for officers only," the young sub proposes to show his friends the barracks, and after seeing the parade ground, goes quietly to the door of the company room and opens it to take his friends in. Instantly a voice is heard shouting "Attention!" and in a moment every man in the room is standing at the foot of his bunk, bareheaded, cap in hand, and stiff as a post. The lieutenant touches one of his buttons with his forefinger and drops it in a careless way, (meant for the return of a salute) looks around the room, makes a few remarks on its condition to his friends, as if the men were insensible blocks who could not hear, and goes out. Thence he takes his friends to the guard-house, full as it is of manacled men, resting from their sentences of labor; and the same scene is repeated. Every prisoner has to stand up and be inspected like a prize ox, while the little sub moves about as if he were a demigod amid slaves.

A visit to a volunteer barrack or the camp of a crack regiment at the close of the war was very different. In the first place, the lieutenant would not have voluntarily taken his friends round to exhibit his men in their bedrooms, neither would he have taken them to the guard-house. If his friends had asked to see the men, he would have gone with them, the men would have stood to attention and saluted, and afterwards the friends might have conversed with the soldiers, who would have received them politely, but as a rule the friends of an officer would have remained with him alone, or viewed the men at such a distance as not to constrain the latter.

In the one case was a constant strain on the reins of discipline, making the men feel the curb all the while, in the other a constant endeavor on the part of the officers to carry a light hand, to make things easy, to insist only on the needful, and not to regard the men as private property. During the war the second system worked well, and the men fought cheerfully for officers whom they loved. Even in the regular regiments the old slavish system of discipline was much relaxed, and principally in consequence of the fact that during the war some promotions were made from the ranks. At the close of hostilities all was changed. It was no longer possible to get men to do duty cheerfully. The duty was disagreeable and irksome, devoid of excitement or glory, promotion had ceased, there was no campaigning, and instead of the cheerful volunteer, fighting for the cause he loved, the hired mercenary was to be the soldier of the future. The change was great, and demanded different discipline. Instead of willing obedience and easy government, absolute servility and rigid authority were needed. The class of men that enlisted in the volunteers would not have entered the regulars for double pay. They had been trained from boyhood to look down on soldiers, as men too lazy to work, and only one remove above criminals. The same feeling exists in England, and in fact in every country where military service is wholly voluntary. It is only in countries where the conscription and the soldier are universal, that the latter is treated with respect by the citizen. The feeling with which the regular soldier is regarded in England and America, is a curious compound of contempt and fear. The hard working artisan, who maintains a family by his labor, looks down on the soldier because the latter is content to live on contemptibly small pay, and is unable comfortably to keep a wife and children; and the same sentiment is common to the clerk, salesman, shopkeeper, and every man who makes a comfortable living above the degree of a common laborer. They all look on the soldier as a poor creature, who cannot make a living. At the same time, whenever they see him drunk, they give him a wide berth, and as a great many "hard cases" enlist in the army, and afterwards become prominent for disorder, the citizen learns to regard the rank and file of the regular army as being made up entirely of the scum of the population. The truth is, that he only sees their worst side, in the cities. The old soldiers, men who have served more than one enlistment without a desertion, are quiet and unobtrusive; he hardly ever sees them, and takes little notice of them when he does: the chronic deserters and re-enlisters, the drunkards, the malingerers, are always thick around the recruiting offices in the cities, and help to give tone to the current idea of the army private.

Were the army, as in France and Germany, constantly in

sight among the people, the citizens would discover that soldiers are men the same as themselves, with all sorts of characters. As a class, a little more inclined to be reticent and silent to strangers than workmen, the best of them have a certain deprecatory air when thrown into a crowd of citizens, dashed with a spice of defiance. They know there is a prejudice against them, and they feel that it is unjust, so they keep among themselves as much as possible, and nourish regimental pride to console them for civil depreciation. All they need to make their position happier, is to be better known.

Another cause of the depreciation is found in the nature of a soldier's duties. There is nothing which is more inexplicable to the ordinary civilian than the true military spirit, that glories in hardships, danger and death, and that despises fine uniforms. He cannot understand it. To be a militia man in a gorgeous uniform, and to march through the streets behind a splendid band is his idea of soldiering, and when he finds that his real soldier friend hates this and loves the excitement of a battle pure and simple, the civilian is puzzled. In a conscriptional country, where every one is liable to service, the feeling of pity and sympathy for men who are forced against their will to endure the hardships of real military life, extends to every member of the population in the country who has a relative in the army, and helps to make the army popular. During the war of the rebellion, when the overpowering necessity of the times operated instead of the conscription, the same feeling tended to make the volunteers popular. They went (according to the public idea) not because they loved a soldier's life, but because it was their *duty*. The men in the regular army after the close of the war, could plead no such excuse. They enlisted either because they loved military life, or because they were too indolent or unskillful to make a living at anything else. In either case, the average citizen disliked the motive and despised the man.

This state of public estimation reacted injuriously on the

army. It was so unpopular a thing to enlist, that no one would do it, save as a last resort, if he had a character to lose. The very worst men of the old volunteers—the bounty jumpers—enlisted by hundreds, and practiced on the regular officers the tricks which they had learned for the purpose of duping provost-marshals in draft times. The percentage of desertions was larger than it had ever been before, and the few good and decent soldiers were lost in the scamps that made up the popular idea of the regular army. It was in the midst of these influences that the bill of 1866, "to increase and fix" the regular army, went into operation. Forty-five regiments of infantry, ten of cavalry, and five of artillery, were announced as the basis of the future army. Half of the regiments of horse and foot were quite new, and others dated from the period of the war. To officer these regiments, about fifteen hundred new officers were required, and here, as in the case of the enlisted men, great difficulties lay in the way of procuring good material.

As with the men, so with the officers, the best and most energetic of the volunteer material had returned to civil life, where it was pushing forward and prospering. There were not enough graduates of West Point to fill the bill. The old army of twelve thousand men had been compelled to rely for officers to a great degree on civil appointments; and out of that old army, at least half of the graduates had passed away, some into the Confederate service, others by death, others on the retired list. The four years of the war had produced about fifty graduates a year, and the coming years would furnish the same proportion. A large residue still remained, that must be filled up by civil appointments. In these latter, the preference was to be given to ex-volunteers, and for the next few years all the so-called "civil appointments" came from the volunteer officers.

This might have been expected to produce a very good class of officers, but it was soon found that this was far from being the case, principally owing to the baneful influence of politics.

Had it been possible for the pick of the old volunteer officers to have been recommended, at the very close of hostilities, by their superior officers, on a strictly military basis, for military aptitude alone, the results might have been good. As it was, the lower appointments were made entirely through the influence of members of congress or senators, who recommended their friends; and only those volunteers possessed of such influence obtained commissions. In many cases they were given to men who had tried civil life for a time, failed therein, and went into the army to make a living. Some actually purchased their commissions through claim agents, who for the price of about five hundred dollars, engaged to procure a senator's influence, and bring the candidate for a commission before the examining board.*

This last-named body was composed of old regular officers, and was authorized to examine the candidates, to see whether they were fit for commissions. The test was chiefly educational. Tactics and regulations had little to do with it. The officers were examined in the ordinary branches of English education, including algebra up to quadratic equations, with a little plane trigonometry, and that was about all. Like all examinations, of whatever character, they failed to touch the real capacity of the applicant, who generally "crammed" for the test. If he failed to pass, and had influence, he secured a second trial, in some instances a third. Influence was sufficient to pull almost any one through.

The consequence of this state of things was that, instead of the best of the volunteer element, the army secured, in too many cases, only the worst, and the incompetency of the new officers to control the army became very painfully evident. Contrary to the general idea, the task of a regimental officer of the United States army in time of peace, is far more difficult than in time

---

* This statement is founded on facts in the knowledge of various gentlemen who shall be nameless, but is not made loosely or from general or hearsay evidence.

of war. Then he is in the midst of comrades, in a brigade, part of a division, a corps, an army. All he has to do, is to keep his men together on the march and in the battle, and to obey orders. His superiors do the thinking.

In time of peace all is changed. The officer is often, nay generally, thrown much on his own responsibility. The troops are scattered in small posts, always short-handed ; and officers are constantly detailed on special duty. Moreover, the army is always in the midst of a population intensely hostile to its spirit and traditions, in active sympathy with all deserters, and exceedingly jealous of military authority. The officer is subject to a code of minute regulations, born of the jealousy of the civil authority, which are all the more vexatious that half the time he does not know what they are. The case in 1866 was even worse than it is now. The old army regulations of 1861 had become obsolete. They were replaced by a host of new laws, new general orders, decisions of departments and what not, none of which were gathered together in an accessible form. The heads of departments and their clerks, who had been grinding away for years in the same mill, had all these laws at their finger-ends. The new officers, whose idea of military life was confined to handling troops in campaign, found that in time of peace they were also expected to be expert lawyers, and in this they failed dismally. They were constantly receiving sharp reprimands from headquarters, as to the improper phraseology of a report or return, the absence of red ink on an endorsement, the bungling manner in which they tied their red tape. In the matters of discipline, they were also constantly in trouble. They had an unruly lot of men to control, desertion to check, and the evil required sharp measures. These they were not allowed to use, under the law. Corporal punishment was abolished, stocks, tying up, bucking and gagging, all those rudely effective methods which had been used among the hard cases of the volunteers. They were compelled to manage their men wholly by moral suasion, or punish them by the slow process of court-martial. They generally preferred the latter, and revenged themselves for their impotence in other directions by excessive punishments in this. At the same time, they retained too much of the old free and easy, hard drinking habits, which the war had induced in them, and found that in time of peace, drunken officers were not allowed. Thus the spectacle was presented of frequent court-martials of men and officers, for substantially the same offence, drunken excesses, and the manifest injustice of the different sentences was almost always visible. A man would be dishonorably discharged, and sent to a military prison at hard labor for two years, for what in an officer would only entail a reprimand or suspension from command for a month or two.

All these circumstances combined to render the regular army of 1866 a very different and far inferior body to that which fought in the Mexican war. The men were discontented and unruly, the officers not fully up to their work, and the amount of trouble that took place during that and the following year, had a great influence on the future of Custer.

Under these circumstances the Seventh Cavalry was formed, and to it Custer was assigned as Lieutenant-Colonel.

It might be supposed that his declension in rank from the proud position of a major-general would be accompanied by some compensations, and that at all events the duty in his new rank would be easier. To a certain extent this is true, and yet in many respects the contrary is the case. It doubtless sounds paradoxical to a civilian, to be told that the command of a regiment is in anything harder than that of a division, while at the same time it is asserted that the position of a general officer demands far more military knowledge and capacity than that of a colonel; and yet both these propositions are held to be true, and have been acted on by the few great commanders whose actions have settled the principles of success in military science. Napoleon, in particular, frequently expressed the opinion that generals ought to be young and colonels old, and always acted on it. By this opinion he intended to convey two important lessons, which are elaborated in other maxims. A short analysis of the conditions of military success may make the reason clear to those who have not studied military history in a professional light.

War requires two elements for its prosecution; troops, and a general. A good general may handle poor troops, so as to beat a poor general with good troops. The troops are the tools, the general the workman. With perfect tools, the perfect workman makes perfect work, and the best general can work better if he has good troops than if he has poor ones. Troops are *made* by their sergeants, captains, and colonels, *handled* by their generals. To *make* them, requires patience and experience, qualities in which the old excel the young; to *handle* them requires adroitness, quickness, and magnetic ardor, qualities in which the young excel the old.

So far Custer had been content to take his troops ready made, good or bad, and to use them as he best could : now he was to try his success at fashioning them out of the raw material. The rest of his life will show what measure of success he attained in his task; for, from first to last, he commanded his regiment whenever it was assembled, and had more to do with its training than almost any other regimental commander with any other regiment of the army since the civil war.

CHAPTER III.

THE SEVENTH CAVALRY

A MONG all the anomalies at the close of the rebellion, none was greater than the position in which the officers of the regular army found themselves. Many field officers of the old army had become major-generals of volunteers, and during the war this office carried all the privileges of command. The sudden end of hostilities showed the real hollowness of the title, and one by one, all the general and other officers of the volunteers, were " mustered out " and paid off. To those who were originally civilians, this did not matter. They had returned to their former stations. The old army officers, however, found it very different. They beheld themselves stripped of the privileges of rank, but still remaining soldiers. In Custer's case, the drop was all the way from Major-General to plain captain of the Fifth Cavalry. This rank was all that really remained to him. He had been brevetted major in the regular army in July, 1863, but brevets amounted to nothing, any more than volunteer commissions.

The formation of the new regiments offered a salve in some respect for the wounded pride of those officers who felt the change too keenly, while the retired list provided for many more. The great chiefs of the war found themselves retained in their rank, and the minor chiefs were consoled by field positions and brevets of general officers in the regular army.

The most conspicuous of these were to be found in the new regiments of cavalry. Sheridan's division commanders in the

22

last campaign, Custer and Devin, also Merritt who had been
their nominal chief, were made lieutenant-colonels, and brevetted
brigadier and major generals in the regular army, all at the
same time, on the recommendation of their chief. It marked
the estimate which he placed on them all, apart from popular
praise or censure. Modest, hard working old Devin, coming
from the militia, with little political influence, and nothing but
his own perseverance and faithful work to recommend him, was
placed on the same plane as Custer and Merritt, who had started
with all the advantages of a West Point education in their favor. The only difference between them was that of seniority.
Merritt had been an officer a year before Custer, and Custer's
army commission ranked him over Devin, otherwise all were
equal. With Merritt and Devin we have finished in this history. Their paths no longer run near Custer's. The latter
was appointed Lieutenant-Colonel of the new Seventh Cavalry,
and henceforward will appear identified with that regiment, of
which it would appear that a short sketch is here proper.

The Seventh U. S. Cavalry was called into existence as a
regiment and its first officers commissioned July 28th, 1866. On
that day, the skeleton of the regiment was as follows: Colonel
A. J. Smith, Lieutenant-Colonel George A. Custer, Major
Alfred Gibbs, all three West Pointers, and Brevet Major Generals U. S. A.

Smith was quite an old soldier, having entered the service
in 1838, and Gibbs dated from before the Mexican war. During the rebellion, Gibbs had latterly commanded the Regular
Cavalry brigade in the First division of the Cavalry Corps.

Eight captains were appointed at the same date, of whom
not one was from the academy. All came from the volunteers,
or had risen from the ranks in the regular army during the war.
Their names were William Thompson, Frederick W. Benteen,
Myles W. Keogh, Edward Myers, Robert M. West, Louis M.
Hamilton, Albert Barnitz, and Michael V. Sheridan. Of these,
Thompson and West had been brigade commanders, Benteen a

colonel, and the rest Lieutenant-Colonels by brevet or otherwise. Six first-lieutenants were commissioned the same day, Samuel M. Robbins, Mathew Berry, Owen Hale, Myles Moylan, F. V. Commagere and Thomas W. Custer. Of these, Custer and Commagere had been Majors, the rest captains of volunteers. T. W. Custer was the brother of the General. He had entered the army on the 23d February, 1866, as second-lieutenant of the First Infantry, an office which he was allowed to resign on the 27th July, being appointed next day in his brother's regiment.

These were the first officers of the Seventh Cavalry appointed just ten years ago. To-day hardly one of them is left. The Colonel was retired from service not long after his appointment, and Major Gibbs died at Fort Leavenworth, a year after the formation of the regiment, from the effects of an old lance-wound received before 1860. Before going any further, it will be well to trace here Custer's official and private career during the time of the formation of the Seventh Cavalry till the opening of his first Indian campaign.

He was mustered out of service as a major-general of volunteers in March, 1866, in Houston, Texas. During the year then past, his position in the regular army had been that of a simple captain in the Fifth Cavalry, on leave of absence. His leave was granted him in April 1865, and read " till further orders." His successes, then, just after Sailor's Creek and Appomattox, were too public and brilliant to be ignored, and as yet he had not excited the envy which afterwards assailed him. In the volunteer service, he had only experienced this envy for a few weeks, at his first elevation, and there were so many prizes in those days that the envy was soon forgotten in hope. Besides this, his services had been so wonderfully successful that he had conquered envy by admiration, in almost all cases. No one therefore seemed to be disposed to shorten his enjoyment of hard earned leisure by intriguing to get him ordered back to his regiment as a captain.

During 1865 and the beginning of 1866 he enjoyed full major-general's pay, and allowances, then about $8000 a year. While in Texas, his expenses for living were very small, as appears from many of his letters home, and he saved a great deal of money. Moreover, there were so many opportunities of making money that he was very sorely tempted at times to leave the service and settle down in Texas.

His muster out, while it sent him home to Monroe, left him in a very different position. He became a captain once more, with only about $2000 a year pay, and a small allowance of quarters. It was a heavy fall in pecuniary circumstances, modified by his savings and by the fact that he was still on leave. He went therefore to New York, and while there, entered into negotiations with the Mexican government to become chief of cavalry for Juarez, in his last struggle with Maximilian. The history of this application will bring out the esteem in which he was then held by General Grant, as evinced in the following letter of introduction.

We append this letter as of special interest, in view of the altered relations of the parties in after days. His letter was written to Senor Romero, the Mexican Minister to Washington. It shows Grant's opinion of Custer in the days when Grant was nothing but an honest soldier.

HEADQUARTERS ARMIES OF THE UNITED STATES,
Washington, D. C., May 16, 1866.

DEAR SIR :—This will introduce to your acquaintance Gen. Custer, who rendered such distinguished service as a cavalry officer during the war. There was no officer in that branch of the service who had the confidence of Gen. Sheridan to a greater degree than Gen. C., and there is no officer in whose judgment I have greater faith than in Sheridan's. Please understand then that I mean by this to endorse Gen. Custer in a high degree.

Gen. Custer proposes to apply for a leave of absence for one year, with permission to leave the country, and to take service while abroad. I propose to endorse his application favorably, and believe that he will get it. Yours truly,

U. S. GRANT.

To Sr. M. Romero, Minister, etc.

Sr. Romero was delighted with the application, as he well might be. Mexico was then in the worst possible state, and the Liberal cause in a desperate condition. The Juarez people had plenty of men, but neither arms, money, nor equipments. Carvajal, the head of the Juarez military government, offered Custer the position of Adjutant General of Mexico, with double the pay of an American Major General, in gold, if he could only come to Mexico with one or two thousand men, Americans; the Mexican Liberal government offering to assume any debt he might incur in raising this force. After events proved that the expedition would have been perfectly feasible, for the hold of Maximilian on Mexico, never strong, was weakening daily, and the arrival of Custer, with his brilliant reputation and the men he could easily have raised, would have ended the war with a blaze of glory. Money and men were both forthcoming, and success was certain. All these bright prospects, however, were destroyed by a simple formality : the American government refused to grant Custer the year's leave he asked for, and he was compelled to choose between the smaller certainty of a captaincy in the American army and the glorious uncertainties of a soldier of fortune. The native good sense and sturdy habits of mind inherited and taught him by family influence saved him from the rôle of the last, and the first was soon bettered for him by the increase of the army.

While his application was still pending, however, he was recalled, together with his wife, to Monroe, by the news of the dangerous illness of Judge Bacon. They arrived there only just in time to witness the Judge's death, which took place May 17th, 1866, and was a heavy blow to both. Long before this time, the good old Judge who had been so careful and anxious about the future of his daughter, had learned to lay aside all fears in that direction, and to feel for her husband a respect and liking, all the stronger for his previous mistrust. He died in Custer's arms, resting on his strong breast, and blessing with his latest breath his two children, finding that instead of losing a daughter he had gained a son, as attentive and affectionate as any of his own could have been, had he possessed one.

While the brilliant deeds of Custer had so far gained him the applause of the world at large, the victory in which he felt the greatest pride of any was that gained during the latter part of his life, over the reluctance and distrust of the Judge, and the conversion of those feelings into the warmest respect and esteem. He had reason to be proud of it, for it was no common victory. It was obtained by a single course of conduct. The Judge, who was the kindest and most idolizing of fathers, full of fears at the future of his daughter on her marriage, was quite overcome by the fact of her entire happiness, and by that alone. The real unselfishness of paternal love, as distinguished from that between lovers, is illustrated by this, that the Judge not only forgave, but learned to love, the man who had taken away his daughter.

The death of Judge Bacon made some difference in the prospects of the young couple, most of the Judge's property, which included the house in Monroe in which she now lives, going to his daughter, but as it was not large, it did not alter their ordinary style of living. They continued to reside at Monroe for the next month or two, till, in July, Custer received his commission from President Johnson, as lieutenant-colonel of the new Seventh Cavalry.

He was still anxious to obtain his year's leave, so as to be able to go to Mexico, and with that object set out for Buffalo, in August, to meet President Johnson, who was then engaged in that celebrated operation known as "swinging round the circle." Mrs. Custer went with him.

Inasmuch as the present book will fall into the hands of many too young to remember distinctly the meaning of the expression "swinging round the circle," it may be well to explain it here. President Johnson, originally a strong Southern Democrat, had been nominated for Vice-President, during the war, on the same ticket with Lincoln, as a "War Democrat" and as a sort of compromise, beating Seymour and McClellan. When the assassination of Lincoln placed Johnson in power, he soon returned to his old *ante-bellum* associations, the result of which was a furious contest between Congress and himself, in which the former had the best of it, through holding the legislative power, with a compact majority. The strife was, at this time, August, 1866, at its very hottest. Congress had adjourned, and the President then indulged in a trip which took him all round the country, and in which he was in the habit of stopping at every railway station to make a political speech to the crowd that gathered on the platform to see the presidential party. He took along with him his whole cabinet and General Grant, and the ludicrous nature of the tour was commemorated by the term "swinging round the circle." When Custer met President Johnson at Buffalo, the young general was still, as far as civil affairs went, a frank, innocent boy. Of political lore he was perfectly guiltless, and an old politician like Johnson could wind him round his finger with his wily tricks. Johnson saw at once what a political and popular help Custer's presence would be to him, and accordingly, instead of granting his request for leave, *ordered* him to accompany the party in its tour, *on duty*. And that is the way Custer came to join Johnson in " swinging round the circle."

To the young couple, the whole jaunt was a pleasure trip, which cost them nothing, where they had delightful times, and nothing to do but enjoy themselves. Of the political aspect of the trip Custer was at first unaware, and as his commission as lieutenant-colonel was already safe, he had " no axe to grind," after his first visit, when the President told him he could not give him leave to go to Mexico. The party travelled by the Lake Shore Railroad to Cleveland, Toledo, then to Monroe, Detroit, Chicago, and so to Springfield, Illinois, the late residence of the murdered President Lincoln.

Johnson had at the time a great idea that his political enemies would try to assassinate him on the road, and insisted on Custer's occupying the next room to his own at every hotel, and keeping loaded revolvers by him, to protect the Executive from murder, a danger which, however, existed chiefly in his own heated imagination. The ostensible cause of the tour was the inauguration of a monument to President Lincoln, which took place at Springfield, the nominal termination of the journey. Political effect and the President's monomania for speeches on the constitution continued the journey to St. Louis, whence the party returned to Washington another way. Custer got tired of the trip at last, when he found that it was entirely a political movement and one productive of ridicule to all the participants, and as soon as the last semblance of danger was removed by their return to the civilized Eastern States, he parted from the President, refusing an invitation to Washington. He refused also, during this trip, the full colonelcy of the Ninth Cavalry, a black regiment, which was offered him, preferring a lower step to a lower grade of service.

On leaving the President, he went to the Soldiers' and Sailors' Convention at Cleveland, and excited quite a commotion by introducing to the meeting the ex-rebel cavalry general Forrest, a rough hewn man, something of his own stamp for fiery energy, and who had been far the most dangerous cavalry commander possessed at any time by the Confederate cause.

Nothing hurt Custer's political and military future like the movements of this summer, all of which were owing to his generous impulsive way of doing things. Honest to the backbone himself, he could not imagine that others could be less so, and he fell, as it were, bound hand and foot, into the midst of a den of hungry political wolves, who would have picked his bones clean had he staid much longer. Like Juvenal refusing to go to Rome, he could reply, when he was asked the cause of his non success in politics, " *Nescio mentire.*" It tells the whole story. He and Sheridan were political failures for the same reason, on opposite sides. Kilpatrick, Slocum, Banning, Logan, Butler, Garfield, and a host of others, were successes for the opposite reason.

At last he was saved from the consequences of his indiscreet utterance of the truth, by receiving orders to report at Fort Riley, Kansas, and assume his command. Never was order more welcome. It found him at Monroe, longing for the plains and the new life which he was to lead there. He was already developing into the sportsman he afterwards became. During his Texan residence he had accumulated a pack of some twenty fox hounds, and had invested in rifles, having become a fair shot. In his letters home from Texas he frequently speaks of his hunting expeditions after deer, rabbits, coons, possums, and other animals. In those days to all appearance he was as innocent as a child about the relative dignity of game, and talks of going on a coon hunt with an old negro, with all the zest of a veteran trapper after a grizzly. He seems to have felt like a regular big boy out of school, eager for anything in the way of game, and making no distinctions.

The foxhound pack of Texas was broken up, except one or two of the finest dogs, which he took to Monroe, but during the "swinging round the circle" trip, he became wonderfully interested in the Scotch deerhound, of which he saw one or two specimens. He ended by buying a pair, bred in Canada from imported dogs, and afterwards received a present of another, an imported dog. From these others were afterwards bred, so that in a few years he possessed quite a pack of these dogs, besides foxhounds, setters, spaniels and others. He had always managed to have dogs, at all periods of his career, even when as a lieutenant he took old "Rose" to Washington with him, but, as soon as he was able to indulge his fancy freely he perfectly revelled in the collection of animals, having as many and varied a pack as used to attend Sir Walter Scott at Abbotsford in days gone by.

The General and Mrs. Custer started for Fort Riley, which they reached when it was yet the terminus of the Pacific Railroad. A year later, in spite of an Indian war, ninety miles more were finished. Fort Riley, when they came there, was a perfect sink of iniquity, as far as concerned the village outside the military post. During the winter and spring, this sink of iniquity was moved on to Fort Hays—cause, extension of the railroad. All the desperate characters of the frontier flocked to the terminus of the railroad, gamblers, thieves, murderers, outcasts of all kinds. In Fort Hays, one year old, were thirty-six graves, every grave that of a man who had died " with his boots on," that is to say killed in a brawl.

The tedium of life inside the post was only relieved by the arrival, from day to day, of the new officers of the Seventh Cavalry, come to report to Custer, in command. On the appointment of these officers, the next thing in order was to provide them a regiment to command, and with that object the rest of the year was occupied in recruiting. The original intention seems to have been to form a regiment of only eight companies, but the Seventh, in common with the other cavalry regiments, was subsequently raised to one of three battalions, each of four companies, necessitating two more majors and four additional captains, besides lieutenants. Major Joel H. Elliot was appointed March 7, 1867, from Indiana. He had been a colonel of volunteers. Major W. S. Abert followed on the 8th June. He had been one of the old army officers, a civil appointment, since 1855, and during the war had been brevetted brigadier-general of volunteers.

The new captains were Thomas M. Dayton, Lee P. Gillette, George W. Yates, and Thomas B. Weir, of whom three had been lieutenant-colonels. The new first-lieutenants were Henry H. Abell, Charles Brewster, James M. Bell, D. W. Wallingford, William W. Cook, and Henry Jackson. All these entered the regiment in 1867.

In the same year the regiment also received five second-lieutenants. Three of these, James T. Leavy, Bradford S. Bassett, and William B. Clark, came from the volunteers, where Bassett had been a captain. The other two, John M. Johnson and Edward S. Godfrey, had just graduated from the " Point." Such was the composition of the Seventh Cavalry when Custer assumed command of the regiment in 1867. Colonel A. J. Smith was the department chief, and therefore never saw his regiment, the whole responsibility falling on Custer. The material of which the men were composed was decidedly bad, as was the case with all the regular regiments at the close of the war. Recruits came from the large towns, and included a great many of the rough classes, men who enlisted with the purpose of shirking as much duty as they could, and of deserting whenever they got tired. We shall see, before long, how much trouble they brought on Custer, and how he at last licked them into shape. There is perhaps to-day no regiment in the army which bears so strongly on itself the imprint of its leader as the Seventh Cavalry. What it is, Custer's name and influence have made it. He found it a crowd of green recruits. He made it into a regiment of veterans and heroes. How he did it, will appear in the course of his life on the plains. Suffice it here to say that he managed to make the regiment too hot for officers who indulged in drunkenness on duty, and either drove them out entirely, induced them to take the pledge, or compelled them to reserve their excesses for places where it concerned themselves alone, and did the least possible injury to the service.

This trait of Custer's character had always been prominent during his volunteer service. He began with it in the Michigan brigade, continued it in the Third division, and now brought it into the Seventh Cavalry. He realized so strongly the dangers of excess in his own nature, that he always sympathized with and aided all whom he found in the same difficulties, trying to escape from evil influence. In all this, he was very far removed from those total abstinence fanatics who have brought so much discredit on the name of " temperance " by their intemperance. He never interfered with the free will of those officers who possessed enough self-control to remain moderate drinkers, and never forced his views on others, unless it became a question of the interest of the service and the career of the individual. He found that his own highstrung, nervous temperament was utterly unfitted to indulge in stimulants, and he totally abandoned the habit. He induced his brother Tom to take the pledge, and abstain from liquors and tobacco, because he saw that their temperaments were very similar; and the result was that Tom Custer became an ornament to his profession, inspired by his brother's example. Whenever Custer found a brave and otherwise capable officer caught in the toils of dipsomania, he always did his best to reform and save him. It was only those wilful and habitual debauchees who gloried in tempting others, on whom Custer was remorselessly severe; and there he had no compassion. To those who know to what an extent the inroads of intemperance have penetrated in the army, and who are frank enough to acknowledge, instead of denying the evil, his conduct needs no excuse. For the opinions of others he never cared. As he began, so he followed to the last, the *right way as it appeared to him,* regardless of consequences.